Mastering CloudForms
Automation

Peter McGowan

Beijing · Boston · Farnham · Sebastopol · Tokyo

Mastering CloudForms Automation

by Peter McGowan

Copyright © 2016 Red Hat, Inc. All rights reserved.

Printed in the United States of America.

Published by O'Reilly Media, Inc., 1005 Gravenstein Highway North, Sebastopol, CA 95472.

O'Reilly books may be purchased for educational, business, or sales promotional use. Online editions are also available for most titles (*http://safaribooksonline.com*). For more information, contact our corporate/institutional sales department: 800-998-9938 or *corporate@oreilly.com*.

Editor: Brian Anderson
Production Editor: Shiny Kalapurakkel
Copyeditor: Rachel Monaghan
Proofreader: Eileen Cohen

Indexer: Angela Howard
Interior Designer: David Futato
Cover Designer: Karen Montgomery
Illustrator: Colleen Cole

July 2016:   First Edition

Revision History for the First Edition
2016-06-21:   First Release

See *http://oreilly.com/catalog/errata.csp?isbn=9781491957226* for release details.

978-1-4919-5722-6

[LSI]

Table of Contents

Part II. Provisioning Virtual Machines

Part IV.   Retirement

Part V.   Integration

Preface

Red Hat CloudForms is a powerful cloud management platform that allows us to efficiently manage our virtual infrastructure and Infrastructure as a Service (IaaS) clouds. Part of this efficient management involves automating many of the day-to-day tasks that would otherwise require manual involvement, or time-consuming and possibly error-prone repetitive steps.

This book is an introduction and how-to guide to working with the *Automate* feature of Red Hat CloudForms.

CloudForms Automate simplifies our lives and increases our operational efficiency. It allows us to do such things as:

- Eliminate many of the manual decisions and operations involved in provisioning virtual machines and cloud instances.

- Load-balance our virtual machines across our virtual infrastructure to match our organization's way of working, be it logical (e.g., cost center, department), operational (e.g., infrastructure lifecycle environment), or categorical (e.g., server role or virtual machine characteristic).

- Create service catalogs to allow our users to provision virtual machines from a single Order button.

- Create autoscalable cloud applications in which new virtual machines are dynamically provisioned on demand.

- Manage our complete virtual machine lifecycle.

- Integrate our virtual machine provisioning workflow with the wider enterprise—for example, automatically registering new virtual machines with a Red Hat Satellite server.

- Implement intelligent virtual machine retirement workflows that de-allocate resources such as IP addresses and unregister from directory services.

A Brief Word on Terminology

This book refers to *Automate* as the CloudForms capability or product feature, and *automation* as the thing that Automate allows us to do. The *Automation Engine* allows us to create intelligent automation workflows and run *automation scripts* written in Ruby.

Who Should Read This Book?

This book will appeal to cloud or virtualization administrators who are interested in automating parts of their virtual infrastructure or cloud computing environment. Although it's primarily aimed at those with some familiarity with Red Hat Cloud-Forms, many of the concepts and terms, such as *orchestration* and *automation workflows*, will be easily understood even to those unfamiliar with the product.

Automate can be one of the more challenging aspects of CloudForms to master. The practitioner requires an unusual blend of skills: a familiarity with traditional "infrastructure" concepts such as virtual machines, hypervisors, and tenant networks, but also a flair for scripting in Ruby and mastery of a programming object model. There is no black magic, however, and all of the skills can be learned if we are shown the way.

The book assumes a reasonable level of competence with the Ruby language on the part of the reader. There are many good online Ruby tutorials available, including Codecademy's "Learn to program in Ruby" (*http://www.codecademy.com/tracks/ruby*).

The book also presumes a comfortable level of working experience and familiarity with the Web User Interface (WebUI) features of CloudForms, particularly Insight, Control, tagging, and provisioning VMs via the Lifecycle → Provision VMs entry point. Many of these features will be automated as we follow the examples in the book, and so an understanding of why tagging is useful (for example) is helpful.

 CloudForms is a web application, so interaction is predominantly via the browser-based WebUI. We only use a command-line terminal when we initially configure a CloudForms appliance, or when troubleshooting or examining logfiles.

Why I Wrote This Book

I was fortunate in having two of the early masters of CloudForms Automate, John Hardy and Brad Ascar from Red Hat, teach me the fundamentals of automation. They opened my eyes to the possibilities and whetted my appetite to learn more. This book is an attempt to pass on that knowledge, supplemented with my real-world experience as an architect at Red Hat, so that others can use this really powerful feature of the product.

I've tried to structure the book around the periodic revelations that I've had while learning CloudForms Automate, the *if only I'd known that weeks ago* moments. In places, this includes some deep code examination and theory, and in-depth logfile analysis, but hopefully this will help the reader's understanding process (it did for me). I also try to illustrate the theory with code snippets and examples.

Versions and Releases

Although the descriptions and screenshots in this book are taken from Red Hat CloudForms 3.2 and 4.0, most of the content also applies to the ManageIQ *Botvinnik* and *Capablanca* releases. CloudForms 4.0 (ManageIQ Capablanca) is the latest release at the time of writing.

Navigating This Book

The book is divided into six parts.

Part I, *Working with CloudForms Automate*

Chapter 1, *Introduction to CloudForms*, sets the scene and describes the capabilities of CloudForms as a cloud management product.

Chapter 2, *Introduction to the Automate Datastore*, takes us on a tour of the objects that we work with when we use the Automate capabilities of CloudForms.

Chapter 3, *Writing and Running Our Own Automation Scripts*, introduces us to writing automation scripts in Ruby, with a simple "Hello, World!" example.

Chapter 4, *Using Schema Variables*, shows how we can use our instance's schema to store and retrieve variables.

Chapter 5, *Working with Virtual Machines*, demonstrates how to work with an Automation Engine virtual machine object, and how to run an automation script from a custom button in the WebUI.

Chapter 6, *Peeping Under the Hood*, introduces some background theory about Rails *models*, and how CloudForms abstracts these as *service models* that we work with when we write our automation scripts.

Chapter 7, *$evm and the Workspace*, takes us on a tour of the useful $evm methods that we frequently use when scripting, such as $evm.vmdb and $evm.object.

Chapter 8, *A Practical Example: Enforcing Anti-Affinity Rules*, is a real-world, full-script example of how we could use the techniques learned so far to implement anti-affinity rules in our virtual infrastructure, based on tags.

Chapter 9, *Using Tags from Automate*, describes in detail how we can create, assign, read, and work with tags from our Ruby automation scripts.

Chapter 10, *Investigative Debugging*, discusses the ways that we can discover which Automate objects are available to us when scripting. This is useful both from an investigative viewpoint when we're developing scripts, and for debugging our scripts when things are not working as expected.

Chapter 11, *Ways of Entering Automate*, shows us the various workflow entry points into the Automate Datastore. It also illustrates how we can determine programmatically the way that our automation script has been called, enabling us to create re-usable scripts.

Chapter 12, *Requests and Tasks*, illustrates how more advanced Automate operations are separated into a *Request* stage, which requires administrative approval to progress into the *Task* stage. The corresponding request and task objects are described and their usage compared.

Chapter 13, *State Machines*, introduces us to state machines and how we can use them to intelligently sequence our workflows.

Chapter 14, *More Advanced Schema Features*, discusses the more advanced but less frequently used schema features: messages, assertions, and collections.

Chapter 15, *Event Processing*, describes the way that CloudForms responds to external events such as a virtual machine shutting down, and traces the event handling sequence through the Automate Datastore. It also shows how Automate manages its own internal events such as `request_started`.

Part II, *Provisioning Virtual Machines*

Chapter 16, *Provisioning a Virtual Machine*, introduces the concept of virtual machine provisioning, the most complex out-of-the-box Automate operation that is performed by CloudForms.

Chapter 17, *The Provisioning Profile*, describes how the provisioning profile is referenced to determine the initial group-specific processing that is performed at the start of a virtual machine provisioning operation.

Chapter 18, *Approval*, shows how the approval workflow operates and how we can adjust auto-approval criteria, such as the number of virtual machines to be provisioned or the amount of storage, to suit our needs.

Chapter 19, *Quota Management*, gives details of the new CloudForms 4.0 quota handling mechanism and how it enables us to establish quotas for tenants or groups.

Chapter 20, *The Options Hash*, explains the importance of a data structure called the *options hash* and how we can use it to retrieve and store variables to customize the virtual machine provisioning operation.

Chapter 21, *The Provisioning State Machine*, discusses the stages in the state machine that governs the sequence of operations involved in provisioning a virtual machine.

Chapter 22, *Customizing Virtual Machine Provisioning*, is a practical example showing how we can customize the state machine and include our own methods to add a second hard disk during the virtual machine provisioning operation.

Chapter 23, *Virtual Machine Naming During Provisioning*, explains how we can customize the *naming* logic that determines the name given to the newly provisioned virtual machine.

Chapter 24, *Virtual Machine Placement During Provisioning*, explains how we can customize the *placement* logic that determines the host, cluster, and datastore locations for our newly provisioned virtual machine.

Chapter 25, *The Provisioning Dialog*, describes the WebUI dialogs that prompt for the parameters that are required before a new virtual machine can be provisioned. The chapter also explains how the dialogs can be customized to expand optional ranges for items like size of memory or to present a cut-down, bespoke dialog to certain user groups.

Chapter 26, *Virtual Machine Provisioning Objects*, details the four main objects that we work with when we write Ruby scripts to interact with the virtual machine provisioning process.

Chapter 27, *Creating Provisioning Requests Programmatically*, shows how we can initiate a virtual machine provisioning operation from an automation script, instead of from the WebUI.

Chapter 28, *Integrating with Satellite 6 During Provisioning*, is a practical example showing how to automate the registration of a newly created virtual machine with Red Hat Satellte 6, both as a *host* and *content host*.

Part III, *Working with Services*

Chapter 29, *Service Dialogs*, introduces the components that make up a *service dialog*, including elements that can be dynamically populated by Ruby methods.

Chapter 30, *The Service Provisioning State Machine*, discusses the stages in the state machine that governs the sequence of operations involved in creating a service.

Chapter 31, *Catalog{Item,Bundle}Initialization*, describes two specific instances of the service-provisioning state machine that have been designed to simplify the process of creating service catalog *items* and *bundles*.

Chapter 32, *Approval and Quota*, shows the approval workflow for services, and how the new consolidated quota-handling mechanism for CloudForms 4.0 also applies to services.

Chapter 33, *Creating a Service Catalog Item*, is a practical example showing how to create a service catalog item to provision a virtual machine.

Chapter 34, *Creating a Service Catalog Bundle*, is a practical example showing how to create a service catalog bundle of three virtual machines.

Chapter 35, *Service Objects*, is an exposé of the various objects that work behind the scenes when a service catalog item is provisioned.

Chapter 36, *Log Analysis During Service Provisioning*, is a step-by-step walk-through, tracing the lines written to *automation.log* at various stages of a service provision operation. This can help our understanding of the several levels of concurrent state-machine activity taking place.

Chapter 37, *Service Hierarchies*, illustrates how services can contain other services and how we can arrange our service groups into hierarchies for organizational and management convenience.

Chapter 38, *Service Reconfiguration*, describes how we can create reconfigurable services. These are capable of accepting configuration parameters at order time via the service dialog and can later be reconfigured with new configuration parameters via the same service dialog.

Chapter 39, *Service Tips and Tricks*, mentions some useful tips to remember when we are developing services.

Part IV, *Retirement*

Chapter 40, *Virtual Machine and Instance Retirement*, discusses the retirement process for virtual machines and instances.

Chapter 41, *Service Retirement*, discusses the retirement process for services.

Part V, *Integration*

Chapter 42, *Calling Automation Using the RESTful API*, shows how we can make external calls *into* CloudForms to run Automate instances via the RESTful API. We can also return results to our caller in this way, enabling us to create our own pseudo-API endpoints within CloudForms.

Chapter 43, *Automation Request Approval*, explains how to customize the default approval behavior for automation requests, so that nonadministrators can submit RESTful API requests without needing administrative approval.

Chapter 44, *Calling External Services*, shows the various ways that we can call *out* from Automate to integrate with our wider enterprise. This includes making outbound REST and SOAP calls, connecting to MySQL databases, and interacting with OpenStack using the fog gem.

Part VI, *Miscellaneous*

Chapter 45, *Distributed Automation Processing*, describes how CloudForms Automate has been designed to be horizontally scalable. The chapter describes the mechanism by which automation requests are distributed among multiple appliances in a region.

Chapter 46, *Argument Passing and Handling*, explains how arguments are passed to, and handled internally by, Automate methods for each of the different ways that we've called them up to this point in the book.

Chapter 47, *Miscellaneous Tips*, closes the book with some useful tips for Automate method development.

Online Resources

There are several online resources that any student of CloudForms Automate should be aware of.

Official Documentation

The official Red Hat documentation for CloudForms is here: *http://red.ht/1rfeDkq*.

Code Repositories

One of the best sources of reference material is the excellent *CloudForms_Essentials* code collection maintained by Kevin Morey from Red Hat (*https://github.com/ramrexx/CloudForms_Essentials*). This contains a wealth of useful code samples, and many of the examples in this book originate from this source.

There is also the very useful Red Hat Consulting (*https://github.com/rhtconsulting*) GitHub repository maintained by several Red Hat consultants.

Forums

The ManageIQ project hosts the *ManageIQ Talk* forum (*http://talk.manageiq.org*).

Blogs

There are several blogs that have good CloudForms-related articles, including some useful "notes from the field." These include:

- CloudForms NOW (*http://cloudformsblog.redhat.com/*)
- Christian's blog (*http://www.jung-christian.de*)
- Laurent Domb OSS blog (*http://blog.domb.net/*)
- ALL THINGS OPEN (*http://allthingsopen.com/*)
- TigerIQ (*http://www.tigeriq.co/*)

Conventions Used in This Book

The following typographical conventions are used in this book:

Italic

Indicates new terms, URLs, email addresses, filenames, and file extensions.

`Constant width`

Used for program listings, as well as within paragraphs to refer to program elements such as variable or function names, databases, data types, environment variables, statements, and keywords.

`Constant width bold`

Shows commands or other text that should be typed literally by the user.

`Constant width italic`

Shows text that should be replaced with user-supplied values or by values determined by context.

This element signifies a tip or suggestion.

This element signifies a general note.

This element indicates a warning or caution.

Using Code Examples

Supplemental material (code examples, exercises, etc.) is available for download at *https://github.com/pemcg/oreilly-mastering-cloudforms-automation*.

This book is here to help you get your job done. In general, if example code is offered with this book, you may use it in your programs and documentation. You do not need to contact us for permission unless you're reproducing a significant portion of the code. For example, writing a program that uses several chunks of code from this book does not require permission. Selling or distributing a CD-ROM of examples from O'Reilly books does require permission. Answering a question by citing this book and quoting example code does not require permission. Incorporating a significant amount of example code from this book into your product's documentation does require permission.

We appreciate, but do not require, attribution. An attribution usually includes the title, author, publisher, and ISBN. For example: "*Mastering CloudForms Automation* by Peter McGowan (O'Reilly). Copyright 2016 Red Hat, Inc., 978-1-4919-5722-6."

If you feel your use of code examples falls outside fair use or the permission given above, feel free to contact us at *permissions@oreilly.com*.

Safari® Books Online

 *Safari Books Online* is an on-demand digital library that delivers expert content in both book and video form from the world's leading authors in technology and business.

Technology professionals, software developers, web designers, and business and creative professionals use Safari Books Online as their primary resource for research, problem solving, learning, and certification training.

Safari Books Online offers a range of plans and pricing for enterprise, government, education, and individuals.

Members have access to thousands of books, training videos, and prepublication manuscripts in one fully searchable database from publishers like O'Reilly Media, Prentice Hall Professional, Addison-Wesley Professional, Microsoft Press, Sams, Que, Peachpit Press, Focal Press, Cisco Press, John Wiley & Sons, Syngress, Morgan Kaufmann, IBM Redbooks, Packt, Adobe Press, FT Press, Apress, Manning, New Riders, McGraw-Hill, Jones & Bartlett, Course Technology, and hundreds more. For more information about Safari Books Online, please visit us online.

How to Contact Us

Please address comments and questions concerning this book to the publisher:

O'Reilly Media, Inc.
1005 Gravenstein Highway North
Sebastopol, CA 95472
800-998-9938 (in the United States or Canada)
707-829-0515 (international or local)
707-829-0104 (fax)

We have a web page for this book, where we list errata, examples, and any additional information. You can access this page at *http://shop.oreilly.com/product/ 0636920050735.do*.

To comment or ask technical questions about this book, send email to *bookques- tions@oreilly.com*.

For more information about our books, courses, conferences, and news, see our web- site at *http://www.oreilly.com*.

Find us on Facebook: *http://facebook.com/oreilly*

Follow us on Twitter: *http://twitter.com/oreillymedia*

Watch us on YouTube: *http://www.youtube.com/oreillymedia*

Acknowledgments

Anyone who works for Red Hat and starts to write a book like this has the advantage of working in an incredible culture of knowledge sharing (one of Red Hat's mottos is "we grow when we share"). There is a long list of people who have helped me in one way or another, but in particular the following people deserve a special mention.

For code samples (many of which have been used in this book), ideas for content, and general sounding-board advice over a long period, thanks goes to Kevin Morey, Bill Helgeson, Cameron Wyatt, Tom Hennessy, Lester Claudio, Brett Thurber, Fabien Dupont, Ed Seymour, and George Goh.

I've lost count of the number of times that Christian Jung, Krain Arnold, Loic Avenal, and Nick Catling from the EMEA CloudForms "Tiger Team" have helped me, and made me wonder *now why didn't I think of that?*

For their patience with my questions and help in proofreading this book for technical correctness, I'd like to thank Tina Fitzgerald, Madhu Kanoor, and Greg McCullough from the CloudForms/ManageIQ engineering Automate team.

For their suggestion of turning a documentation hobby project borne of frustration into a real book, and for the behind-the-scenes organization to make it happen, I am indebted to the CloudForms marketing team members Marty Wesley and Geert Jensen.

I would like to thank Brian Anderson from O'Reilly for his encouragement and patience with a new and naive author, and Mark Reynolds from HPE for reviewing the book from a useful non–Red Hat point of view.

And finally, a big thank you to my wife Sarah, for her tireless support and encouragement, and tolerance of the *other woman* in my life for the past two years, named Ruby.

Working with CloudForms Automate

Part I introduces the objects and concepts that we work with when we develop our automation scripts. Some of the chapters contain practical coding examples to assist the learning process, while others are more theoretical and contain background information to help build an overall understanding of the object model.

## CHAPTER 1

Introduction to CloudForms

Welcome to this guide to mastering the Automate feature of Red Hat CloudForms. Before we begin our journey through Automate, it's worth taking a general tour of CloudForms to establish a context for all that we'll be learning.

What Is CloudForms?

Red Hat CloudForms is a *cloud management platform* that is also rather good at managing traditional server virtualization products such as VMware vSphere or Red Hat Enterprise Virtualization (RHEV). This broad capability makes it ideal as a *hybrid cloud manager*, able to manage both public clouds, and on-premises private clouds and virtual infrastructures. It provides a single management interface into a hybrid environment, enabling cross-platform orchestration to be achieved with relative simplicity.

Although originally a virtualization and *Infrastructure as a Service* (IaaS) cloud manager, CloudForms 4.0 introduced support for Docker container management, including Red Hat's OpenShift Enterprise 3.x *Platform as a Service* (PaaS) cloud solution (see Figure 1-1).

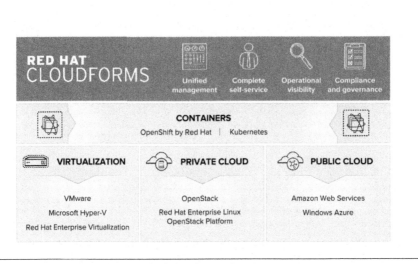

Figure 1-1. Red Hat CloudForms high-level overview

Requirements of a Cloud Management Platform

Cloud management platforms (CMPs) are software tools that allow for the integrated management of public, private, and hybrid cloud environments. There are several requirements that are generally considered necessary for a product to be classified as a cloud management platform. These are:

- Self-service catalog-based ordering of services
- Metering and billing of cloud workloads
- Policy-based workload optimization and management
- Workflow orchestration and automation
- The capability to integrate with external tools and systems
- Role-based access control (RBAC) and multitenancy

Providers

CloudForms manages each cloud, container, or virtual environment using modular subcomponents called *providers*. Each provider contains the functionality required to connect to and monitor its specific target platform, and this provider specialization enables common cloud management functionality to be abstracted into the core product. In keeping with the *manager of managers* concept, CloudForms providers communicate with their respective underlying cloud or infrastructure platform using the native APIs published for the platform manager (such as VMware vCenter Server using the vSphere SOAP API).

The pluggable nature of the provider architecture makes it relatively straightforward to develop new providers to support additional cloud and infrastructure platforms. For example, the last two versions of CloudForms have added five new providers, with more currently under development.

Providers are broadly divided into categories, and with CloudForms 4.0 these are *cloud*, *infrastructure*, *configuration management*, and *container*.

Cloud Providers

CloudForms 4.0 ships with cloud providers that connect to and manage two *public* clouds: Amazon Web Services and Microsoft Azure. It also has a cloud provider that can connect to and manage a *private* or *on-premises* Red Hat OpenStack Platform (OSP) cloud (this is the *OverCloud* in the case that OSP is managed by the Red Hat OpenStack Platform 7 Director).

Infrastructure Providers

CloudForms 4.0 ships with infrastructure providers that connect to and manage VMware vCenter Server, Red Hat Enterprise Virtualization Manager, and Microsoft System Center Virtual Machine Manager. It also has an infrastructure provider that can connect to and manage a private or on-premises Red Hat OpenStack Platform 7 Director *UnderCloud*.

Configuration Management Providers

CloudForms 4.0 ships with a configuration management provider that can connect to and manage Red Hat Satellite 6. This enables CloudForms to import and use Satellite 6 *host groups*, and extends the provisioning capability to include *bare-metal* (i.e., non-virtual) servers.

Container Providers

CloudForms 4.0 ships with container providers that can connect to and manage two Docker container managers: Red Hat Atomic Platform and Red Hat OpenShift Enterprise.

Mixing and Matching Providers

When deploying CloudForms in our enterprise we often connect to several providers. We can illustrate this with an example company.

Company XYZ Inc.

Our example organization has an established VMware vSphere 5.5 virtual environment, containing many hundreds of virtual machines. This virtual infrastructure is typically used for the stable, long-lived virtual machines, and many of the organization's critical database, directory services, and file servers are situated here. Approximately half of the VMware virtual machines run Red Hat Enterprise Linux,[1] and to facilitate the patching, updating, and configuration management of these VMs, the organization has a Satellite 6 server.

Company XYZ is a large producer of several varieties of widget, and the widget development test cycle involves creating many short-lived instances in an OpenStack private cloud, to cycle through the test suites. The developers like to have a service catalog from which they can order one of the many widget test environments, and at any time there can be several hundred instances running various test configurations.

The web developers in the company are in the process of redeveloping the main Internet web portal as a scalable public cloud workload hosted in Amazon Web Services (AWS). The web portal provides a rich product catalog, online documentation, knowledge base, and ecommerce shopping area to customers.

In this organization, CloudForms manages the workflows that provision virtual machines into the vSphere virtual infrastructure, AWS, and OpenStack. The users have a self-service catalog to provision individual virtual machine workloads into either VMware or Amazon, or entire test suites into OpenStack. CloudForms orchestration workflows help with the maintenance of an *image factory* that keeps virtual machine images updated and published as VMware templates, Amazon Machine Images (AMIs), and OpenStack *Glance* images.

As part of the provisioning process CloudForms also manages the integration workflows that allow newly provisoned virtual machines to be automatically registered with the Satellite 6 server, and an in-house configuration management database (see Figure 1-2). This ensures that newly provisioned virtual machines are configured by Puppet according to server role and patched with the latest updates, with a full inventory visible to the help-desk system.

---

1 CloudForms is virtual machine operating system neutral; it can manage Windows, Red Hat, Fedora, Debian, Ubuntu, or SUSE VMs (or their derivatives) with equal ease.

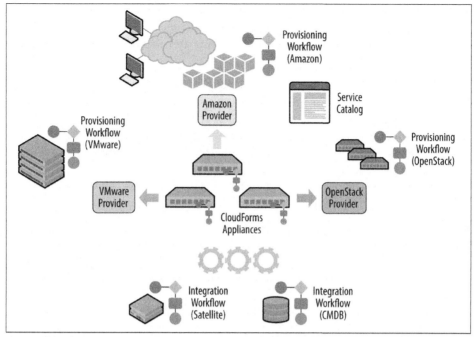

Figure 1-2. Red Hat CloudForms providers and workflows

The Capabilities of CloudForms

We've already mentioned some of the capabilities of CloudForms such as *orchestration*, a *service catalog*, and *integration workflows*. Let's have a look at the four main areas of capability: insight, control, automate, and integrate.

Insight

Insight is the process of gathering intelligence on our virtual or cloud infrastructure so that we can manage it effectively. It is one of the most fundamental but important capabilities of the product.

When we first connect a provider, CloudForms begins a process of *discovery* of the virtual or cloud infrastructure. An infrastructure provider will collect and maintain details of the entire virtual infrastructure, including clusters, hypervisors, datastores, virtual machines, and the relationships among them. Cloud vendors do not typically expose infrastructure details, so cloud providers will typically gather and monitor tenant-specific information on cloud components such as instances, images, availability zones, networks, and security groups.

CloudForms also stores and processes any real-time or historical performance data that the provider exposes. It uses the historical data to calculate useful trend-based analytics such as image or VM right-sizing suggestions and capacity-planning recommendations. It uses the real-time performance statistics and power-on/off events to give us insight into workload utilization and also uses this information to calculate metering and chargeback costs.

One of the roles of a CloudForms server is that of *Smart Proxy*. A server with this role has the ability to initiate a *SmartState Analysis* on a virtual machine, template, instance, or even Docker container. SmartState Analysis (also known as *fleecing*) is a patented technology that scans the container or virtual machine's disk image to examine its contents. The scan discovers users and groups that have been added and applications that have been installed, and searches for and optionally retrieves the contents of specified configuration files or Windows Registry settings. This is an agentless operation that doesn't require the virtual machine to be powered on.

CloudForms allows us to apply tags to infrastructure or cloud components to help us identify and classify our workloads or resources in a way that makes sense to our organization. These tags might specify an owning department, cost center, operating system type, location, or workload classification, for example. We can create powerful filters in the WebUI that allow us to display managed components such as VMs along organizational and business lines, rather than physical placement or characteristic.

To round off the summary of its insight ability, CloudForms also has a powerful reporting capability that can be used to create online or exportable CSV or PDF reports.

Control

We can use the *Control* functionality of CloudForms to enforce security and configuration policies, using the information retrieved from insight. For example, the SmartState Analysis of a virtual machine might discover a software package containing a known critical security vulnerability. We could implement a control policy to shut down the VM, or migrate it to a hypervisor in a quarantine network so that it can be patched.

Using real-time performance statistics, we might configure alerts to warn us when critical virtual machines are running at unusually high utilization levels. Many monitoring tools can do this, but with CloudForms we could also use such an alert to trigger an Automate workflow to dynamically scale out the application workload by provisioning more servers.

We can monitor for compliance with corporate security policies, by gathering and intelligently processing the contents of selected configuration files. In this way we might detect if SELinux has been disabled, for example, or that sshd is running with an insecure configuration. We can run such compliance rules automatically and mark a virtual machine as *noncompliant*, whereupon its status will be immediately visible in the WebUI.

Automate

One of the most powerful features of CloudForms is its ability to *automate* the orchestration of workloads and resources in our virtual infrastructure or cloud. Automate allows us to create and use powerful workflows using the Ruby scripting language and features provided by the *Automation Engine*, such as *state machines* and *service models*.

CloudForms comes preconfigured with a large number of out-of-the-box workflows, to orchestrate such things as:

- Provisioning or scaling out of *workloads*, such as virtual machines or cloud instances
- Provisioning or scaling out of *infrastructure*, such as bare-metal hypervisors or *compute nodes*
- Scaling back or retirement of virtual machine or cloud instances

Each of these is done in the context of comprehensive role-based access control, with administrator-level approval of selected Automate operations required where appropriate.

We can extend or enhance these default workflows and create whole new orchestration workflows to meet our specific requirements.

Service catalog

We can create self-service catalogs to permit users to order our orchestration workflows with a single button click. CloudForms Automate comes with an interactive service dialog designer that we use to build rich dialogs, containing elements such as text boxes, radio buttons, or drop-down lists. These elements can be dynamically prepopulated with values that are specific and relevant to the logged-in user or workload being ordered.

Integrate

As an extension of its Automate capability, CloudForms is able to connect to and *integrate* with many enterprise tools and systems. The system comes with Ruby gems to enable automation scripts to connect to both RESTful and SOAP APIs, as well as libraries to connect to several SQL and LDAP databases, and the ability to run remote PowerShell scripts on Windows servers.

Typical integration actions might be to extend the virtual machine provisioning workflow to retrieve and use an IP address from a corporate IP address management (IPAM) solution; to create a new configuration item (CI) record in the central configuration management database (CMDB), or to create and update tickets in the enterprise service-management tool, such as ServiceNow.

The CloudForms Appliance

To simplify installation, CloudForms is distributed as a fully installed virtual machine, known as the *CloudForms Management Engine* (often referred to as *appliance* for convenience).

A CloudForms 4.0 appliance comes preconfigured with everything we need. It runs Red Hat Enterprise Linux 7.2, with PostgreSQL 9.4, Rails 4.2.5, the CloudForms application, and all associated Ruby gems installed. An appliance is downloadable as a virtual machine image template in formats suitable for VMware, Red Hat Enterprise Virtualization, OpenStack, or Microsoft System Center Virtual Machine Manager.

All software packages in a CloudForms appliance are installed from RPM files, just as with any other Red Hat Enterprise Linux server. The packages can be updated with yum update from a Satellite 6 server or the Red Hat content delivery network.

Ruby and Rails

CloudForms is a Ruby on Rails application that uses PostgreSQL as its database. When we use the Automate functionality of CloudForms, we work extensively with the Ruby language and write scripts that interact with a Ruby object model defined for us by the Automation Engine. We certainly don't need to be Rails developers, however (we don't really *need* to know anything about Rails), but as we'll see in Chapter 6, some understanding of Rails concepts can make it easier to understand the object model and what happens behind the scenes when we run our scripts.

Why Rails? Ruby on Rails is a powerful development framework for database-centric web-based applications. It is popular for open source product development; for example, *Foreman*, one of the core components of Red Hat's Satellite 6.x product, is also a Rails application.

Projects, Products, and Some History

Red Hat is an open source company, and its *products* are derived from one or more "upstream" open source *projects*. In the case of CloudForms, the upstream project is ManageIQ. [2]

ManageIQ (the Project)

The ManageIQ project releases a new version every six months (approximately). Each version is named alphabetically after a chess Grand Master, and so far these have been Anand, Botvinnik, and Capablanca. At the time of writing, Capablanca is the current release.

Red Hat CloudForms (the Product)

Red Hat CloudForms 1.0 was originally a suite of products comprising CloudForms System Engine, CloudForms Cloud Engine, and CloudForms Config Server, each with its own upstream project.

When Red Hat acquired ManageIQ (a privately held company) in late 2012, it decided to discontinue development of the original CloudForms 1.0 projects[3] and base a new version, CloudForms 2.0, on the much more capable and mature ManageIQ Enterprise Virtualization Manager (EVM) 5.x product. EVM 5.1 was rebranded as CloudForms Management Engine 5.1.

It took Red Hat approximately 18 months from the time of the ManageIQ acquisition to make the source code ready to publish as an open source project. Once completed, the ManageIQ project was formed, and development was started on the Anand release.

CloudForms Management Engine (the Appliance)

CloudForms Management Engine is the name of the CloudForms virtual appliance that we download from redhat.com. The most recent versions of CloudForms Management Engine have been based on corresponding ManageIQ project releases. The relative versions and releases are summarized in Table 1-1.

---

2 The ManageIQ home is at *http://manageiq.org/*.

3 CloudForms System Engine didn't completely disappear. It was based on the upstream *Katello* project, which now forms a core part of Red Hat's Satellite 6.x product.

Table 1-1. Summary of the relative project and product versions

ManageIQ project release	CloudForms Management Engine version	CloudForms version
	5.1	2.0
	5.2	3.0
Anand	5.3	3.1
Botvinnik	5.4	3.2
Capablanca	5.5	4.0

Summary

This chapter has introduced CloudForms at a fairly high level but has hopefully established a product context. The remainder of the book focuses specifically on the Automate functionality of CloudForms. Let's roll up our sleeves and get started!

Further Reading

Red Hat CloudForms (*http://red.ht/1XcHYK2*)

A Technical Overview of Red Hat Cloud Infrastructure (RHCI) (*http://bit.ly/1YgGKwY*)

The Forrester Wave™: Hybrid Cloud Management Solutions, Q1 2016 (*http://bit.ly/22WpTQx*)

ManageIQ Architecture Guides—Provider Overview (*http://bit.ly/1PMCq6Z*)

## CHAPTER 2

Introduction to the Automate Datastore

When we use the Automate capability of CloudForms, we write scripts in the Ruby language and use objects that the CloudForms Automation Engine makes available to us. The CloudForms Web User Interface (WebUI) allows us to access the Automate functionality via the Automate top-level menu (see Figure 2-1).

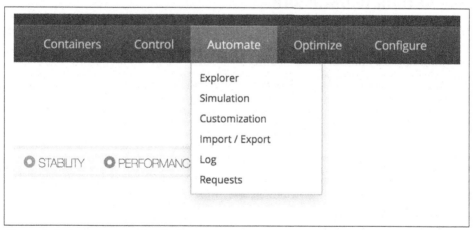

Figure 2-1. Automate top-level menu

The Automate Explorer

The first menu item that we see takes us to the *Explorer*. This is our visual interface into the Automate Datastore, and it contains the various kinds of Automate objects that we'll use throughout this book (see Figure 2-2).

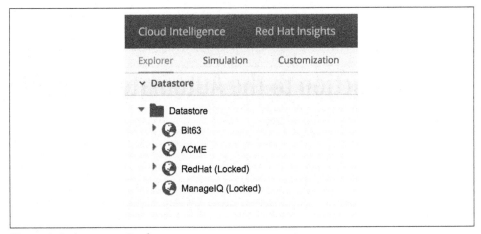

Figure 2-2. Automate Explorer

Before we start our journey into learning CloudForms Automate, we'll take a tour of the Automate Datastore to familiarize ourselves with the objects that we'll find there.

The Automate Datastore

The Automate Datastore has a directory-like structure, consisting of several types of organizational units arranged in a hierarchy (see Figure 2-3).

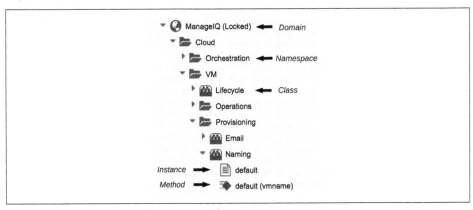

Figure 2-3. Automate Datastore icon styles

Next, we'll look at each type of object in more detail.

Domains

A *domain* is a collection of namespaces, classes, instances, and methods. The ManageIQ project provides a single *ManageIQ* domain for all supplied automation code, while Red Hat adds the supplemental *RedHat* domain containing added-value code for the CloudForms product. Both the *ManageIQ* and *RedHat* domains are locked, indicating their read-only nature, but we can create new domains for our own custom automation code. Figure 2-2 shows the two default domains and two custom domains: *Bit63* and *ACME*.

Organizing our own code into custom domains greatly simplifies the task of exporting and importing code (simplifying code portability and reuse). It also leaves ManageIQ or Red Hat free to update the locked domains through minor releases without fear of overwriting our customizations.

Domain Priority

User-added domains can be individually enabled or disabled and can be ordered by priority such that if code exists in the same path in multiple domains (for example, /*Cloud/VM/Provisioning/StateMachines*), the code in the highest-priority enabled domain will be executed. We can change the priority order of our user-added domains using the Configuration → Edit Priority Order of Domains menu (see Figure 2-4).

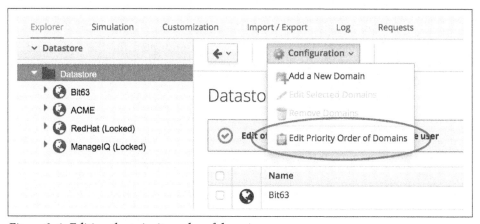

Figure 2-4. Editing the priority order of domains

Importing/Exporting Domains

We can export domains using rake from the command line and import them either using rake or from the WebUI. (Using rake enables us to specify more import and export options.) A typical rake import line is as follows:

```
bin/rake evm:automate:import YAML_FILE=bit63.yaml IMPORT_AS=Bit63 SYSTEM=false \
ENABLED=true DOMAIN=Export PREVIEW=false
```

Copying Objects Between Domains

We frequently need to customize code in the locked RedHat or ManageIQ domains—for example, when implementing our own custom VM placement method. Fortunately, we can easily copy any object from the locked domains into our own, using Configuration → Copy this (see Figure 2-5).

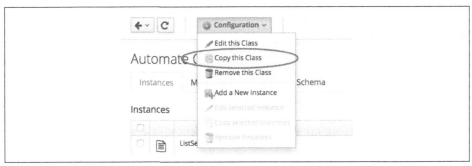

Figure 2-5. Copying a class

When we copy an object such as a class, we are prompted for the From and To domains. We can optionally deselect "Copy to same path" and specify our own destination path for the object (see Figure 2-6).

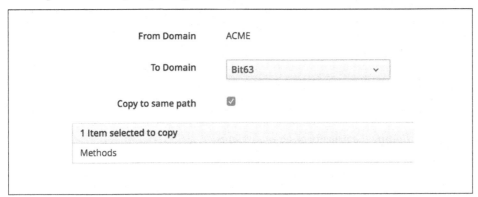

Figure 2-6. Specifying the destination domain and path

Importing Old Format Exports

Domains were a new feature of the Automate Datastore in CloudForms 3.1. Prior to this release, all factory-supplied and user-created automation code was contained in a common structure, which made updates difficult when any user-added code was introduced (the user-supplied modifications needed exporting and reimporting/merging whenever an automation update was released).

To import a Datastore backup from a CloudForms 3.0 and prior format Datastore, we must convert it to the new Datastore format first, like so:

```
cd /var/www/miq/vmdb
bin/rake evm:automate:convert FILE=database.xml DOMAIN=SAMPLE \
ZIP_FILE=/tmp/sample_converted.zip
```

Namespaces

A *namespace* is a folder-like container for classes, instances, and methods, and is used purely for organizational purposes. We create namespaces to arrange our code logically, and namespaces often contain other namespaces (see Figure 2-7).

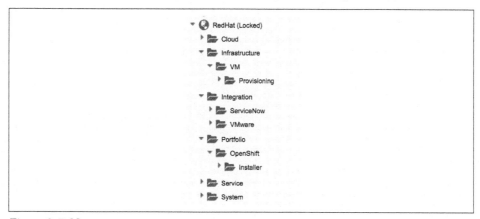

Figure 2-7. Namespaces

Classes

A *class* is similar to a template: it contains a generic definition for a set of automation operations. Each class has a *schema* that defines the variables, states, relationships, or methods that instances of the class will use.

The Automate Datastore uses object-oriented terminology for these objects. A *class* is a generic definition for a set of automation operations, and these classes are *instantiated* as specific instances. The classes that we work with in the Automate Datastore are not the same as Ruby classes that we work with in our automation scripts.

Schemas

A *schema* is made up of a number of elements, or *fields*, that describe the properties of the class. A schema often has just one entry—to run a single method—but in many cases it has several components. Figure 2-8 shows the schema for a *placement* class, which has several different field types.

Fields	
Name	**Value**
placement	${/#miq_provision.placement_auto}
vm	
host	
storage	
storage_max_vms	
storage_max_pct_used	
redhat	redhat_best_fit_cluster
vmware	vmware_best_fit_least_utilized
microsoft	microsoft_best_fit_least_utilized

Figure 2-8. A more complex schema

Adding or Editing a Schema

We add or edit each schema field in the schema editor by specifying the *field type* from a drop-down list (see Figure 2-9).

Figure 2-9. Schema field type

Each field type has an associated *data type*, which is also selectable from a drop-down list (see Figure 2-10).

Figure 2-10. Schema field data type

We can define default values for fields in a class schema. These will be inherited by all instances created from the class but can be optionally overridden in the schema of any particular instance.

Relationships

One of the schema field types is a *relationship*, which links to other instances elsewhere in the Automate Datastore. We often use relationships as a way of chaining instances together, and relationship values can accept variable substitutions for flexibility (see Figure 2-11).

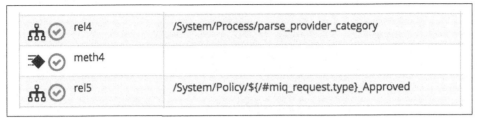

	rel4	/System/Process/parse_provider_category
	meth4	
	rel5	/System/Policy/${/#miq_request.type}_Approved

Figure 2-11. Relationship fields showing variable substitutions

Instances

An *instance* is a specific *instantiation* or "clone" of the generic class and is the entity run by the Automation Engine. An instance contains a copy of the class schema but with actual values of the fields filled in (see Figure 2-12).

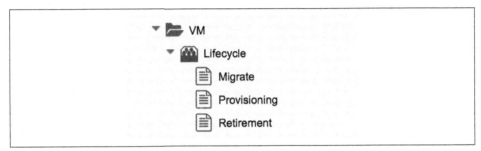

Figure 2-12. Single class definition with three instances

Methods

A *method* is a self-contained block of Ruby code that gets executed when we run any automation operation. A typical method looks like this:

```
#
# Description: This method checks to see if the VM has been powered off or
# suspended
#

# Get vm from root object
vm = $evm.root['vm']

if vm
  power_state = vm.attributes['power_state']
  ems = vm.ext_management_system
  $evm.log('info', "VM:<#{vm.name}> on provider:<#{ems.try(:name)} has Power \
          State:<#{power_state}>")

  # If VM is powered off or suspended exit
```

```
if %w(off suspended).include?(power_state)
  # Bump State
  $evm.root['ae_result']          = 'ok'
elsif power_state == "never"
  # If never then this VM is a template so exit the retirement state machine
  $evm.root['ae_result']          = 'error'
else
  $evm.root['ae_result']          = 'retry'
  $evm.root['ae_retry_interval'] = '60.seconds'
end
end
```

Methods can have one of three *location* values: *inline*, *built-in*, or *URI*. In practice most of the methods that we create are inline methods, which means they run as a separate Ruby process outside of Rails.

Summary

In this chapter we've learned about the fundamental objects or organizational units that we work with in the Automate Datastore: domains, namespaces, classes, instances, and methods.

We are now ready to use this information to write our first automation script.

Further Reading

Scripting Actions in CloudForms, Chapter 2—Automate Model (*http://red.ht/1YekXFN*)

CloudForms 3.1 Exporting Automate Domains (*https://access.redhat.com/solutions/1225313*)

CloudForms 3.1 Importing Automate Domains (*https://access.redhat.com/solutions/1225383*)

CloudForms 3.1 Automate Model Conversion (*https://access.redhat.com/solutions/1225413*)

## CHAPTER 3

Writing and Running Our Own Automation Scripts

Let's jump right in and start writing our first automation script. In time-honored fashion we'll write "Hello, World!" to the Automate Engine logfile.

Before we do anything, we need to ensure that the Automation Engine server role is selected on our CloudForms appliance. We do this from the Configure → Configuration menu, selecting the CloudForms server in the Settings accordion (see Figure 3-1).

The Automation Engine server role is now enabled by default in CloudForms 4.0, but it's still worthwhile to check that this role is set on our CloudForms appliance.

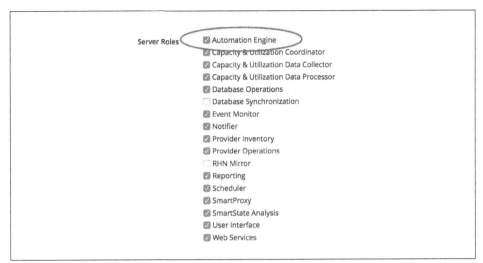

Figure 3-1. Setting the Automation Engine server role

The Automation Engine Role

Setting the Automation Engine role is necessary to be able to run *queued* Automate tasks (this includes anything that starts off as an automation *request*, which we'll cover in Chapter 12). Automate actions initiated directly from the WebUI—such as running instances from Simulation, or processing methods to populate dynamic dialogs—are run on the WebUI appliance itself, regardless of whether it has the Automation Engine role enabled.

Our first Automate examples in the book will be run from Simulation, so we don't need the Automation Engine role to be set for these to work. When we move on to more advanced ways of running our scripts, however, we will need the role enabled, so by checking that it's set now, we'll have one less thing to troubleshoot as we progress through the book.

Creating the Environment

Before we create our first automation script, we need to put some things in place. We'll begin by adding a new domain called *ACME*. We'll add all of our automation code into this new domain.

Adding a New Domain

In the Automate Explorer, highlight the Datastore icon in the sidebar, and click Configuration → Add a New Domain (see Figure 3-2).

Figure 3-2. Adding a new domain

We'll give the domain the name **ACME**, give it the description **ACME Corp.**, and ensure that the Enabled checkbox is selected.

Adding a Namespace

Now we'll add a namespace into this domain, called *General*. Highlight the *ACME* domain icon in the sidebar, and click Configuration → Add a New Namespace (see Figure 3-3).

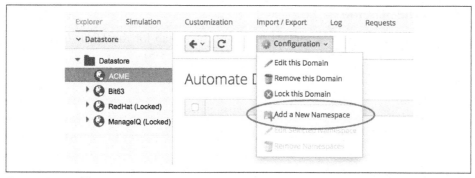

Figure 3-3. Adding a new namespace

Give the namespace the name **General** and the description **General Content**.

Adding a Class

Now we'll add a new class, called *Methods*.

> Naming a class Methods may seem somewhat confusing, but many of the generic classes in the ManageIQ and RedHat domains in the Automate Datastore are called Methods to signify their general-purpose nature.

Highlight the *General* domain icon in the sidebar, and click Configuration → Add a New Class (see Figure 3-4).

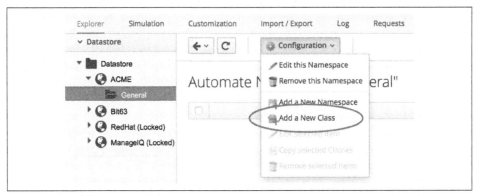

Figure 3-4. Adding a new class

Give the class the name **Methods** and the description **General Instances and Meth ods**. We'll leave the display name empty for this example.

Editing the Schema

Now we'll create a simple schema. Click the Schema tab for the *Methods* class, and click Configuration → Edit selected Schema (see Figure 3-5).

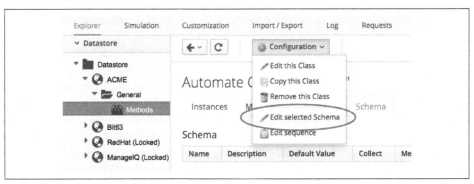

Figure 3-5. Editing the schema

Click New Field, and add a single field with name **execute**, type **Method**, and data type **String** (see Figure 3-6).

Figure 3-6. Adding a new schema field

Click the checkmark in the lefthand column to save the field entry, and click the Save button to save the schema. We now have our generic class definition called *Methods* set up, with a simple schema that executes a single method.

Hello, World!

Our first Automate method is very simple; we'll write an entry to the *automation.log* file using this two-line script:

```
$evm.log(:info, "Hello, World!")
exit MIQ_OK
```

Adding a New Instance

First we need to create an instance from our class. In the Instances tab of the new *Methods* class, select Configuration → Add a New Instance (see Figure 3-7).

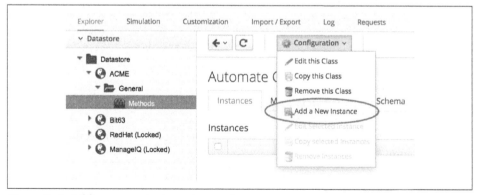

Figure 3-7. Adding a new instance to our class

We'll call the instance **HelloWorld**, and it'll run (execute) a method called *hello_world* (see Figure 3-8).

Figure 3-8. Entering the instance details

Click the Add button.

Adding a New Method

In the Methods tab of the new *Methods* class, select Configuration → Add a New Method (see Figure 3-9).

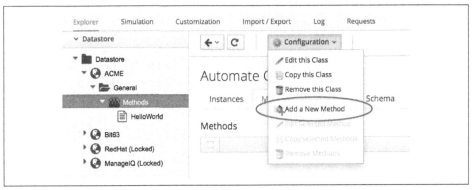

Figure 3-9. Adding a new method to our class

Name the method **hello_world**, and paste our two lines of code into the Data window (see Figure 3-10).

Figure 3-10. Entering the method details

Click Validate and then Add.

Get into the habit of using the Validate button; it can save you a lot of time catching Ruby syntactical typos when you develop more complex scripts.

Running the Instance

We'll run our new instance using the *Simulation* functionality of Automate, but before we do that, log in to CloudForms again from another browser or a private browsing tab, and navigate to Automate → Log in the WebUI.[1]

The CloudForms WebUI uses browser session cookies, so if we want two or more concurrent login sessions (particularly as different users), it helps to use different web browsers or private/incognito windows.

In the simulation, we actually run an instance called *Call_Instance* in the */System/ Request/* namespace of the *ManageIQ* domain, and this in turn calls our *HelloWorld* instance using the namespace, class, and instance attribute/value pairs that we pass to it (see Chapter 11).

From the Automate → Simulation menu, complete the details (see Figure 3-11).

---

1 Alternatively, `ssh` into the CloudForms appliance as *root* and enter `tail -f /var/www/miq/vmdb/log/automa` `tion.log`.

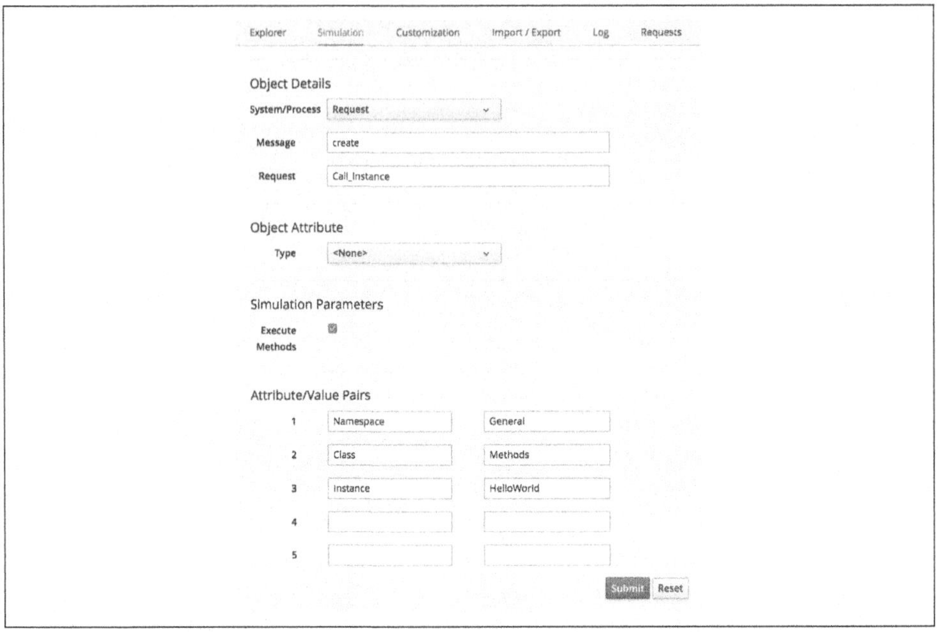

Figure 3-11. Completing the Simulation details

Click Submit.

If all went well, we should see our "Hello, World!" message appear in the *automation.log* file:

```
Invoking [inline] method [/ACME/General/Methods/hello_world] with inputs [{}]
<AEMethod [/ACME/General/Methods/hello_world]> Starting
<AEMethod hello_world> Hello, World!
<AEMethod [/ACME/General/Methods/hello_world]> Ending
Method exited with rc=MIQ_OK
```

Success!

Exit Status Codes

In our example we used an exit status code of MIQ_OK. Although with simple methods such as this we don't strictly need to specify an exit code, it's good practice to do so. When we build more advanced multimethod classes and state machines, an exit code can signal an error condition to the Automation Engine so that action can be taken.

There are four exit codes that we can use:

`MIQ_OK (0)`

> Continues normal processing. This is logged to *automation.log* as:

```
Method exited with rc=MIQ_OK
```

`MIQ_WARN(4)`

> Warning message, continues processing. This is logged to *automation.log* as:

```
Method exited with rc=MIQ_WARN
```

`MIQ_ERROR / MIQ_STOP (8)`

> Stops processing current object. This is logged to *automation.log* as:

```
Stopping instantiation because [Method exited with rc=MIQ_STOP]
```

`MIQ_ABORT (16)`

> Aborts entire automation instantiation. This is logged to *automation.log* as:

```
Aborting instantiation because [Method exited with rc=MIQ_ABORT]
```

The difference between `MIQ_STOP` and `MIQ_ABORT` is subtle but comes into play as we develop more advanced Automate workflows.

`MIQ_STOP` stops the currently running instance, but if this instance was called via a reference from another "parent" instance, the subsequent steps in the parent instance would still complete.

`MIQ_ABORT` stops the currently running instance and any parent instance that called it, thereby terminating the Automate task altogether.

Summary

In this chapter we've seen how simple it is to create our own domain, namespace, class, instance, and method, and run our script from Simulation. These are the fundamental techniques that we use for all of our automation scripts, and we'll use this knowledge extensively as we progress through the book.

We've also discovered the status codes that we should use to pass our exit status back to the Automation Engine.

## CHAPTER 4

Using Schema Variables

Our simple *HelloWorld* instance in the previous chapter had a very simple schema, containing a single field that ran a simple self-contained method. As we become more adventurous with Automate, we'll find that the schema can be used to associate variables or *attributes* with an instance. Any Automate method run by the instance can read these instance attributes, allowing us to define variables or constants outside of our Ruby scripts. This simplifies maintenance and promotes code reuse. Methods can also write to these instance attributes, allowing a degree of data sharing between multiple methods that might be run in sequence from the same instance.

In our next Automate example, we'll add some attribute fields to our class schema, set values for those attributes in our instance, and read them from our method.

Preparing the Schema

Let's edit the schema of the *Methods* class (see Figure 4-1).

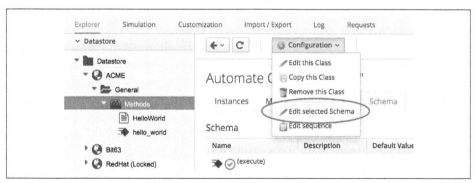

Figure 4-1. Editing the schema of the Methods class

We'll add three attributes: `servername`, `username`, and `password`. The `servername` and `username` attributes will be simple text strings, but the `password` attribute will have a data type of `Password`, meaning it will be stored in an encrypted form in the database (see Figure 4-2).

Figure 4-2. Adding attributes

Click Save.

We need to ensure that the schema method (our **execute** field) is listed *after* the three new schema attributes in the field list; otherwise, the attributes won't be visible to the method when it runs. If necessary, run Configuration → Edit sequence to shuffle the schema fields up or down (see Figure 4-3).

Figure 4-3. Editing a class schema sequence

The Instance

Now we'll create a new instance in our *Methods* class as before, but this time called *GetCredentials*. We'll also fill in some values for the `servername`, `username`, and `pass word` schema attributes (see Figure 4-4).

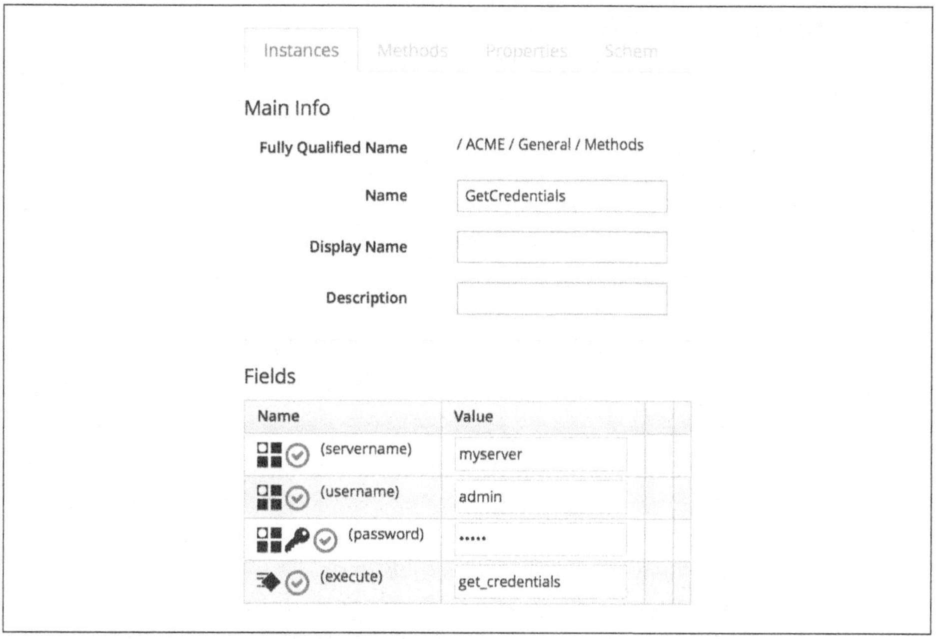

Figure 4-4. Entering the instance schema field details

Notice that our `password` schema value has been obfuscated.

The Method

Each of the schema attributes will be available to our method as hash key/value pairs from `$evm.object`, which is the Automate object representing our currently running instance.

Our code for this example will be as follows:

```
$evm.log(:info, "get_credentials started")

servername = $evm.object['servername']
username   = $evm.object['username']
password   = $evm.object.decrypt('password')

$evm.log(:info, "Server: #{servername}, Username: #{username}, Password: \
#{password}")
exit MIQ_OK
```

We'll create a method in our *Methods* class as we did before, but this time called *get_credentials*. We'll add our code to the Data box, click Validate, and then click Save.

Running the Instance

Finally, we'll run the new instance through Automate → Simulation again, invoking *Call_Instance* once more with the appropriate attribute/value pairs (see Figure 4-5).

Attribute/Value Pairs

1	Namespace	General
2	Class	Methods
3	Instance	GetCredentials
4		
5		

Submit Reset

Figure 4-5. Argument name/value pairs for Call_Instance

We check *automation.log* and see that the attributes have been retrieved from the instance schema and the password has been decrypted:

```
Invoking [inline] method [/ACME/General/Methods/get_credentials] with inputs [{}]
<AEMethod [/ACME/General/Methods/get_credentials]> Starting
<AEMethod get_credentials> get_credentials started
<AEMethod get_credentials> Server: myserver, Username: admin, Password: guess
<AEMethod [/ACME/General/Methods/get_credentials]> Ending
Method exited with rc=MIQ_OK
```

 The password value is encrypted using the v2_key created when the CloudForms database is initialised and is unique to that Cloud-Forms region. If we export an Automate Datastore containing encrypted passwords and import it into a different CloudForms region, we won't be able to decrypt the password.

Summary

In this chapter we've seen how we can store instance variables called *attributes* in our schema and that they can be accessed by the methods run from that instance.

Using class or instance schema variables like this is very common. One example is when we use CloudForms to provision virtual machines. The out-of-the-box virtual machine provisioning workflow includes an approval stage (see Chapter 18) that allows us to define a default for the number of VMs and their sizes (CPUs and memory), which can be autoprovisioned without administrative approval. The max_vms, `max_cpus`, and `max_memory` values used at this workflow stage are stored as schema attributes in the approval instance and are therefore available to us to easily customize without changing any Ruby code.

When writing our own integration methods, we often need to specify a valid username and password to connect to other systems outside of CloudForms—for example, if we're making a SOAP call to a hardware load balancer (see Chapter 44 for an example). We can use the technique shown in this example to securely store and retrieve credentials to connect to anything else in our enterprise.

## CHAPTER 5

Working with Virtual Machines

Our two Automate examples so far have been slightly abstract, but in this chapter we'll work with a real virtual machine. Our script will find and use the Automation Engine object representing the virtual machine, and we'll call one of the object's methods. Rather than running our script from Simulation as we have up to now, we'll customize the WebUI display for our virtual machine and add a new toolbar button to run our script.

Custom Attributes

CloudForms naturally collects a large amount of data about each virtual machine or instance that it manages and displays this in the WebUI. We can examine such attributes as IP address, operating system, CPU count, or disk configuration, for example, but sometimes it is useful to be able to add our own comments or notes to the virtual machine. CloudForms allows us to do this in the form of *custom attributes*, which have two parts: a name (sometimes called the *key*) and a text string value (see Figure 5-1).

Custom Attributes	
CMDB CI	1344782-RH6-21
Configuration Status	Configured, last Puppet run 16:30 03-06-16
Project Owner	imogen.irving@bit63.com

Figure 5-1. Example custom attributes

Custom attributes are a useful way to store any related free-text information with an object, particularly a virtual machine. We might store a CMDB configuration item ID, for example, or perhaps some text describing the configuration status. Virtual machine custom attributes are visible in the WebUI and readable from an automation script.

In this example we'll create an Automate method that adds a custom attribute to a virtual machine. The attribute will be visible to any user who clicks on the virtual machine details in the WebUI.

We'll launch the Automate instance from a custom button that we'll add to the toolbar in the virtual machine details web frame, and we'll include a dialog to prompt for the text to add to the custom attribute.

Creating the Service Dialog

The first thing we must do is create the *service dialog* to be displayed when our custom button is clicked. Creating a service dialog is a multistage process, involving the addition of tabs, boxes, and dialog elements such as text boxes, radio buttons, or drop-down lists.

Navigate to Automate → Customization, and select Service Dialogs in the accordion. Highlight All Dialogs, then select Configuration → Add a new Dialog (don't click the Add button yet). See Figure 5-2.

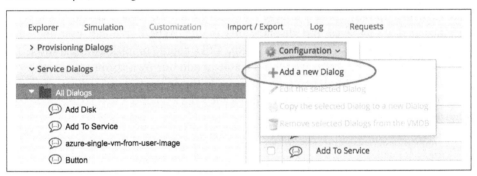

Figure 5-2. Adding a new service dialog

Enter **Button** for the dialog information label and description, select the Submit and Cancel options, and click + → Add a new Tab to this Dialog (don't click the Add button yet). See Figure 5-3.

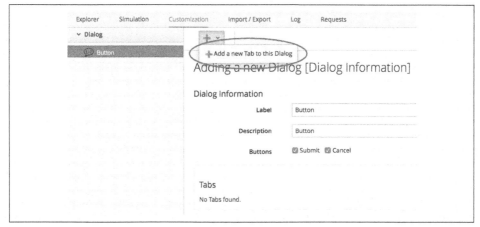

Figure 5-3. Adding a new tab to the dialog

Enter **Main** for the tab information label and description, and click + → Add a new Box to this Tab (don't click the Add button yet). Notice how the shape of the dialog dynamically builds in the lefthand accordion pane (see Figure 5-4).

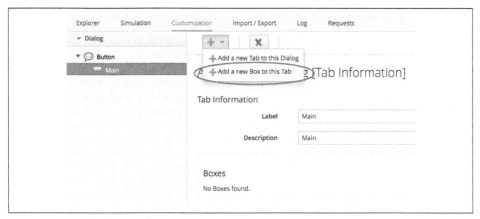

Figure 5-4. Adding a new box to the tab

Enter **Custom Attribute** for the box information label and description, and click + → Add a new Element to this Box (don't click the Add button yet). The dialog continues to take shape in the accordion (see Figure 5-5).

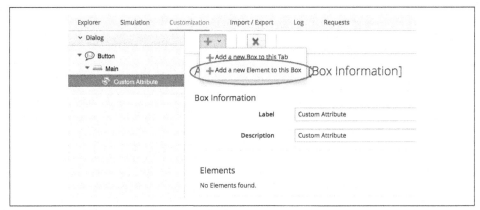

Figure 5-5. Adding a new element to the box

We'll give the first element the label of **Key**, the name of **key**, and a type of Text Box. Leave the other values as the default (don't click the Add button yet). The Key attribute appears in the accordion as soon as we add the element name (see Figure 5-6).

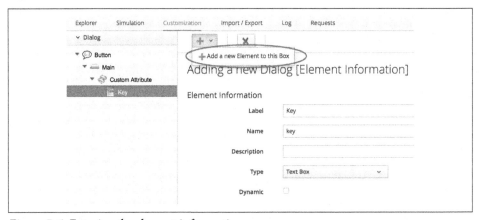

Figure 5-6. Entering the element information

Click + → Add a new Element to this Box to create a second element. We'll give the second element the label of **Value**, the name of **value**, and a type of Text Box. Leave the other values as the default, and now, finally, click the Add button. The completed dialog is saved and displayed (see Figure 5-7).

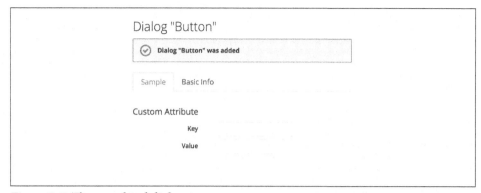

Figure 5-7. The completed dialog

Creating the Instance and Method

We create a new instance in our *Methods* class just as we did before, called `AddCusto
mAttribute`. We leave the password, servername, and username schema fields blank
but add the value **add_custom_attribute** in the execute field.

> As we see here, defining attributes in our class schema doesn't
> mean that we have to use them in every instance created from the
> class. We can create generic class schemas that contain a number of
> attributes that the instances may need to use.

The Code

Values entered into a dialog box are available to our method through `$evm.root`. The
Automation Engine prefixes the dialog element names with `dialog_`, so the values
that we want to read are `$evm.root['dialog_key']` and `$evm.root['dia
log_value']`.

Our code for this example will be as follows:

```
$evm.log(:info, "add_custom_attribute started")
#
# Get the VM object
#
vm = $evm.root['vm']
#
# Get the dialog values
#
key   = $evm.root['dialog_key']
value = $evm.root['dialog_value']
#
# Set the custom attribute
#
vm.custom_set(key, value)
exit MIQ_OK
```

We create a new method in our *Methods* class as we did before and call it *add_custom_attribute*. We paste the code into the Data box, click Validate, and then click Save.

Creating the /System Entry Point

To illustrate an alternative way of calling an instance, we're going to be creating our own entry point directly in the */System/* namespace, rather than redirecting through *Call_Instance* as before.[1]

First we must copy the *ManageIQ/System/Request* class into our own domain (see Figure 5-8).

---

1 Most automation operations enter the Automate Datastore at */System/Request*. *Call_Instance* is already there as a "convenience" instance that we can call with arguments to redirect straight to our own instance, which is why we've used that up to now. There are occasions, however, when we need to create our own entry point directly in */System/Request*, so this example illustrates how we do that.

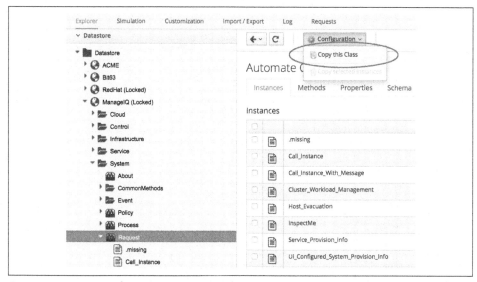

Figure 5-8. Copying the /System/Request class

Copy the class into the *ACME* domain, and ensure that "Copy to same path" is selected.

Now we have to create a new instance of the class (see Figure 5-9).

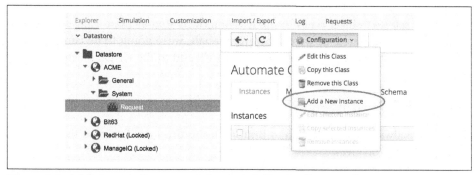

Figure 5-9. Adding a new instance to the copied /System/Request class

For the new instance, enter the name **AddCustomAttribute**, and then enter **/General/Methods/AddCustomAttribute** into the rel1 field (see Figure 5-10).

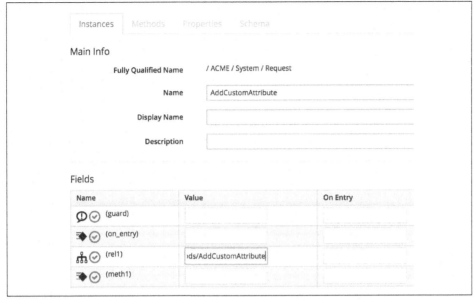

Figure 5-10. Setting the new instance name and rel1 field

Running Automation Scripts from a Button

CloudForms allows us to extend the WebUI functionality by adding our own custom buttons to selected object types in the user interface. Rather than using the Simulation feature of Automate as we did before, though, we're going to be launching this automation script from a custom button that we'll add to the virtual machine display object.

Creating the Button Group

Buttons are always displayed from a Button Group drop-down list, so first we must create a new button group.

Navigate to Automate → Customization, and select Buttons in the accordion. Now highlight Object Types → VM and Instance, then select Configuration → Add a new Button Group (see Figure 5-11).

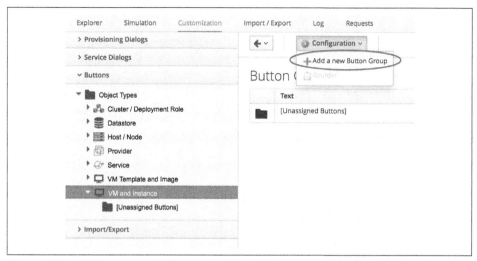

Figure 5-11. Adding a new button group

Set the Button Group Text and Button Group Hover Text to be `VM Operations`. Select a suitable Button Group Image from the available drop-down list, and click the Add button to create the button group.

Creating the Button

Now that we have our button group, we can add a button to it to call our script.

Highlight the new VM Operations button group in the accordion, and select Configuration → Add a new Button (see Figure 5-12).

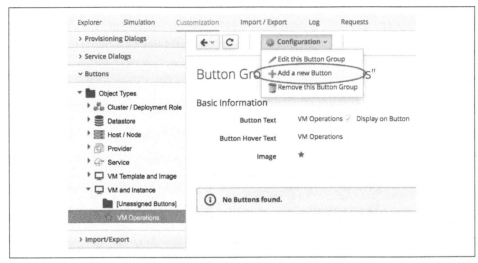

Figure 5-12. Adding a new button to the button group

Set the Button Text and Button Hover Text to **Add Custom Attribute**. Select a suitable Button Image from the available drop-down list, and pick our new Button dialog from the Dialog drop-down list. In the Object Details section we'll select the new / *System/Request* instance that we created called **AddCustomAttribute** (see Figure 5-13).

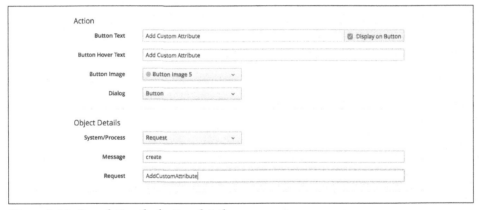

Figure 5-13. Completing the button details

Running the Instance

If we navigate to a virtual machine in the WebUI and examine its details, we should see our new VM Operations button group displayed in the toolbar. If we click the Button Group icon, we should see the button displayed as a drop-down (see Figure 5-14).

Figure 5-14. The new button group and button added to the toolbar

If we click on the Add Custom Attribute button, we should be presented with our dialog (see Figure 5-15).

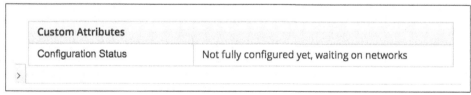

Figure 5-15. Completing the service dialog

Enter some text, click Submit, and wait a few seconds. We should see the new custom attribute displayed at the botton of the VM details pane (see Figure 5-16).

Custom Attributes	
Configuration Status	Not fully configured yet, waiting on networks

Figure 5-16. The newly added custom attribute

Summary

In this chapter we've learned several new useful skills. In our automation script we've seen how to work with the Automation Engine object representing a virtual machine. We've extended the WebUI functionality by creating a custom button, and we've added a service dialog to prompt our user for input. To top it off we've discovered the utility of custom attributes. Good work!

This has been a useful introduction to "real world" automation. Adding a custom button in this way to run a short automation script is fairly common in production environments. We would typically use a custom button to start a virtual machine backup, add a disk, reconfigure the number of CPUs, or extend memory, for example.

We can add buttons to the WebUI display toolbars for clusters, datastores, hosts, and providers, but we most frequently add them to virtual machines as we have in this chapter, and to services (which we cover in Part III).

Further Reading

ManageIQ: Using Custom Attributes (*https://access.redhat.com/articles/311753*)

## CHAPTER 6

Peeping Under the Hood

We've now worked with an Automation Engine object that represents a virtual machine, and we've called one of its methods to add a custom attribute to the VM.

In this chapter we'll take a deeper look at these Automation Engine objects and at some of the technology that exists behind the scenes in Rails when we run automation scripts. It is useful background information but can be skipped on first read if required.

A Little Rails Knowledge (Goes a Long Way)

Firstly, by way of reassurance…

> We do not need to know Ruby on Rails to write CloudForms Automation scripts.

It can, however, be useful to have an appreciation of Rails *models*, and how the Automation Engine encapsulates these as Ruby objects that we can program with. The objects represent the things that we are typically interested in when we write automation code, such as VMs, clusters, guest applications, or even provisioning requests.

Plain Old Ruby

The Ruby scripts that we write are just plain Ruby 2.2, although the Active Support core extensions to Ruby are available if we wish to use them.

The Active Support extensions can make our lives easier. For example, rather than adding math to our Automation script to work out the number of seconds in a two-month time span (perhaps to specify a VM retirement period), we can just specify `2.months`.

Our automation scripts access Ruby objects, made available to us by the Automation Engine via the $evm variable ($evm is described in more detail in Chapter 7). Behind the scenes these are Rails objects, which is why having some understanding of Rails can help our investigation into how we can use these objects to our maximum benefit.

Model-View-Controller

Rails is a model-view-controller (MVC) application (see Figure 6-1).[1]

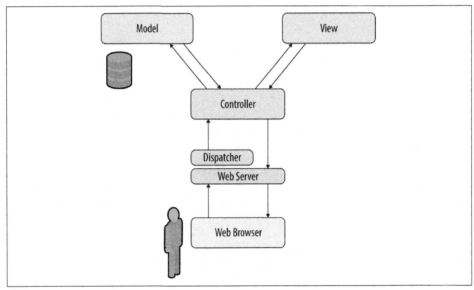

Figure 6-1. An MVC application

The *model* is a representation of the underlying logical structure of data from the database (which in the case of CloudForms is PostgreSQL). When writing automation scripts, we work with models extensively (although we may not necessarily realize it).

Rails models are called *active records*. They always have a singular *CamelCase* name (e.g., GuestApplication), and their corresponding database tables have a plural *snake_case* name (e.g., guest_applications).

Active Record Associations

Active record *associations* link the models together in one-to-many or one-to-one relationships that allow us to traverse objects.

---

1 See also Ruby on Rails/Getting Started/Model-View-Controller (*http://bit.ly/1TZftd8*).

We can illustrate this by looking at some of the Rails code that defines the *host* (i.e., hypervisor) active record:

```
class Host < ActiveRecord::Base
  ...
  belongs_to             :ext_management_system, :foreign_key => "ems_id"
  belongs_to             :ems_cluster
  has_one                :operating_system, :dependent => :destroy
  has_one                :hardware, :dependent => :destroy
  has_many               :vms_and_templates, :dependent => :nullify
  has_many               :vms
  ...
```

We see that there are several associations from a host object, including to the cluster of which it's a member, and to the virtual machines that run on that host.

Although these associations are defined in Rails, they are available to us when we work with the corresponding *service model* objects from the Automation Engine (see "Service Models" on page 54).

Rails Helper Methods (.find_by_*)

Rails does a lot of things to make our lives easier, including dynamically creating *helper methods*. The most useful ones to us as CloudForms automation scripters are the find_by_*columnname* methods:

```
owner = $evm.vmdb('user').find_by_id(ownerid.to_i)
vm = $evm.vmdb('vm').find_by_name(vm_name)
```

We can .find_by_ any column name in a database table. For example, in PostgreSQL we can look at the services table that represents services created via a service catalog:

```
vmdb_production=# \d services
                                Table "public.services"
        Column         |          Type          |         Modifiers
-----------------------+------------------------+---------------------------
 id                    | bigint                 | not null default nextva...
 name                  | character varying(255) |
 description           | character varying(255) |
 guid                  | character varying(255) |
 type                  | character varying(255) |
 service_template_id   | bigint                 |
 options               | text                   |
 display               | boolean                |
 ...
```

We see that there is a description column, so if we wanted we could call:

```
$evm.vmdb('service').find_by_description('My New Service')
```

Don't try searching the CloudForms sources for def find_by_description; these are not statically defined methods and so don't exist in the CloudForms code. In a future version of CloudForms they will be deprecated in favor of a more current Rails-like syntax using where—for example:

```
$evm.vmdb('service').where(:description =>'My New Service')
```

Service Models

We saw earlier that Rails data models are called active records. We can't access these directly from an automation script, but fortunately most of the useful ones are made available to us as Automation Engine service model objects.

The objects that we work with in the Automation Engine are all service models—instances of an MiqAeService class that abstract and make available to us their corresponding Rails active record.

For example, if we're working with a *user* object (representing a person, such as the owner of a virtual machine), we might access that object in our script via $evm.root['user']. This is actually an instance of an MiqAeServiceUser class, which represents the corresponding Rails user active record. There are service model objects representing all of the things that we need to work with when we write automation scripts. These include the traditional components in our infrastructure, such as virtual machines, hypervisor clusters, operating systems, or Ethernet adapters, but also the intangible objects, such as provisioning requests or automation tasks.

All of the MiqAeService objects extend a common MiqAeServiceModelBase class that contains some common methods available to all objects (also see Chapter 9), such as:

```
.tagged_with?(category, name)
.tags(category = nil)
.tag_assign(tag)
```

Many of the service model objects have several levels of superclass—for example:

```
MiqAeServiceMiqProvisionRedhatViaPxe <
            MiqAeServiceMiqProvisionRedhat <
                        MiqAeServiceMiqProvision <
                                    MiqAeServiceMiqRequestTask <
                                                MiqAeServiceModelBase
```

The following list shows the class definition for some of the CloudForms 3.2 MiqAe Service model classes, showing their immediate superclass:

```
class MiqAeServiceAuthentication < MiqAeServiceModelBase
class MiqAeServiceAuthPrivateKey < MiqAeServiceAuthentication
class MiqAeServiceAuthKeyPairCloud < MiqAeServiceAuthPrivateKey
class MiqAeServiceAuthKeyPairOpenstack < MiqAeServiceAuthKeyPairCloud
...
```

```
class MiqAeServiceAutomationRequest < MiqAeServiceMiqRequest
class MiqAeServiceAutomationTask < MiqAeServiceMiqRequestTask
...
class MiqAeServiceAvailabilityZone < MiqAeServiceModelBase
class MiqAeServiceAvailabilityZoneAmazon < MiqAeServiceAvailabilityZone
class MiqAeServiceAvailabilityZoneOpenstack < MiqAeServiceAvailabilityZone
...
class MiqAeServiceHost < MiqAeServiceModelBase
class MiqAeServiceHostMicrosoft < MiqAeServiceHost
class MiqAeServiceHostOpenstackInfra < MiqAeServiceHost
class MiqAeServiceHostRedhat < MiqAeServiceHost
class MiqAeServiceHostVmware < MiqAeServiceHost
class MiqAeServiceHostVmwareEsx < MiqAeServiceHostVmware
...
class MiqAeServiceMiqProvision < MiqAeServiceMiqProvisionTask
class MiqAeServiceMiqProvisionAmazon < MiqAeServiceMiqProvisionCloud
class MiqAeServiceMiqProvisionCloud < MiqAeServiceMiqProvision
class MiqAeServiceMiqProvisionConfiguredSystemRequest < MiqAeServiceMiqRequest
class MiqAeServiceMiqProvisionMicrosoft < MiqAeServiceMiqProvision
class MiqAeServiceMiqProvisionOpenstack < MiqAeServiceMiqProvisionCloud
class MiqAeServiceMiqProvisionRedhat < MiqAeServiceMiqProvision
class MiqAeServiceMiqProvisionRedhatViaIso < MiqAeServiceMiqProvisionRedhat
class MiqAeServiceMiqProvisionRedhatViaPxe < MiqAeServiceMiqProvisionRedhat
class MiqAeServiceMiqProvisionRequest < MiqAeServiceMiqRequest
class MiqAeServiceMiqProvisionRequestTemplate < MiqAeServiceMiqProvisionRequest
class MiqAeServiceMiqProvisionTask < MiqAeServiceMiqRequestTask
...
class MiqAeServiceServiceTemplateProvisionTask < MiqAeServiceMiqRequestTask
...
class MiqAeServiceVmOrTemplate < MiqAeServiceModelBase
class MiqAeServiceVm < MiqAeServiceVmOrTemplate
class MiqAeServiceVmCloud < MiqAeServiceVm
class MiqAeServiceVmInfra < MiqAeServiceVm
class MiqAeServiceVmMicrosoft < MiqAeServiceVmInfra
class MiqAeServiceVmOpenstack < MiqAeServiceVmCloud
class MiqAeServiceVmAmazon < MiqAeServiceVmCloud
class MiqAeServiceVmRedhat < MiqAeServiceVmInfra
```

Service Model Object Properties

The service model objects that the Automation Engine makes available to us have four properties that we frequently work with: *attributes, virtual columns, associations,* and *methods*.

Attributes

Just like any other Ruby object, the service model objects that we work with have *attributes* that we often use. A service model object represents a record in a database table, and the object's attributes correspond to the columns in the table for that record.

For example, some attributes for a Red Hat Enterprise Virtualization (RHEV) host (i.e., hypervisor) object (`MiqAeServiceHostRedhat`), with typical values, are:

```
host.connection_state = connected
host.created_on = 2014-11-13 17:53:34 UTC
host.ems_cluster_id = 1000000000001
host.ems_id = 1000000000001
host.ems_ref = /api/hosts/b959325b-c667-4e3a-a52e-fd936c225a1a
host.ems_ref_obj = /api/hosts/b959325b-c667-4e3a-a52e-fd936c225a1a
host.guid = fcea82c8-6b5d-11e4-98ac-001a4aa01599
host.hostname = 192.168.1.224
host.hyperthreading = nil
host.id = 1000000000001
host.ipaddress = 192.168.1.224
host.last_perf_capture_on = 2015-06-05 10:25:46 UTC
host.name = rhelh03.bit63.net
host.power_state = on
host.settings = {:autoscan=>false, :inherit_mgt_tags=>false, :scan_frequency=>0}
host.smart = 1
host.type = HostRedhat
host.uid_ems = b959325b-c667-4e3a-a52e-fd936c225a1a
host.updated_on = 2015-06-05 10:43:00 UTC
host.vmm_product = rhel
host.vmm_vendor = RedHat
```

We can enumerate an object's attributes using:

```
this_object.attributes.each do |key, value|
```

Virtual Columns

In addition to the standard object attributes (which correspond to *real* database columns), Rails dynamically adds a number of virtual columns to many of the service models.

A *virtual column* is a computed database column that is not physically stored in the table. Virtual columns often contain more dynamic values than attributes, such as the number of VMs currently running on a hypervisor.

Some virtual columns for our same RHEV host object, with typical values, are:

```
host.authentication_status = Valid
host.derived_memory_used_avg_over_time_period = 790.1026640002773
host.derived_memory_used_high_over_time_period = 2586.493300608264
host.derived_memory_used_low_over_time_period = 0
host.os_image_name = linux_generic
host.platform = linux
host.ram_size = 15821
host.region_description = Region 1
```

```
host.region_number = 1
host.total_cores = 4
host.total_vcpus = 4
host.v_owning_cluster = Default
host.v_total_miq_templates = 0
host.v_total_storages = 3
host.v_total_vms = 7
```

We access these virtual columns just as we would access attributes, using *object.vir
tual_column_name* syntax. If we want to enumerate through all of an object's virtual
columns getting the corresponding values, we must use `.send`, specifying the virtual
column name, like so:

```
this_object.virtual_column_names.each do |virtual_column_name|
  virtual_column_value = this_object.send(virtual_column_name)
```

Associations

We saw earlier that there are associations between many of the active records (and
hence service models), and we use these extensively when scripting.

For example, we can discover more about the hardware of our virtual machine by following associations between the VM object (`MiqAeServiceVmRedhat`), and its hardware   and   guest   device   objects   (`MiqAeServiceHardware`   and
`MiqAeServiceGuestDevice`), as follows:

```
hardware = $evm.root['vm'].hardware
hardware.guest_devices.each do |guest_device|
  if guest_device.device_type == "ethernet"
    nic_name = guest_device.device_name
  end
end
```

Fortunately, we don't need to know anything about the active records or service models behind the scenes; we just magically follow the association. See Chapter 10 to find
out what associations there are to follow.

Continuing our exploration of our RHEV host object (`MiqAeServiceHostRedhat`),
the associations available to this object are:

```
host.datacenter
host.directories
host.ems_cluster
host.ems_events
host.ems_folder
host.ext_management_system
host.files
host.guest_applications
host.hardware
host.lans
host.operating_system
```

```
host.storages
host.switches
host.vms
```

We can enumerate an object's associations using:

```
this_object.associations.each do |association|
```

Methods

Most of the objects that we work with have useful methods defined that we can use, either in their own class or one of their parent superclasses. For example, the methods available to call for our RHEV host object (`MiqAeServiceHostRedhat`) are:

```
host.authentication_password
host.authentication_userid
host.credentials
host.current_cpu_usage
host.current_memory_headroom
host.current_memory_usage
host.custom_get
host.custom_keys
host.custom_set
host.domain
host.ems_custom_get
host.ems_custom_keys
host.ems_custom_set
host.event_log_threshold?
host.get_realtime_metric
host.scan
host.ssh_exec
host.tagged_with?
host.tags
host.tag_assign
```

Enumerating a service model object's methods is more challenging, because the actual object that we want to enumerate is running in the Automation Engine on the remote side of a dRuby call (see the following section, "Distributed Ruby"), and all we have is the local `DRb::DRbObject` accessible from `$evm`. We can use `method_missing`, but we get returned the entire method list, which includes attribute names, virtual column names, association names, superclass methods, and so on:

```
this_object.method_missing(:class).instance_methods
```

Distributed Ruby

The Automation Engine runs in a CloudForms *worker* thread, and it launches one of our automation scripts by spawning it as a child Ruby process. We can see this from the command line using **ps** to check the PID of the worker processes and its children:

```
\_ /var/www/miq/vmdb/lib/workers/bin/worker.rb
|   \_ /opt/rh/rh-ruby22/root/usr/bin/ruby  <-- automation script running
```

An automation script runs in its own process space, but it must somehow access the
service model objects that reside in the Automation Engine process. It does this using
Distributed Ruby.

Examining CloudForms Workers

We can use `rake evm:status` to see which workers are running on a CloudForms
appliance:

```
vmdb
bin/rake evm:status


...
Worker Type                                                        | Status  |
-------------------------------------------------------------------+---------+
ManageIQ::Providers::Redhat::InfraManager::EventCatcher            | started |
ManageIQ::Providers::Redhat::InfraManager::MetricsCollectorWorker  | started |
ManageIQ::Providers::Redhat::InfraManager::MetricsCollectorWorker  | started |
ManageIQ::Providers::Redhat::InfraManager::RefreshWorker           | started |
MiqEmsMetricsProcessorWorker                                       | started |
MiqEmsMetricsProcessorWorker                                       | started |
MiqEventHandler                                                    | started |
MiqGenericWorker                                                   | started |
MiqGenericWorker                                                   | started |
MiqPriorityWorker                                                  | started |
MiqPriorityWorker                                                  | started |
MiqReportingWorker                                                 | started |
MiqReportingWorker                                                 | started |
MiqScheduleWorker                                                  | started |
MiqSmartProxyWorker                                                | started |
```

Distributed Ruby (dRuby) is a distributed client-server object system that allows a client Ruby process to call methods on a Ruby object located in another (server) Ruby
process. This can even be on another machine.

The object in the remote dRuby server process is locally represented in the dRuby client by an instance of a `DRb::DRbObject` object. In the case of an automation script,
this object is our `$evm` variable.

The Automation Engine cleverly handles everything for us. When it runs our automation script, the Engine sets up the dRuby session automatically, and we access all of
the service model objects seamlesssly via `$evm` in our script. Behind the scenes the
dRuby library handles the TCP/IP socket communication with the dRuby server in
the Automation Engine worker.

We gain insight into this if we examine some of these $evm objects using object_walker—for example:

```
$evm.root['user'] => #<MiqAeMethodService::MiqAeServiceUser:0x0000000c5431c8>  \
                     (type: DRb::DRbObject, URI: druby://127.0.0.1:38842)
```

Although the use of dRuby is mostly transparent to us, it can occasionally produce unexpected results. Perhaps we are hoping to find some useful user-related method that we can call on our user object, which we know we can access as $evm.root['user']. We might try to call a standard Ruby method, such as:

```
$evm.root['user'].instance_methods
```

If we were to do this we would actually get a list of the instance methods for the local DRb::DRbObject object, rather than the remote MiqAeServiceUser service model—probably not what we want.

When we get more adventurous in our scripting, we also occasionally get a DRb::DRbUnknown object returned to us, indicating that the class of the object is unknown in our dRuby client's namespace.

Summary

This chapter has given us some good insight into the Rails active records that Cloud-Forms uses internally to represent our virtual infrastructure, and how these are made available to us as service model objects. We've also seen how these service model objects have four specific properties that we frequently make use of: attributes, virtual columns, associations, and methods.

Further Reading

Methods Available for Use with CloudForms Management Engine (*http://red.ht/1syq2Nv*)

Change Automate Methods to Communicate via REST API (*https://github.com/ManageIQ/manageiq/issues/2215*)

Support 'where' Method for Service Models (*https://github.com/ManageIQ/manageiq/pull/6046*)

Masatoshi Seki, *The dRuby Book* (Pragmatic)

$evm and the Workspace

When we write automation scripts, we access the Automation Engine and all of its objects through a single $evm variable.[1] This is sometimes referred to as the *workspace*.

As discussed in Chapter 6, the $evm variable is a DRb::DRbObject object representing a dRuby client connection back to the Automation Engine. The object at the dRuby server side of our $evm variable is an instance of an MiqAeService object, which contains over 40 methods. In practice we generally use only a few of these methods, most commonly:

```
$evm.root
$evm.object
$evm.current (this is equivalent to calling $evm.object(nil))
$evm.parent
$evm.log
$evm.vmdb
$evm.execute
$evm.instantiate
```

We will look at these methods in more detail in the next sections.

$evm.log

$evm.log is a simple method that we've used already. It writes a message to *automation.log* and accepts two arguments: a log level and the text string to write. The log level can be written as a Ruby symbol (e.g., :info, :warn), or as a text string (e.g., "info", "warn").

---

1 The original ManageIQ product was called *Enterprise Virtualization Manager*, often abbreviated to EVM.

$evm.root

$evm.root, illustrated in Figure 7-1, is the method that returns to us the root object in the workspace (environment, variables, linked objects, etc.). This is the instance whose invocation took us into the Automation Engine. From $evm.root we can access other service model objects, such as $evm.root['vm'], $evm.root['user'], or $evm.root['miq_request'] (the actual objects available depend on the context of the Automate tasks that we are performing).

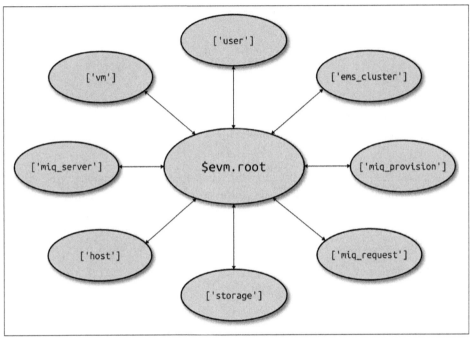

Figure 7-1. The object model

$evm.root contains a lot of useful information that we use programmatically to establish our running context—for example, to see if we've been called by an API call or from a button (see also Chapter 10):

```
$evm.root['vmdb_object_type'] = vm    (type: String)
...
$evm.root['ae_provider_category'] = infrastructure    (type: String)
...
$evm.root.namespace = ManageIQ/SYSTEM    (type: String)
$evm.root['object_name'] = Request    (type: String)
$evm.root['request'] = Call_Instance    (type: String)
$evm.root['instance'] = ObjectWalker    (type: String)
```

`$evm.root` also contains any variables that were defined on our entry into the Automation Engine, such as the `$evm.root['dialog*']` variables that were defined from our service dialog.

$evm.object, $evm.current, and $evm.parent

As we saw, `$evm.root` returns to us the object representing the instance that was launched when we entered Automate. Many instances have schemas that contain relationships to other instances, and as each relationship is followed, a new child object is created under the calling object to represent the called instance. Fortunately, we can access any of the objects in this parent-child hierarchy using `$evm.object`.

Calling `$evm.object` with no arguments returns the currently instantiated/running instance. As automation scripters we can think of this as "our currently running code," and we can access it using the alias `$evm.current`. When we wanted to access our `username` schema variable, we accessed it using `$evm.object['username']`.

We can access our parent object (the one that called us) using `$evm.object("..")`, or the alias `$evm.parent`.

 `$evm.root` is the same as `$evm.object("/")`.

When we ran our first example script, *HelloWorld* (from Simulation), we specified an entry point of */System/Process/Request*, and our request was to an instance called *Call_Instance*. We passed to this the namespace, class, and instance that we wanted it to run (via a relationship).

This would have resulted in an object hierarchy (when viewed from the *hello_world* method) as follows:

```
--- object hierarchy ---
$evm.root = /ManageIQ/SYSTEM/PROCESS/Request
  $evm.parent = /ManageIQ/System/Request/Call_Instance
    $evm.object = /ACME/General/Methods/HelloWorld
```

$evm.vmdb

`$evm.vmdb` is a useful method that can be used to retrieve any service model object (see "Service Models" on page 54). The method can be called with one or two arguments.

Single-Argument Form

When called with a single argument, the method returns the generic service model object type, and we can use any of the Rails helper methods (see Chapter 6) to search by database column name:

```
vm = $evm.vmdb('vm').find_by_id(vm_id)
clusters = $evm.vmdb(:EmsCluster).find(:all)
$evm.vmdb(:VmOrTemplate).find_each do | vm |
```

The service model object name can be specified in CamelCase (e.g., `Availability Zone`) or snake_case (e.g., `availability_zone`) and can be a string or symbol.

Two-Argument Form

When called with two arguments, the second argument should be the service model ID to search for:

```
owner = $evm.vmdb('user', evm_owner_id)
```

We can also use more advanced query syntax to return results based on multiple conditions, like so:

```
$evm.vmdb('CloudTenant').find(:first,
                        :conditions => ["ems_id = ? AND name = ?",
                                        src_ems_id, tenant_name])
```

VM or Template?

Question: When should we use *vm* (`:Vm`) or *vm_or_template* (`:VmOrTemplate`) in our `$evm.vmdb` searches?

Answer: Searching for a *vm_or_template* (`MiqAeServiceVmOrTemplate`) object will return both virtual machines *and* templates that satisfy the search criteria, whereas searching for a *vm* object (`MiqAeServiceVm`) will return only virtual machines. Think about whether you need both returned.

There are some subtle differences between the objects. `MiqAeServiceVm` is a subclass of `MiqAeServiceVmOrTemplate` that adds two further methods that are not relevant for templates: `add_to_service` and `remove_from_service`.

Both `MiqAeServiceVmOrTemplate` and `MiqAeServiceVm` have a Boolean attribute, `template`, which is `true` for an image or template, and `false` for a VM.

$evm.execute

We can use $evm.execute to call one of 13 miscellaneous but useful methods. The methods are defined in a service model called *Methods* (MiqAeServiceMethods) and are as follows:

- send_email(to, from, subject, body, content_type = nil)
- snmp_trap_v1(inputs)
- snmp_trap_v2(inputs)
- category_exists?(category)
- category_create(options = {})
- tag_exists?(category, entry)
- tag_create(category, options = {})
- service_now_eccq_insert(server, username, password, agent, queue, topic, name, source, *params)
- service_now_task_get_records(server, username, password, *params)
- service_now_task_update(server, username, password, *params)
- service_now_task_service(service, server, username, password, *params)
- create_provision_request(*args)
- create_automation_request(options, userid = "admin", auto_approve = false)

Examples

Let's look at some examples of calling these methods.

Creating a tag if one doesn't already exist

```
unless $evm.execute('tag_exists?', 'cost_center', '3376')
  $evm.execute('tag_create', "cost_center", :name => '3376',
                                       :description => '3376')
end
```

In this example we call the tag_exists? method to see if the cost_center/3376 tag exists. If it doesn't (i.e., tag_exists? returns false), then we call the tag_create method to create the tag, passing the tag category arguments, :name and :description.

Sending an email

```
to = 'pemcg@redhat.com'
from = 'cloudforms01@uk.bit63.com'
subject = 'Test Message'
body = 'What an awesome cloud management product!'
$evm.execute('send_email', to, from, subject, body)
```

Here we define the to, from, subject, and body arguments, and call the send_email method.

Creating a new automation request

The create_automation_request method is new with CloudForms 4.0, and it enables us to chain automation requests together. This is also very useful when we wish to explicitly launch an automation task in a different zone than the one in which our currently running script resides:

```
options = {}
options[:namespace]     = 'Stuff'
options[:class_name]    = 'Methods'
options[:instance_name] = 'MyInstance'
options[:user_id]       = $evm.vmdb(:user).find_by_userid('pemcg').id
# options[:attrs]        = attrs
# options[:miq_zone]     = zone
auto_approve            = true

$evm.execute('create_automation_request', options, 'admin', auto_approve)
```

In this example we define the namespace, class, and instance names to be used for the automation request, and we look up the service model object of the user as whom we want to run the automation task. The admin user in the argument list is the *requester* to be used for approval purposes.

$evm.instantiate

We can use $evm.instantiate to launch another Automate instance programmatically from a running method, by specifying its URI within the Automate namespace, like so:

```
$evm.instantiate('/Discovery/Methods/ObjectWalker')
```

Instances called in this way execute synchronously, so the calling method waits for completion before continuing. The called instance also appears as a child object of the caller (it sees the caller as its $evm.parent).

Summary

This has been a more theoretical chapter, examining the eight most commonly used $evm methods.[2] In our simple scripts so far, we have already used three of them: $evm.log, $evm.object, and $evm.root. Our next example in Chapter 8 uses two others, and we will use the remaining three as we progress through the book. These methods form a core part of our scripting toolbag, and their use will become second nature as we advance our automation scripting skills.

Further Reading

MiqAeService class (*http://bit.ly/1TZilqg*)

---

2 There are a further three state-machine specific $evm methods that we frequently use, but we'll cover those in Chapter 13

## CHAPTER 8

A Practical Example:
Enforcing Anti-Affinity Rules

We can use the techniques that we've learned so far to write an automation script to solve a realistic task.

Task

Write an Automate method that enforces anti-affinity rules for virtual machines, based on a `server_role` tag applied to each VM. There should be only one VM of any `server_role` type running on any host in the cluster.

The Automate method should be run from a button visible on the VM details page. If another VM with the same `server_role` tag is found running on the same host (hypervisor) as the displayed VM, then we live-migrate the current VM to another host with no other such tagged VMs. We also email all users in the `EvmGroup-administrator` group to notify them that the migration occurred.

Solution

We can achieve the task in the following way (the entire script is also available on Git-Hub (*http://bit.ly/1YhSRd0*)). We'll define two methods internally within our Ruby script, `relocate_vm` and `send_email`. Our main code will be a simple iteration loop.

relocate_vm

The first method, `relocate_vm`, makes use of a virtual column (`vm.host_name`), and several associations to find a suitable host (hypervisor) to migrate the virtual machine to. These associations are `vm.ems_cluster` to find the cluster that our VM is running on, `ems_cluster.hosts` to find the other hypervisors in the cluster, and `host.vms` to get the list of VMs running on a hypervisor. Finally, it calls a method (`vm.migrate`) to perform the VM migration.

```ruby
def relocate_vm(vm)
  #
  # Get our host name
  #
  our_host = vm.host_name                          # <-- Virtual column
  #
  # Loop through the other hosts in our cluster
  #
  target_host = nil
  vm.ems_cluster.hosts.each do |this_host|         # <-- Two levels of association
    next if this_host.name == our_host
    host_invalid = false
    this_host.vms.each do |this_vm|                # <-- Association
      if this_vm.tags(:server_role).first == our_server_role
        host_invalid = true
        break
      end
    end
    next if host_invalid
    #
    # If we get to here then no duplicate server_role VMs have been found
    # on this host
    #
    target_host = this_host
    break
  end
  if target_host.nil?
    raise "No suitable Host found to migrate VM #{vm.name} to"
  else
    $evm.log(:info, "Migrating VM #{vm.name} to host: #{target_host.name}")
    #
    # Migrate the VM to this host
    #
    vm.migrate(target_host)                        # <-- Method
  end
  return target_host.name
end
```

send_email

The second method, send_email, sends an email to all members of a user group. It uses the `group.users` association to find all users in a particular group, uses the `user.email` attribute to find a user's email address, and calls `$evm.execute` to run the internal `:send_email` method:

```
def send_email(group_name, vm_name, new_host)
  #
  # Find the group passed to us, and pull out the user emails
  #
  recipients = []
  group = $evm.vmdb('miq_group').find_by_description(group_name)
  group.users.each do |group_member|          # <-- Association
    recipients << group_member.email          # <-- Attribute
  end
  #
  # 'from' is the current logged-user who clicked the button
  #
  from = $evm.root['user'].email
  subject = "VM migration"
  body = "VM Name: #{vm_name} was live-migrated to Host: #{new_host}"
  body += " in accordance with anti-affinity rules"
  #
  # Send emails
  #
  recipients.each do |recipient|
    $evm.log(:info, "Sending email to <#{recipient}> from <#{from}> \
                    subject: <#{subject}>")
    $evm.execute(:send_email, recipient, from, subject, body)
  end
end
```

Main Code

We'll wrap our main section of code in a begin/rescue block so that we can catch and handle any exceptions:

```
begin
  #-------------------------------------------------------------------------
  # Main code
  #-------------------------------------------------------------------------
  #
  # We've been called from a button on the VM object, so we know that
  # $evm.root['vm'] will be loaded
  #
  vm = $evm.root['vm']
  #
  # Find out this VM's server_role tag
  #
  our_server_role = vm.tags(:server_role).first
  $evm.log(:info, "VM #{vm.name} has a server_role tag of: #{our_server_role}")
  #
  # Loop through the other VMs on the same host
  #
  vm.host.vms.each do |this_vm|                # <-- Two levels of Association
    next if this_vm.name == vm.name
    if this_vm.tags(:server_role).first == our_server_role
      $evm.log(:info, "VM #{this_vm.name} also has a server_role tag of: \
```

```
                              #{our_server_role}, taking remedial action")
        new_host = relocate_vm(vm)
        send_email('EvmGroup-administrator', vm.name, new_host)
      end
    end
    exit MIQ_OK

rescue => err
  $evm.log(:error, "[#{err}]\n#{err.backtrace.join("\n")}")
  exit MIQ_STOP
end
```

The main code determines the virtual machine service model object from
$evm.root['vm'], and retrieves the first server_role tag applied to the VM (see
Chapter 9 for more details on using tags from Automate). It then chains two associations together (vm.host and host.vms) to determine the other VMs running on the
same hypervisor as our VM. If any of these VMs has the same server_role tag as our
VM, we call the relocate_vm method and notify the EvmGroup-administrator group
via email that the VM has been relocated.

Summary

Here we've shown how we can achieve a realistic task with a relatively simple Ruby
script, using many of the concepts that we've learned so far in the book. We've worked
with service model objects representing a user, a group, a virtual machine, a cluster,
and a hypervisor, and we've traversed the associations between some of them. We've
read from an object's attribute and virtual column, and called an object's method to
perform the migrate operation. Finally, we've explored working with tags, and we've
used $evm.execute to send an email.

Although most modern virtualization platforms have an anti-affinity capability built
in, this is still a useful example of how we can achieve selected workload placement
based on tags. When we implement this kind of tag-based placement, we need to
ensure that our VM workloads aren't tagged multiple times with possibly conflicting
results—for example, one tag implying affinity, and another anti-affinity.

Further Reading

Workload Placement by Type (Not Near That) (*http://red.ht/1WIjxV0*)

Using Tags from Automate

Tags are a very powerful feature of CloudForms. They allow us to add *Smart Management* capabilities to the objects in the WebUI such as virtual machines, hosts, or clusters; to create tag-related filters; and to group, sort, or categorize items by tag.

For example, we might assign a tag to a virtual machine to identify which department or cost center owns the VM. We could then create a chargeback rate for billing purposes and assign the rate to all VMs tagged as being owned by a particular department or cost center.

We might also tag virtual machines with a *Location* or *Data Center* tag. We could create a filter view in the WebUI to display all VMs at a particular location so that we instantly can see which systems might be affected if we run a data center failover or power test.

Tags are not only applied to virtual machines. We often tag our virtual infrastructure components—such as hosts, clusters, or datastores—with a *Provisioning Scope* tag. When we provision new virtual machines, our Automate workflow must determine where to put the new VM (a process known as *placement*). We can use the Provisioning Scope tag to determine a *best fit* for a particular virtual machine, based on a user's group membership. In this way we might, for example, place all virtual machines provisioned by users in a development group on a nonproduction cluster.

These are just three examples of how tags can simplify systems administration and help our Automate workflows. Fortunately, Automate has comprehensive support for tag-related operations.

Tag or Custom Attribute?

We've already seen the use of a custom attribute on a virtual machine. At first glance tags and custom attributes seem to be similar, but there are good reasons to use one over the other.

Tags are better if we wish to categorize, sort, or filter an object based on its tag. We could, for example, quickly search for all items tagged with a particular value. A tag must exist within a category before it can be used, however, so we have to consider the manageability of tag categories that contain many hundreds of different tags.

Custom attributes are better if we just wish to assign a generic text string to an object but don't need to sort or categorize objects by the attribute name or string.

Creating Tags and Categories

Tags are defined and used within the context of tag *categories*. We can check whether a category exists, and if not, create it:

```
unless $evm.execute('category_exists?', 'data_center')
  $evm.execute('category_create',
                :name => 'data_center',
                :single_value => false,
                :perf_by_tag => false,
                :description => "Data Center")
end
```

We can also check whether a tag exists within a category, and if not, create it:

```
unless $evm.execute('tag_exists?', 'data_center', 'london')
  $evm.execute('tag_create',
                'data_center',
                :name => 'london',
                :description => 'London East End')
end
```

 Tag and category *names* must be lowercase, and optionally contain underscores. They have a maximum length of 30 characters. The tag and category *descriptions* can be free text.

Assigning and Removing Tags

We can assign a category/tag to an object (in this case, a virtual machine) as follows:

```
vm = $evm.root['vm']
vm.tag_assign("data_center/london")
```

We can remove a category/tag from an object like so:

```
vm = $evm.root['vm']
vm.tag_unassign("data_center/paris")
```

Testing Whether an Object Is Tagged

We can test whether an object (in this case, a user group) is tagged with a particular tag, like so:

```
ci_owner = 'engineering'
groups = $evm.vmdb(:miq_group).find(:all)
groups.each do |group|
  if group.tagged_with?("department", ci_owner)
    $evm.log("info", "Group #{group.description} is tagged")
  end
end
```

Retrieving an Object's Tags

We can use the `tags` method to retrieve the list of all tags assigned to an object:

```
group_tags = group.tags
```

This method also enables us to retrieve the tags in a particular category (in this case, using the tag name as a symbol):

```
all_department_tags = group.tags(:department)
first_department_tag = group.tags(:department).first
```

 When called with no argument, the `tags` method returns the tags as *"category/tag"* strings. When called with an argument of tag category, the method returns the tag name as the string.

Searching for Specifically Tagged Objects

We use the `find_tagged_with` method to search for objects tagged with a particular tag:

```
tag = "/managed/department/legal"
hosts = $evm.vmdb(:host).find_tagged_with(:all => tag, :ns => "*")
```

This example shows that categories themselves are organized into namespaces behind the scenes. In practice the only namespace that seems to be in use is */managed*, and we rarely need to specify this.

The `find_tagged_with` method has a slightly ambiguous past. It was present in CloudForms 3.1 but returned active records rather than `MiqAeService` objects. It disappeared as an Automate method in CloudForms 3.2 but thankfully is back with CloudForms 4.0 and now returns service model objects as expected.

Practical Example

We could discover all infrastructure components tagged with `/department/engineer ing`. We might wish to find out the service model class name of the object and the object's name, for example. We could achieve this using the following code snippet:

```
tag = '/department/engineering'
[:vm_or_template, :host, :ems_cluster, :storage].each do |service_object|
  these_objects = $evm.vmdb(service_object).find_tagged_with(:all => tag,
                                                             :ns => "/managed")
  these_objects.each do |this_object|
    service_model_class = "#{this_object.method_missing(:class)}".demodulize
    $evm.log("info", "#{service_model_class}: #{this_object.name}")
  end
end
```

On a small CloudForms 4.0 system, this prints:

```
MiqAeServiceManageIQ_Providers_Redhat_InfraManager_Template: rhel7-generic
MiqAeServiceManageIQ_Providers_Redhat_InfraManager_Vm: rhel7srv010
MiqAeServiceManageIQ_Providers_Openstack_CloudManager_Vm: rhel7srv031
MiqAeServiceManageIQ_Providers_Redhat_InfraManager_Host: rhelh03.bit63.net
MiqAeServiceStorage: Data
```

This code snippet shows an example of where we need to work with or around Distributed Ruby (dRuby). The following loop enumerates through these_objects, substituting this_object on each iteration:

```
these_objects.each do |this_object|
  ...
end
```

Normally this is transparent to us and we can refer to the object methods, such as name, and all works as expected.

Behind the scenes, however, our automation script is accessing all of these objects remotely via its dRuby client object. We must bear this in mind if we also wish to find the class name of the remote object.

If we call this_object.class, we get the string "DRb::DRbObject", which is the correct class name for a dRuby client object. We have to tell dRuby to forward the class method call on to the dRuby server, and we do this by calling this_object.method_miss ing(:class). Now we get returned the full *module::class* name of the remote dRuby object (such as MiqAeMethodService::MiqAe ServiceStorage), but we can call the demodulize method on the string to strip the MiqAeMethodService:: module path from the name, leaving us with MiqAeServiceStorage.

Getting the List of Tag Categories

On versions prior to CloudForms 4.0, getting the list of tag categories was slightly challenging. Both tags and categories are listed in the same classifications table, but tags also have a nonzero parent_id value that ties them to their category. To find the categories from the classifications table, we had to search for records with a parent_id of zero:

```
categories = $evm.vmdb('classification').find(:all,
                                        :conditions => ["parent_id = 0"])
categories.each do |category|
  $evm.log(:info, "Found category: #{category.name} (#{category.description})")
end
```

With CloudForms 4.0 we now have a categories association directly from an MiqAe ServiceClassification object, so we can say:

```
$evm.vmdb(:classification).categories.each do |category|
  $evm.log(:info, "Found category: #{category.name} (#{category.description})")
end
```

Getting the List of Tags in a Category

We occasionally need to retrieve the list of tags in a particular category, and for this we have to perform a double lookup—once to get the classification ID, and again to find MiqAeServiceClassification objects with that parent_id:

```
classification = $evm.vmdb(:classification).find_by_name('cost_center')
cost_center_tags = {}
$evm.vmdb(:classification).find_all_by_parent_id(classification.id).each do |tag|
  cost_center_tags[tag.name] = tag.description
end
```

Finding a Tag's Name, Given Its Description

Sometimes we need to add a tag to an object, but we only have the tag's free-text description (perhaps this matches a value read from an external source). We need to find the tag's snake_case name to use with the tag_apply method, but we can use more Rails syntax in our find call to look up two fields at once:

```
department_classification = $evm.vmdb(:classification).find_by_name('department')
tag = $evm.vmdb('classification').find(
                        :first,
                        :conditions => ["parent_id = ? AND description = ?",
                        department_classification.id, 'Systems Engineering'])
tag_name = tag.name
```

The tag names aren't in the classifications table (just the tag description). When we call tag.name, Rails runs an implicit search of the tags table for us, based on the tag.id:

```
irb(main):051:0> tag.name
  Tag Load (0.6ms)  SELECT "tags".* FROM "tags" WHERE "tags"."id" = 44 LIMIT 1
  Tag Inst Including Associations (0.1ms - 1rows)
    => "syseng"
```

Finding a Specific Tag (MiqAeServiceClassification) Object

We can just search for the tag object that matches a given category/tag, as follows:

```
tag = $evm.vmdb(:classification).find_by_name('department/hr')
```

 Anything returned from $evm.vmdb(:classification) is a MiqAe ServiceClassification object, not a text string.

Deleting a Tag Category

With CloudForms 4.0 we can now delete a tag category using the RESTful API:

```ruby
require 'rest-client'
require 'json'
require 'openssl'
require 'base64'

begin

  def rest_action(uri, verb, payload=nil)
    headers = {
      :content_type  => 'application/json',
      :accept        => 'application/json;version=2',
      :authorization => "Basic #{Base64.strict_encode64("#{@user}:#{@pass}")}"
    }
    response = RestClient::Request.new(
      :method       => verb,
      :url          => uri,
      :headers      => headers,
      :payload      => payload,
      verify_ssl: false
    ).execute
    return JSON.parse(response.to_str) unless response.code.to_i == 204
  end

  servername   = $evm.object['servername']
  @user        = $evm.object['username']
  @pass        = $evm.object.decrypt('password')

  uri_base = "https://#{servername}/api/"

  category = $evm.vmdb(:classification).find_by_name('network_location')
  rest_return = rest_action("#{uri_base}/categories/#{category.id}", :delete)
  exit MIQ_OK

rescue RestClient::Exception => err
  unless err.response.nil?
    $evm.log(:error, "REST request failed, code: #{err.response.code}")
    $evm.log(:error, "Response body:\n#{err.response.body.inspect}")
  end
  exit MIQ_STOP
rescue => err
  $evm.log(:error, "[#{err}]\n#{err.backtrace.join("\n")}")
  exit MIQ_STOP
end
```

In this example we define a generic method called `rest_action` that uses the Ruby `rest-client` gem to handle the RESTful connection. We extract the CloudForms server's credentials from the instance schema just as we did in Chapter 4, and we retrieve the service model of the tag category that we wish to delete, to get its ID.

Finally, we make a RESTful DELETE call to the */api/categories* URI, specifying the tag category ID to be deleted.

Summary

In this chapter we've seen how we can work with tags from our Automation scripts, and we'll use these techniques extensively as we progress through the book.

Further Reading

Creating and Using Tags in Red Hat CloudForms (*https://access.redhat.com/articles/421423*)

## CHAPTER 10

Investigative Debugging

As we saw in Chapter 6, there is a lot of useful information in the form of service model object attributes and virtual columns, links to other objects via associations, and service model methods that we can call. The challenge is sometimes knowing which objects are available to us at any particular point in our workflow, and how to access their properties and traverse associations to find the information that we need.

Fortunately there are several ways of exploring the object structure in the Automation Engine, both to investigate what might be available to use, and to debug and trouble-shoot our own automation code. This chapter will discuss the various tools that we can use to reveal the service model object structure available during any Automate operation.

InspectMe

InspectMe is an instance/method combination supplied out-of-the-box that we can call to dump some attributes of $evm.root and its associated objects. As an example, we can call *InspectMe* from a button on a "VM and Instance" object as we did when running our *AddCustomAttribute* instance in Chapter 5. As both the instance and method are in the *ManageIQ/System/Request* namespace, we can call *InspectMe* directly rather than calling *Call_Instance* as an intermediary.

We can view the *InspectMe* output in *automation.log*:

```
# vmdb
# grep inspectme log/automation.log | awk 'FS="INFO -- :" {print $2}'
Root:<$evm.root> Attributes - Begin
   Attribute - ae_provider_category: infrastructure
   Attribute - miq_server: #<MiqAeMethodService::MiqAeServiceMiqServer:0x00000...
   Attribute - miq_server_id: 1000000000001
   Attribute - object_name: Request
   Attribute - request: InspectMe
   Attribute - user: #<MiqAeMethodService::MiqAeServiceUser:0x0000000b86b540>
   Attribute - user_id: 1000000000001
   Attribute - vm: rhel7srv001
   Attribute - vm_id: 1000000000025
   Attribute - vmdb_object_type: vm
Root:<$evm.root> Attributes - End
...
```

This log snippet shows the section of a typical *InspectMe* output that dumps the attributes of $evm.root.

Kevin Morey from Red Hat has written an improved version of *InspectMe*, available from *https://github.com/ramrexx/Cloud Forms_Essentials*. His *InspectMe* provides a very clear output of the attributes, virtual columns, associations, and tags that are available for the object on which it was launched. For example, if called from a button on a virtual machine, *InspectMe* will list all of that VM's properties, including hardware, operating system, and the provisioning request and task details.

object_walker

object_walker[1] is a slightly more exploratory tool that walks and dumps the objects, attributes, and virtual columns of $evm.root and its immediate objects. It also recursively traverses associations to walk and dump any objects that it finds, much like a web crawler would explore a website. It prints the output in a Ruby-like syntax that can be copied and pasted directly into an automation script to access or walk the same path.

Black or Whitelisting Associations

One of the features of *object_walker* is the ability to selectively choose which associations to "walk" to limit the output. We do so by setting a @walk_association_policy to :whitelist or :blacklist, and then defining a @walk_association_whitelist or

---

1 *object_walker* is available from *https://github.com/pemcg/object_walker*, along with instructions for use.

`@walk_association_blacklist` to list the associations to be walked (whitelist), or not walked (blacklist).

In practice a `@walk_association_policy` of `:blacklist` produces so much output that it's rarely used, and so a `:whitelist` is more often defined, like so:

```
@walk_association_whitelist =
  'MiqAeServiceVmRedhat'     => ['ems_cluster',
                                 'ems_folder',
                                 'resource_pool',
                                 'storage',
                                 'service',
                                 'hardware'
                                 ],
  'MiqAeServiceUser'         => ['current_group'],
  'MiqAeServiceGuestDevice' => ['hardware',
                                 'lan',
                                 'network']
```

object_walker_reader

There is a companion script, *object_walker_reader*, that can be copied to the Cloud-Forms appliance to extract the *object_walker* outputs from *automation.log*. The reader script can also list all outputs by timestamp, dump a particular output by timestamp, and even *diff* two outputs—useful when we are running *object_walker* before and after a built-in method (for example, in a state machine) to see what the method has changed:

```
Object Walker 1.7 Starting
    --- $evm.current_* details ---
    $evm.current_namespace = Bit63/stuff   (type: String)
    $evm.current_class = methods   (type: String)
    $evm.current_instance = objectwalker   (type: String)
    $evm.current_message = create   (type: String)
    $evm.current_object = /Bit63/stuff/methods/objectwalker   (type: DRb::DRb...
    $evm.current_object.current_field_name = Execute   (type: String)
    $evm.current_object.current_field_type = method   (type: String)
    $evm.current_method = object_walker   (type: String)
    --- automation instance hierarchy ---
    /ManageIQ/SYSTEM/PROCESS/Request   ($evm.root)
    |   /ManageIQ/System/Request/call_instance   ($evm.parent)
    |   |   /Bit63/stuff/methods/objectwalker   ($evm.object)
    --- walking $evm.root ---
    $evm.root = /ManageIQ/SYSTEM/PROCESS/Request   (type: DRb::DRbObject)
    |   --- attributes follow ---
    |   $evm.root['ae_provider_category'] = infrastructure   (type: String)
    |   $evm.root.class = DRb::DRbObject   (type: Class)
    |   $evm.root['dialog_walk_association_whitelist'] =   (type: String)
    |   $evm.root['instance'] = objectwalker   (type: String)
    |   $evm.root['miq_group'] => #<MiqAeMethodService::MiqAeServiceMiqGro...
    |   |   --- attributes follow ---
```

```
        |   |   $evm.root['miq_group'].created_on = 2015-09-23 12:39:48 UTC
        |   |   $evm.root['miq_group'].description = EvmGroup-super_administrator
        |   |   $evm.root['miq_group'].group_type = system   (type: String)
  ...
        |   |   --- end of attributes ---
        |   |   --- virtual columns follow ---
        |   |   $evm.root['miq_group'].allocated_memory = 59055800320   (type: ...
        |   |   $evm.root['miq_group'].allocated_storage = 560493232128   (type: .
        |   |   $evm.root['miq_group'].allocated_vcpu = 27   (type: Fixnum)
  ...
        |   $evm.root['vm'] => intraweb005   (type: DRb::DRbObject, URI: dru...
        |   |   --- attributes follow ---
        |   |   $evm.root['vm'].boot_time = 2016-04-06 14:51:52 UTC   (type: ...
        |   |   $evm.root['vm'].cloud = false   (type: FalseClass)
        |   |   $evm.root['vm'].connection_state = connected   (type: String)
        |   |   $evm.root['vm'].cpu_limit = -1   (type: Fixnum)
        |   |   $evm.root['vm'].cpu_reserve = 0   (type: Fixnum)
  ...
        |   |   ems_cluster = $evm.root['vm'].ems_cluster
        |   |   (object type: MiqAeServiceEmsCluster, object ID: 1000000000001)
        |   |   |   --- attributes follow ---
        |   |   |   ems_cluster.created_on = 2015-09-23 13:21:59 UTC
        |   |   |   ems_cluster.drs_automation_level = fullyAutomated
        |   |   |   ems_cluster.drs_enabled = true   (type: TrueClass)
        |   |   |   ems_cluster.drs_migration_threshold = 3   (type: Fixnum)
  ...
        |   |   |   --- methods follow ---
        |   |   |   ems_cluster.register_host
        |   |   |   ems_cluster.tag_assign
        |   |   |   ems_cluster.tag_unassign
        |   |   |   ems_cluster.tagged_with?
        |   |   |   ems_cluster.tags
```

Here we see a partial output from *object_walker_reader*, showing the traversal of the associations between objects, and a list of attributes, virtual columns, associations, and methods for each object encountered.

Rails Console

We can connect to the Rails console to have a look around.

When we're working with the Rails command line, we have full read/write access to the objects and tables that we find there. We should use this technique purely for read-only investigation, and at our own risk. Making any additions or changes may render our CloudForms appliance unstable, and unsupported by Red Hat.

On the CloudForms appliance itself:

```
# vmdb    # alias vmdb='cd /var/www/miq/vmdb/' is defined on the appliance
# source /etc/default/evm
# bin/rails c
Loading production environment (Rails 3.2.17)
irb(main):001:0>
```

Once in the Rails console, there are many things that we can do, such as use Rails object syntax to look at all host active records:

```
irb(main):002:0> Host.all
   (3.6ms)  SELECT version()
  Host Load (0.7ms)  SELECT "hosts".* FROM "hosts"
  Host Inst (85.2ms - 2rows)
=> [#<HostRedhat id: 1000000000002, name: "rhelh02.bit63.net", \
                     hostname: "192.168.12.22", ipaddress: "192.168.12.22",...

irb(main):003:0>
```

We can even generate our own $evm variable that matches the Automation Engine default:

```
$evm=MiqAeMethodService::MiqAeService.new(MiqAeEngine::MiqAeWorkspaceRuntime.new)
```

With our $evm variable we can emulate actions that we perform from an automation script:

```
irb(main):002:0> $evm.log(:info, "test from the Rails console")
=> true
```

As with a "real" automation method, this writes our message to *automation.log*:

```
...8:45:11.223058 #2109:eb9998]  INFO -- : <AEMethod > test from the Rails console
```

Rails db

It is occasionally useful to be able to examine some of the database tables (such as to look for column headers that we can find_by_* on).[2] We can connect to Rails db, which puts us directly into a psql session:

```
[root@cloudforms ~]# vmdb
[root@cloudforms03 vmdb]# source /etc/default/evm
[root@cloudforms03 vmdb]# bin/rails db
psql (9.4.5)
Type "help" for help.

vmdb_production=#
```

Once in the Rails db session, we can freely examine the VMDB database. For example, we could look at the columns in the guest_devices table:

---

2 A diagram of the database layout is available from *http://people.redhat.com/~mmorsi/cfme_db.png*.

```
vmdb_production=# \d guest_devices
                                 Table "public.guest_devices"
        Column         |          Type          |            Modifiers
-----------------------+------------------------+---------------------------------
 id                    | bigint                 | not null default nextval('guest_...
 device_name           | character varying(255) |
 device_type           | character varying(255) |
 location              | character varying(255) |
 filename              | character varying(255) |
 hardware_id           | bigint                 |
 mode                  | character varying(255) |
 controller_type       | character varying(255) |
 size                  | bigint                 |
 free_space            | bigint                 |
 size_on_disk          | bigint                 |
 address               | character varying(255) |
 switch_id             | bigint                 |
 lan_id                | bigint                 |
 ...
```

We could list all templates on our appliance (templates are in the vms column, but have a Boolean `template` attribute that is `true`):

```
vmdb_production=# select id,name from vms where template = 't';
        id        |                   name
------------------+------------------------------------------
 1000000000014 | RedHat_CFME-5.5.0.13
 1000000000015 | rhel7-generic
 1000000000016 | rhel-guest-image-7.0-20140930.0.x86_64
 1000000000017 | RHEL 7
 1000000000029 | ManageIQ_Capablanca
 1000000000053 | Fedora 23
(6 rows)
```

Summary

In this chapter we've learned four very useful ways of investigating the object model. We can use *InspectMe* or *object_walker* to print the structure to *automation.log*, or we can interactively use the Rails command line.

We use these tools and techniques extensively when developing our scripts, both to find out the available objects that we might use, and also to debug our scripts when things are not working as expected.

Further Reading

inspectXML—Dump Objects as XML (*http://cloudformsblog.redhat.com/tag/xml-format/*)

## CHAPTER 11

Ways of Entering Automate

We are starting to see how powerful CloudForms Automate can be, so let's look at the various ways that we can initiate an automation operation.

There are six methods that we generally use to launch into Automate to run our instances or initiate our custom workflows. The method that we choose determines the Automate Datastore entry point and the objects that are available to our method when it runs.

Buttons and Simulation

So far we have launched automation scripts in two ways: from Simulation and from a custom button. With either of these methods we were presented with a drop-down list of entry points under */System/Process* into the Automate Datastore (see Figure 11-1).

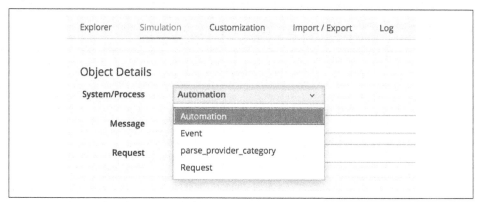

Figure 11-1. Entry points into the Automate Datastore from Simulation

In practice we only use */System/Process/Request* to launch our own automation requests from a button or Simulation. Entries at */System/Process/Request* get redirected to the **Request** instance name that we specified with the call, which should be an instance in the */System/Request* namespace. In our examples so far, we've used **Request** instances of *Call_Instance* and *AddCustomAttribute* (which we added to our *ACME* domain).

 The usage of */System/Process/Event* has changed with CloudForms 4.0. We would need to pass an EventStream object with our request to use this entry point.

The */System/Process/Automation* entry point is used internally when *tasks* are created for such operations as virtual machine provisioning or retirement:

```
Instantiating [/System/Process/AUTOMATION? \
MiqProvision%3A%3Amiq_provision=1000000000091& \
MiqServer%3A%3Amiq_server=1000000000001& \
User%3A%3Auser=1000000000001& \
object_name=AUTOMATION& \
request=vm_provision& \
vmdb_object_type=miq_provision]
```

RESTful API

We can initiate an Automate operation using the RESTful API (see Chapter 42 for more details). In this case we can directly invoke any instance anywhere in the Automate Datastore; we do not need to call */System/Process/Request*.

Control Policy Actions

We can create *control policy action* that launches a custom automation instance (see Figure 11-2).

Figure 11-2. Launching a custom automation as a control action

This can launch any instance in */System/Request,* but as before we can use *Call_Instance* to redirect the call via the built-in `rel2` relationship to an instance in our own domain and namespace.

Alerts

We can create an *alert* that sends a management event. The Event Name field corresponds to the name of an instance that we create to handle the alert (see Figure 11-3).

Figure 11-3. Creating an alert that sends a management event called ScaleOut

In CloudForms 3.2 and prior, this called an instance under */System/Event* in the Automate Datastore that corresponds to the management event name. In CloudForms 4.0 the new location name corresponds to the position in the event switchboard */System/Event/CustomEvent/Alert.* We can clone the */System/Event/CustomEvent/Alert* namespace into our own domain and add the corresponding instance (see Figure 11-4).

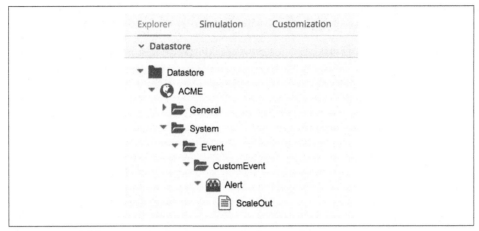

Figure 11-4. Adding an instance to process an alert management event

This instance will now be run when the alert is triggered.

Service Dialog Dynamic Elements

We can launch an Automate instance anywhere in the Automate Datastore from a dynamic service dialog element. In practice this type of script is designed specifically to populate the element, and we wouldn't launch a general workflow in this manner. We cover dynamic service dialog elements more in Chapter 29.

Finding Out How Our Method Has Been Called

Our entry point into Automate governs the content of $evm.root—this is the object whose instantiation took us into Automate. If we write a generically useful method such as one that adds a disk to a virtual machine, it might be useful to be able to call it in several ways, without necessarily knowing what $evm.root might contain.

For example, we might wish to add a disk during the provisioning workflow for the VM, from a button on an existing VM object in the WebUI, or even from an external RESTful call into the Automate Engine, passing the VM ID as an argument. The content of $evm.root is different in each of these cases.

For each case we need to access the target VM object in a different way, but we can use the $evm.root['vmdb_object_type'] key to help us establish context:

```
case $evm.root['vmdb_object_type']
when 'miq_provision'                    # called from a VM provision workflow
  vm = $evm.root['miq_provision'].destination
  ...
when 'vm'
  vm = $evm.root['vm']                  # called from a button
  ...
when 'automation_task'                  # called from a RESTful automation request
  attrs = $evm.root['automation_task'].options[:attrs]
  vm_id = attrs[:vm_id]
  vm = $evm.vmdb('vm').find_by_id(vm_id)
  ...
end
```

Summary

In this chapter we've learned the various ways that we can enter Automate and start running our scripts. We've also learned how to create generically useful methods that can be called in several ways, and how to establish their running context using `$evm.root['vmdb_object_type']`.

Many of the Automate methods that we write are usable in several different contexts —as part of a virtual machine provisioning workflow or from a button, for example. They can be run from the first instance called when we enter Automate, or via a relationship in another instance already running in the Automation Engine. This instance might even be a state machine (we discuss state machines in Chapter 13), in which case we might need to signal an exit condition using `$evm.root['ae_result']`:

```
# Normal exit
$evm.root['ae_result'] = 'ok'
exit MIQ_OK
rescue => err
  $evm.root['ae_result'] = 'error'
  $evm.root['ae_reason'] = "Unspecified error, see automation.log for backtrace"
  exit MIQ_STOP
```

If we take all of these possible factors into account when we write our scripts, we add flexibility in how they can be used and called. We also increase code reuse and reduce the sprawl of multiple similar scripts in our custom domains.

Further Reading

Scripting Actions in CloudForms Chapter 3—Invoking Automate (*http://red.ht/ 21cx2uB*)

## CHAPTER 12

Requests and Tasks

We have seen several references to automation requests and tasks so far in the book. This chapter explains what they are, their differences, and why it's useful to understand them. This is a *deep-dive* chapter, so feel free to skip it for now and return later if curious.

The Need for Approval

Some relatively simple automation operations result in the Automate instance being run directly with no need for approval by an administrator. Examples of these are:

- Running an Automate instance from simulation
- Automate instances that run to populate dynamic dialog elements
- Running an Automate instance from a button
- Automate instances entered as a result of a control policy action type of Invoke a Custom Automation
- Alerts that send a management event

The automation scripts that we've developed so far fall into ths first category.

Other, more complex automation operations—such as provisioning virtual machines or cloud instances—can alter or consume resources in our virtual or cloud infrastructure. For this type of operation, CloudForms allows us to insert an approval stage into the Automate workflow. It does this by separating the operation into two distinct stages—the *request* and the *task*—with an administrative approval being required to progress from one to the other.

Examples of these are:

- Calling an automation request via the RESTful API
- Provisioning a host
- Provisioning a virtual machine
- Requesting a service
- Reconfiguring a virtual machine
- Reconfiguring a service
- Migrating a virtual machine

Let's now look at these in more detail.

Request and Task Objects

There are Automation Engine objects representing the two stages of each of these more complex operations. Each type of object holds information relevant to its particular stage (see Table 12-1). The *request object* contains information about the requester and the operation to be performed. The *task object* holds the details about and status of the actual automation operation (the "task"):

Table 12-1. Object stages

Operation	Request object	Task object
Generic operation	`miq_request`	`miq_request_task`
Automation request	`automation_request`	`automation_task`
Provisioning a host	`miq_host_provision_request`	`miq_host_provision`
Provisioning a VM	`miq_provision_request`	`miq_provision`
Reconfiguring a VM	`vm_reconfigure_request`	`vm_reconfigure_task`
Requesting a service	`service_template_provision_request`	`service_template_provision_task`
Reconfiguring a service	`service_reconfigure_request`	`service_reconfigure_task`
Migrating a VM	`vm_migrate_request`	`vm_migrate_task`

In addition to those listed here, a kind of pseudo–request object is created when we add a service catalog item to provision a VM.

When we create the catalog item, we fill out the Request Info fields, as if we were provisioning a VM interactively via the Infrastructure → Virtual Machines → Lifecycle → Provision VMs menu (see Chapter 33).

The values that we select or enter are added to the options hash in a newly created `miq_provision_request_template` object (see Table 12-2). This then serves as the "request" template for all subsequent VM provision operations from this service catalog item.

Table 12-2. Adding values to the options hash

Operation	Request object	Task object
VM ordered from a service catalog Item	`miq_provision_request_template`	`miq_provision`

Approval

Automation requests must be approved before the task object that handles the automation workflow is created. Admin users can auto-approve their own requests, whereas standard users need their requests explicitly approved by anyone in an access-control group with the roles `EvmRole-super_administrator`, `EvmRole-administrator`, or `EvmRole-approver`.

Some automation workflows have an *approval* stage that can auto-approve requests, even from standard users. The most common automation operation that standard users frequently perform is to provision a virtual machine, and for this there are approval thresholds in place (`max_vms`, `max_cpus`, `max_memory`, `max_retirement_days`). VM provision requests specifying numbers or sizes below these thresholds are auto-approved, whereas requests exceeding these thresholds are blocked, pending explicit approval.

Object Class Ancestry

If a request is approved, one or more task objects will be created from information contained in the request object (a single request for three VMs will result in three task objects, for example).

We can examine the class ancestry for the CloudForms 3.2 request objects:

```
MiqAeServiceAutomationRequest < MiqAeServiceMiqRequest
MiqAeServiceMiqHostProvisionRequest < MiqAeServiceMiqRequest
MiqAeServiceMiqProvisionRequest < MiqAeServiceMiqRequest
MiqAeServiceMiqProvisionRequestTemplate < MiqAeServiceMiqProvisionRequest
MiqAeServiceMiqRequest < MiqAeServiceModelBase
MiqAeServiceServiceTemplateProvisionRequest < MiqAeServiceMiqRequest
MiqAeServiceVmMigrateRequest < MiqAeServiceMiqRequest
MiqAeServiceVmReconfigureRequest < MiqAeServiceMiqRequest
```

and for the task objects:

```
MiqAeServiceAutomationTask < MiqAeServiceMiqRequestTask
MiqAeServiceMiqHostProvision < MiqAeServiceMiqRequestTask
MiqAeServiceMiqProvision < MiqAeServiceMiqRequestTask
MiqAeServiceMiqProvisionAmazon < MiqAeServiceMiqProvisionCloud
MiqAeServiceMiqProvisionCloud < MiqAeServiceMiqProvision
MiqAeServiceMiqProvisionOpenstack < MiqAeServiceMiqProvisionCloud
MiqAeServiceMiqProvisionRedhat < MiqAeServiceMiqProvision
MiqAeServiceMiqProvisionRedhatViaIso < MiqAeServiceMiqProvisionRedhat
MiqAeServiceMiqProvisionRedhatViaPxe < MiqAeServiceMiqProvisionRedhat
MiqAeServiceMiqProvisionVmware < MiqAeServiceMiqProvision
MiqAeServiceMiqProvisionVmwareViaNetAppRcu < MiqAeServiceMiqProvisionVmware
MiqAeServiceMiqProvisionVmwareViaPxe < MiqAeServiceMiqProvisionVmware
MiqAeServiceMiqRequestTask < MiqAeServiceModelBase
MiqAeServiceServiceTemplateProvisionTask < MiqAeServiceMiqRequestTask
MiqAeServiceVmReconfigureTask < MiqAeServiceMiqRequestTask
```

We see that there are twice as many types of task object. This is because a request to perform an action (e.g., provision a VM) can be converted into one of several types of workflow (e.g., provision a VMware VM via PXE, or clone from template).

Context

When we develop our own automation scripts, we may be working with either a request *or* a task object, depending on the workflow stage of the operation that we're interacting with (for example, provisioning a VM). Sometimes we have to search for one and if that fails, fall back to the other, like so:

```
prov = $evm.root['miq_provision_request'] ||
       $evm.root['miq_provision'] ||
       $evm.root['miq_provision_request_template']
```

If we have a request object, there may not necessarily be a task object (yet), but if we have one of these more complex task objects, we can always follow an association to find the request object that preceded it.

When we're developing Automate methods, having an understanding of whether we're running in a request or task context can be really useful. Think about what stage in the automation flow the method will be running—before or after approval.

Example scenario: we wish to set the number of VMs to be provisioned as part of a VM provisioning operation. We know that a :number_of_vms options hash key can be set, but this appears in the options hash for both the task and request objects. (See Chapter 20 for more details.) Where should we set it?

Answer: the *task* objects are created after the *request* is approved, and the number of VMs to be provisioned is one of the criteria that auto-approval uses to decide whether or not to approve the request. The :number_of_vms key also determines how many task objects are created (it is the task object that contains the VM-specific options hash keys such as :vm_target_name, :ip_addr, etc.).

We must therefore set :number_of_vms in the request options hash, *before* the task objects are created.

Object Contents

The request object contains details about the requester (person), approval status, approver (person), and reason, and the parameters to be used for the resulting task in the form of an *options hash*. The options hash contains whatever optional information is required for the automation operation to complete, and its size depends on the automation request type. In the case of an miq_provision_request, the options hash has over 70 key/value pairs, specifying the characteristics of the VM to be provisioned—for example:

```
...
miq_provision_request.options[:vlan] = ["rhevm", "rhevm"]   (type: Array)
miq_provision_request.options[:vm_auto_start] = [true, 1]   (type: Array)
miq_provision_request.options[:vm_description] = nil
miq_provision_request.options[:vm_memory] = ["2048", "2048"]   (type: Array)
miq_provision_request.options[:vm_name] = rhel7srv003   (type: String)
...
```

Much of the information in the request object is propagated to the task object, including the options hash.

Dumping the Object Contents

We can use *object_walker* to show the difference between an automation request and task object, by setting the following @walk_association_whitelist:

```
@walk_association_whitelist = \
    { "MiqAeServiceAutomationTask" => ["automation_request", "miq_request"]}
```

We can call the *ObjectWalker* instance from the RESTful API, using the */api/automation_requests* URI.

The request object

When the Automate instance (in this case, *ObjectWalker*) runs, the request has already been approved, and so our $evm.root only has a direct link to the task object. The request object is still reachable via an association from the task object, however:

```
automation_request = $evm.root['automation_task'].automation_request
(object type: MiqAeServiceAutomationRequest, object ID: 2000000000003)
|    automation_request.approval_state = approved   (type: String)
|    automation_request.created_on = 2015-06-07 09:14:03 UTC (type: ...
|    automation_request.description = Automation Task   (type: String)
|    automation_request.id = 2000000000003   (type: Fixnum)
|    automation_request.message = Automation Request initiated   (type: String)
|    automation_request.options[:attrs] = {:userid=>"admin"}   (type: Hash)
|    automation_request.options[:class_name] = Methods   (type: String)
|    automation_request.options[:delivered_on] = 2015-06-07 09:14:10 UTC
|    automation_request.options[:instance_name] = ObjectWalker   (type: String)
|    automation_request.options[:namespace] = Bit63/Discovery   (type: String)
|    automation_request.options[:user_id] = 2000000000001   (type: Fixnum)
|    automation_request.request_state = active   (type: String)
|    automation_request.request_type = automation   (type: String)
|    automation_request.requester_id = 2000000000001   (type: Fixnum)
|    automation_request.requester_name = Administrator   (type: String)
|    automation_request.status = Ok   (type: String)
|    automation_request.type = AutomationRequest   (type: String)
|    automation_request.updated_on = 2015-06-07 09:14:13 UTC   (type: ActiveSup...
|    automation_request.userid = admin   (type: String)
|    --- virtual columns follow ---
|    automation_request.reason = Auto-Approved   (type: String)
|    automation_request.region_description = Region 2   (type: String)
|    automation_request.region_number = 2   (type: Fixnum)
|    automation_request.request_type_display = Automation   (type: String)
|    automation_request.resource_type = AutomationRequest   (type: String)
|    automation_request.stamped_on = 2015-06-07 09:14:04 UTC   (type: ActiveSup...
|    automation_request.state = active   (type: String)
|    automation_request.v_approved_by = Administrator   (type: String)
|    automation_request.v_approved_by_email =    (type: String)
|    --- end of virtual columns ---
|    --- associations follow ---
|    automation_request.approvers (type: Association (empty))
|    automation_request.automation_tasks (type: Association)
|    automation_request.destination (type: Association (empty))
|    automation_request.miq_request (type: Association)
|    automation_request.miq_request_tasks (type: Association)
|    automation_request.requester (type: Association)
|    automation_request.resource (type: Association)
|    automation_request.source (type: Association (empty))
|    --- end of associations ---
|    --- methods follow ---
```

```
|    automation_request.add_tag
|    automation_request.approve
|    automation_request.authorized?
|    automation_request.clear_tag
|    automation_request.deny
|    automation_request.description=
|    automation_request.get_classification
|    automation_request.get_classifications
|    automation_request.get_option
|    automation_request.get_option_last
|    automation_request.get_tag
|    automation_request.get_tags
|    automation_request.pending
|    automation_request.set_message
|    automation_request.set_option
|    automation_request.user_message=
|    --- end of methods ---
```

The task object

The task object is available directly from $evm.root:

```
$evm.root['automation_task'] => #<MiqAeMethodService::MiqAeServiceAutomation \
  Task:0x0000000800a0c0>  (type: DRb::DRbObject, URI: druby://127.0.0.1:35...)
|    $evm.root['automation_task'].created_on = 2015-06-07 09:14:10 UTC
|    $evm.root['automation_task'].description = Automation Task   (type: String)
|    $evm.root['automation_task'].id = 2000000000003   (type: Fixnum)
|    $evm.root['automation_task'].message = Automation Request initiated
|    $evm.root['automation_task'].miq_request_id = 2000000000003 (type: Fixnum)
|    $evm.root['automation_task'].options[:attrs] = {:userid=>"admin"}
|    $evm.root['automation_task'].options[:class_name] = Methods (type: String)
|    $evm.root['automation_task'].options[:delivered_on] = 2015-06-07 09:14:10
|    $evm.root['automation_task'].options[:instance_name] = ObjectWalker
|    $evm.root['automation_task'].options[:namespace] = Bit63/Discovery
|    $evm.root['automation_task'].options[:user_id] = 2000000000001
|    $evm.root['automation_task'].phase_context = {}   (type: Hash)
|    $evm.root['automation_task'].request_type = automation   (type: String)
|    $evm.root['automation_task'].state = active   (type: String)
|    $evm.root['automation_task'].status = retry   (type: String)
|    $evm.root['automation_task'].type = AutomationTask   (type: String)
|    $evm.root['automation_task'].updated_on = 2015-06-07 09:14:13 UTC
|    $evm.root['automation_task'].userid = admin   (type: String)
|    --- virtual columns follow ---
|    $evm.root['automation_task'].region_description = Region 2   (type: String)
|    $evm.root['automation_task'].region_number = 2   (type: Fixnum)
|    --- end of virtual columns ---
|    --- associations follow ---
|    $evm.root['automation_task'].automation_request (type: Association)

     <as above>

|    automation_request = $evm.root['automation_task'].automation_request
     (object type: MiqAeServiceAutomationRequest, object ID: 2000000000003)
```

```
|     automation_request.approval_state = approved   (type: String)
|     automation_request.created_on = 2015-06-07 09:14:03 UTC  (type: Ac...
|     automation_request.description = Automation Task   (type: String)
|     automation_request.id = 2000000000003   (type: Fixnum)
|     automation_request.message = Automation Request initiated
|     ...
</as above>

|  $evm.root['automation_task'].destination (type: Association (empty))
|  $evm.root['automation_task'].miq_request (type: Association)
|  miq_request = $evm.root['automation_task'].miq_request
|  (object type: MiqAeServiceAutomationRequest, object ID: 2000000000003)
|  $evm.root['automation_task'].miq_request_task (type: Association (empty))
|  $evm.root['automation_task'].miq_request_tasks (type: Association (empty))
|  $evm.root['automation_task'].source (type: Association (empty))
|  --- end of associations ---
|  --- methods follow ---
|  $evm.root['automation_task'].add_tag
|  $evm.root['automation_task'].clear_tag
|  $evm.root['automation_task'].execute
|  $evm.root['automation_task'].finished
|  $evm.root['automation_task'].get_classification
|  $evm.root['automation_task'].get_classifications
|  $evm.root['automation_task'].get_option
|  $evm.root['automation_task'].get_option_last
|  $evm.root['automation_task'].get_tag
|  $evm.root['automation_task'].get_tags
|  $evm.root['automation_task'].message=
|  $evm.root['automation_task'].set_option
|  $evm.root['automation_task'].statemachine_task_status
|  $evm.root['automation_task'].user_message=
|  --- end of methods ---
$evm.root['automation_task_id'] = 2000000000003   (type: String)
```

Comparing the Objects

We can see some interesting things when we compare these two objects:

- From the task object, the request object is available from either of two associations: its specific object type `$evm.root['automation_task'].automation_request` and the more generic `$evm.root['automation_task'].miq_request`. These both link to the same request object, and this is the case with all of the more complex task objects—we can always follow an `miq_request` association to get back to the request, regardless of request object type.

- We see that the request object has several approval-specific methods that the task object doesn't have (or need):

```
automation_request.approve
automation_request.authorized?
automation_request.deny
automation_request.pending
```

We can use these methods to implement our own approval workflow mechanism if we wish (see Chapter 43 for an example).

Summary

The chapter has illustrated how more complex automation workflows are split into a *request* stage and a *task* stage. This allows us to optionally insert an administrative approval "gate" between them and thus maintain a level of control over our standard users to prevent them from running uncontrolled automation operations in our virtual infrastructure.

We have discussed request and task objects, and why it can be beneficial to keep track of whether our automation scripts are running in request or task context (and therefore which of the two objects to make use of).

This has been quite a detailed analysis, but they are very useful concepts to grasp.

Further Reading

Methods Available for Automation—Requests (Miq_Request) (*http://red.ht/1Ul0I8b*)

## CHAPTER 13

State Machines

We have mentioned *workflows* several times in the preceding chapters. A workflow can be simply defined as a sequence of operations or steps that make up a work process. Many tasks that we perform as cloud or systems administrators can be broken down into simple workflow steps:

1. Do something.

2. Do something.

3. Do something.

CloudForms Automate allows us to add intelligence to our workflow steps by defining steps as *states*. Each state is capable of performing pre and postprocessing around the main task, and can handle and potentially recover from errors that occur while performing the task (see Table 13-1). Individual states can enter a retry loop, with the maximum number of retries and overall timeout for the state being definable.

Table 13-1. Adding intelligence to workflow steps via states

Step	On entry	Task	On exit	On error
1	Preprocess before doing something.	Do something.	Postprocess after doing something.	Handle any errors while doing something.
2	Preprocess before doing something.	Do something.	Postprocess after doing something.	Handle any errors while doing something.
3	Preprocess before doing something.	Do something.	Postprocess after doing something.	Handle any errors while doing something.

When we assemble several of these intelligent states together, it becomes an Automate *state machine*. The logic flow through an Automate state machine is shown in Figure 13-1.

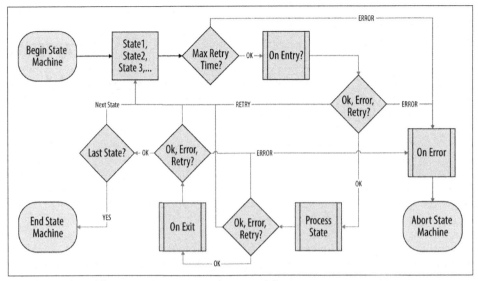

Figure 13-1. Simple Automate state machine workflow

Building a State Machine

We build an Automate state machine in much the same way that we define any other class schema. One of the types of schema field is a state, and if we construct a class schema definition comprising a sequence of states, this then becomes a state machine.

> A state machine schema should comprise *only* assertions, attributes, or states. We should not have any schema lines that have a Type field of Relationship in a state machine.

State Machine Schema Field Columns

If we look at all of the attributes that we can add for a schema field, in addition to the familar Name, Description, and Value headings, we see a number of column headings that we haven't used so far (see Figure 13-2).

Figure 13-2. Schema field column headings

The schema columns for a state machine are the same as in any other class schema, but we use more of them.

Value (instance)/Default Value (schema)

As in any other class schema, this value is a relationship to an *instance* to be run to perform the main processing of the state. Surprising as it may seem, we don't necessarily need to specify a value here for a state machine (see On Entry, next), although it is good practice to do so.

On Entry

We can optionally define an On Entry method to be run before the "main" method (the Value entry) is run. We can use this to set up or test for preconditions to the state; for example, if the "main" method adds a tag to an object, the On Entry method might check that the category and tag exist.

The method name can be specified as a relative path to the local class (i.e., just the method name), or in namespace/class/method syntax.

Note that some older state machines, such as */Infrastructure/VM/Provisoning/State-Machines/ProvisionRequestApproval/*, use an On Entry method instead of a Value relationship to perform the main work of the state. This usage is deprecated, and we should always use a Value relationship in our state machines.

On Exit

We can optionally define an On Exit method to be run if the "main" method (the Value relationship/instance or On Entry method) returns $evm.root['ae_result'] = *ok*.

On Error

We can optionally define an On Error method to be run if the "main" method (the Value relationship/instance or On Entry method) returns $evm.root['ae_result'] = *error*.

Max Retries

We can optionally define a maximum number of retries that the state is allowed to attempt. Defining this in the state rather than the method itself simplifies the method coding and makes it easier to write generic methods that can be reused in a number of state machines.

Max Time

We can optionally define a maximum time (in seconds) that the state will be permitted to run for, before being terminated.

State Machine Example

We can look at the out-of-the-box */Infrastructure/VM/Provisoning/StateMachines/ ProvisionRequestApproval/Default* state machine instance as an example and see that it defines four attributes and has just two states: `ValidateRequest` and `ApproveRe quest` (see Figure 13-3).

Fields									
Name	Value	On Entry	On Exit	On Error	Collect	Max Retries	Max Time	Message
max_cpus								create
max_vms	1							create
max_memory								create
max_retirement_days								create
ValidateRequest		validate_request		pending_request		100		create
ApproveRequest		approve_request				100		create

Figure 13-3. The /ProvisionRequestApproval/Default state machine

Neither state has a Value relationship, but each runs a locally defined class method to perform the main processing of the state.

The `ValidateRequest` state runs the *validate_request* On Entry method and *pending_request* as the On Error method.

The `ApproveRequest` state runs the *approve_request* On Entry method.

State Variables

There are several state variables that can be read or set by state methods to control the processing of the state machine.

Setting State Result

We can run a method within the context of a state machine to return a completion status to the Automation Engine, which then decides which next action to perform (such as whether to advance to the next state).

We do this by setting one of three values in the `ae_result` hash key:

```
# Signal an error
$evm.root['ae_result'] = 'error'
$evm.root['ae_reason'] = "Failed to do something"

# Signal that the step should be retried after a time interval
$evm.root['ae_result']         = 'retry'
$evm.root['ae_retry_interval'] = '1.minute'
```

```
# Signal that the step completed successfully
$evm.root['ae_result'] = 'ok'
```

State Retries

We can find out whether we're in a step that's being retried by querying the `ae_state_retries` key:

```
state_retries = $evm.root['ae_state_retries'] || 0
```

Getting the State Machine Name

We can find the name of the state machine that we're running in, as follows:

```
state_machine = $evm.current_object.class_name
```

Getting the Current Step in the State Machine

We can find out which step (state) in the state machine we're executing in (useful if we have a generic error-handling method):

```
step = $evm.root['ae_state']
```

Getting the on_entry, on_exit, on_error Status State

A method can determine which status state (on_entry, on_exit, or on_error) it's currently executing in, as follows:

```
if $evm.root['ae_status_state'] == "on_entry"
  ...
```

State Machine Enhancements in CloudForms 4.0

Several useful additions to state machine functionality were added in CloudForms 4.0.

Error Recovery

Rather than automatically aborting the state machine (the behavior prior to Cloud-Forms 4.0), an on_error method now has the capability to take recovery action from an error condition and set $evm.root['ae_result'] = 'continue' to ensure that the state machine continues.

Skipping States

To allow for intelligent on_entry preprocessing, and to advance if preconditions are already met, an on_entry method can set $evm.root['ae_result'] = 'skip' to advance directly to the next state, without calling the current state's Value method.

Jumping to a Specific State

Any of our state machine methods can set $evm.root['ae_next_state'] = <state_name> to allow the state machine to advance several steps.

Note that setting ae_next_state allows us only to go forward in a state machine. If we want to go back to a previous state, we can restart the state machine but set ae_next_state to the name of the state at which we want to restart. When issuing a restart, if we do not specify ae_next_state, the state machine will restart at the first state:

```
# Currently in state4
$evm.root['ae_result'] = 'restart'
$evm.root['ae_next_state'] = 'state2'
```

Nested State Machines

As has been mentioned, the Value field of a state machine should be a relationship to an instance. Prior to CloudForms 4.0 this could not be another state machine, but with 4.0 this requirement has been lifted, so now we can call an entire state machine from a step in a *parent* state machine (see Figure 13-4).

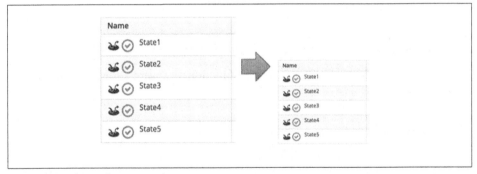

Figure 13-4. Nested state machines

Saving Variables Between State Retries

When a step is retried in a state machine, the Automation Engine reinstantiates the entire state machine, starting from the state issuing the retry.

 This is why state machines should not contain lines that have a Type field of Relationship. A state is a special kind of relationship that can be skipped during retries. If we had a Relationship line anywhere in our state machine, then it would be rerun every time a later state issued a `$evm.root['ae_result'] = 'retry'`.

This reinstantiation makes life difficult if we want to store and retrieve variables between steps in a state machine (something we frequently want to do). Fortunately, there are three `$evm` methods that we can use to test for the presence of, save, and read variables between reinstantiations of our state machine:

```
$evm.set_state_var(:server_name, "myserver")
if $evm.state_var_exist?(:server_name)
  server_name = $evm.get_state_var(:server_name)
end
```

We can save most types of variables, but because of the dRuby mechanics behind the scenes, we can't save hashes that have default initializers—for example:

```
my_hash=Hash.new { |h, k| h[k] = {} }
```

Here the `|h, k| h[k] = {}` is the initializer function.

Summary

State machines are incredibly useful, and we often use them to create our own intelligent, reusable workflows. They allow us to focus on the logic of our state methods, while the Automation Engine handles the complexity of the on-entry and on-exit condition handling and the state retry logic.

When deciding whether to implement a workflow as a state machine, consider the following:

- Could I skip any of my workflow steps by intelligently preprocessing?
- Would my code be cleaner if I could assume that preconditions had been set up or tested before entry?
- Might any of my workflow steps result in an error that could possibly be handled and recovered from?
- Do any of my workflow steps require me to retry an operation in a wait loop?

- Do I need to put a timeout on my workflow completing?

If the answer to any of these questions is yes, then a state machine is a good candidate for implementation.

Further Reading

Automate State Machine Enhancements (*http://bit.ly/1TZL0f1*)

## CHAPTER 14

More Advanced Schema Features

Our Automate examples so far have used relatively simple class schema features. We have used the attribute and method field types, and we've seen how to store attributes as strings or encrypted passwords. We've called our instances using simple URI pathnames such as *General/Methods/HelloWorld*, and our instances have run single methods. This simple type of schema allows us to create many different and useful instances, but there are times when we need additional flexibility. For example, it is sometimes useful to be able to select which of several methods in our schema to run, based on criteria established at runtime.

There are three more class schema features that we can use to extend the usefulness of our instances: *messages*, *assertions*, and *collections*.

Messages

Each schema field has a Message column/value that we can optionally use to identify a particular field to execute or evaluate when we call the instance. We can think of this as a filter to determine which schema values to process.

The default message is *create*, and if we look at the schema that we created for our */ACME/General/Methods* class, we see that the default message value of *create* was automatically set for us for all fields (see Figure 14-1).

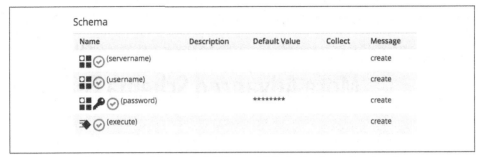

Figure 14-1. The schema of the /ACME/General/Methods class, showing the message

We specify the message when we create a relationship to an instance, by appending #message after the URI to the instance. If we don't explicitly specify a message, then #create is implicitly used.

For example, we could create a relationship to run our first HelloWorld instance, using a URI of either:

    /ACME/General/Methods/HelloWorld

or:

    /ACME/General/Methods/HelloWorld#create

In both cases, the *hello_world* method would execute, as this is the *method* schema field "filtered" by the *create* message.

Specifying Our Own Messages

It can be useful to create a class/instance schema that allows for one of several methods to be executed, depending on the message passed to the instance at runtime. For example, the schema for the */Infrastructure/VM/Provisioning/Placement* class allows for a provider-specific VM placement algorithm to be created (see Figure 14-2).

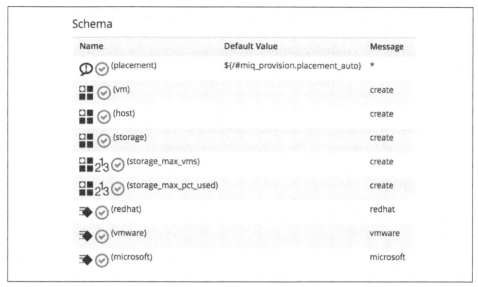

Figure 14-2. Schema for the /Infrastructure/VM/Provisioning/Placement class

We can therefore call any instance of the class as part of the VM provisioning state machine, by appending a message created from a variable substitution corresponding to the provisioning source vendor (i.e., redhat, vmware, or microsoft):

```
/Infra.../VM/Provisioning/Placement/default#${/#miq_provision.source.vendor}
```

In this way we are able to create a generic class and instance definition that contains several methods, and we can choose which method to run dynamically at runtime by using a message.

Assertions

One of the schema field types that we can use is an *assertion*. This is a Boolean check that we can put anywhere in our class schema (assertions are always processed first in an instance). If the assertion evaluates to true, the remaining instance schema fields are processed. If the assertion evaluates to false, the remainder of the instance fields are not processed.

We can see an example of an assertion (called placement) at the start of the schema for the Placement class in Figure 14-2. Placement methods are relevant only if the Automatic checkbox has been selected at provisioning time, and this checkbox sets a Boolean value, miq_provision.placement_auto. The placement assertion checks that this value is true and prevents the remainder of the instance from running if automatic placement has not been selected.

Another use for assertions is to put a "guard" field in an instance whose methods are applicable only to a single provider. For example, we might have an instance that configures VMware NSX software-defined networking during the provisioning of a virtual machine. The methods would fail if called during an OpenStack provisioning operation, but we can add an assertion field to the instance, as follows:

```
'${/#miq_provision.source.vendor}' == 'VMware'
```

This will return `true` if the provisioning operation is to a VMware provider but `false` otherwise, thereby preventing the methods from running in a non-VMware context.

Collections

As we have seen, there is a parent-child relationship between the `$evm.root` object (the one whose instantiation took us into the Automation Engine) and subsequent objects created as a result of following schema relationships or by calling `$evm.instantiate`.

If a child object has schema attribute values, it can read or write to them by using its own `$evm.object` hash (e.g., we saw the use of `$evm.object['username']` in Chapter 4). Sometimes we need to propagate these values back up the parent `$evm.root` object, and we do this using *collections*.

We define a value to collect in the Collect schema column, using this syntax (see Figure 14-3):

```
/root_variable_name = schema_variable_name
```

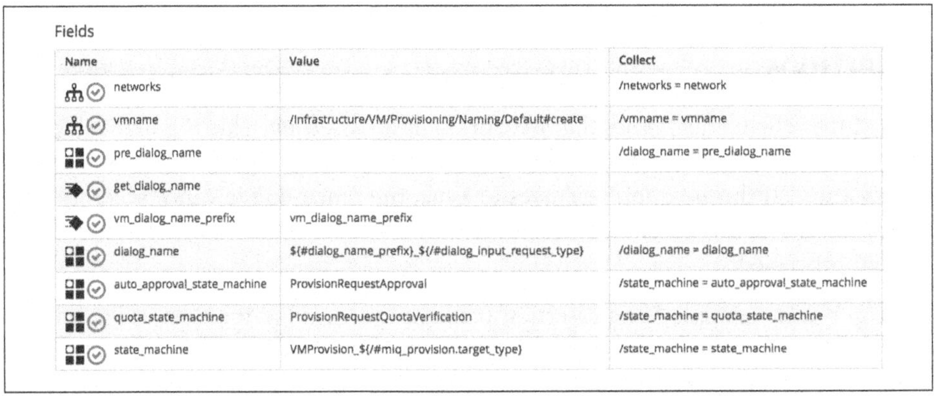

Fields		
Name	Value	Collect
networks		/networks = network
vmname	/Infrastructure/VM/Provisioning/Naming/Default#create	/vmname = vmname
pre_dialog_name		/dialog_name = pre_dialog_name
get_dialog_name		
vm_dialog_name_prefix	vm_dialog_name_prefix	
dialog_name	${#dialog_name_prefix}_${/#dialog_input_request_type}	/dialog_name = dialog_name
auto_approval_state_machine	ProvisionRequestApproval	/state_machine = auto_approval_state_machine
quota_state_machine	ProvisionRequestQuotaVerification	/state_machine = quota_state_machine
state_machine	VMProvision_${/#miq_provision.target_type}	/state_machine = state_machine

Figure 14-3. Collections defined in the schema of a provisioning profile

This provisioning profile has several schema attributes defined, such as `dialog_name` and `auto_approval_state_machine`. The Collect value makes these attribute values available to this instance's caller as `$evm.root['dialog_name']` and `$evm.root['state_machine']`.

Summary

This chapter completes our coverage of the objects that we work with in the Automate Datastore. The three schema features that we've learned about here are used less frequently but are still very useful tools to have in our scripting toolbag.

## CHAPTER 15

Event Processing

One of the most powerful features of CloudForms Automate is its capability to process *events*. CloudForms can monitor and respond to external (provider) events, such as a virtual machine starting or stopping, or a hypervisor going into maintenance. These events can then be used as triggers for Automate operations. We might wish to initiate a SmartState Analysis scan on a new VMware virtual machine when a `VmCrea tedEvent` event is detected, for example. Perhaps we'd like to intercept and cancel a `USER_INITIATED_SHUTDOWN_VM` event being detected on a critical Red Hat Enterprise Virtualization (RHEV) virtual machine that we've tagged as `do_not_shutdown`.

CloudForms Automate also raises its own events internally, which can then be used as workflow triggers. We see an example of this when we provision a new virtual machine (we cover VM provisioning in Part II of the book). The workflow for provisioning a virtual machine includes an approval stage—we can optionally allow administrators to approve large VM requests—followed by a quota-checking stage to ensure that users are not exceeding their quota. The successful approval of the VM provisioning request results in Automate raising a `request_approved` internal event. This `request_approved` event is then used as the trigger to automatically start the quota-checking workflow (see Chapter 19 for more details on this workflow).

In this chapter we'll examine in detail how events are processed by the Automation Engine. This is a *deep-dive* chapter containing useful background information but can be skipped for now if required. Event handling happens automatically in Cloud-Forms, and an understanding of the event processing workflow can help us as we advance our Automate skills. In Chapter 43 we create an entirely new approval workflow, based largely on our knowledge of event processing.

To improve the scalability of event handling, particularly with the advent of new providers and provider types, the event processing mechanism has been substantially rewritten in CloudForms 4.0. We'll first look at the new component parts of Automate's event processing, and then we'll study how external events are caught and internal events are raised and handled.

Event Processing Component Parts

The are several new components involved in processing events in CloudForms 4.0, including an event stream object type, the Event Switchboard, and event handlers.

The Event Stream Object

Events are now handled by an `EventStream` object, derived from a parent `EventStream` class. An `EventStream` object is created in response to an external or internal event, and this object is sent to Automate to initiate the event handling process.

Events enter Automate at the */System/Process/Event* instance, and this contains a `rel5` relationship that redirects the handling of the event into the Event Switchboard. The root of the Event Switchboard is at */System/Event* (see Figure 15-1).

Figure 15-1. Entry relationship into the Event Switchboard

The Event Switchboard

The *Event Switchboard* is a new set of namespaces, classes, instances, and methods, written to handle the processing of events in a scalable manner.

/System/Process/Event contains a `rel5` relationship into the switchboard, and this relationship URI comprises three parts: the event namespace, the event source, and the event type. Each is selected from the substitution of a runtime variable:

```
/System/Event/${/#event_stream.event_namespace} /
${/#event_stream.source} /
${/#event_type}
```

The substituted values are taken from attributes of the `EventStream` object representing the event and the event type.

Event stream namespace

The `${/#event_stream.event_namespace}` part of the relationship translates to one of three *event stream namespaces*:

- `EmsEvent` if the event's origin was an *external management system* (i.e., a provider). An `EmsEvent` instance contains all information about its virtual machine, host, and provider related to the event.

- `MiqEvent` if the event's origin was an internal CloudForms/ManageIQ-initiated policy event.

- `RequestEvent` if the event is related to an automation request (e.g., `request_cre ated`).

These can be seen in Figure 15-2.

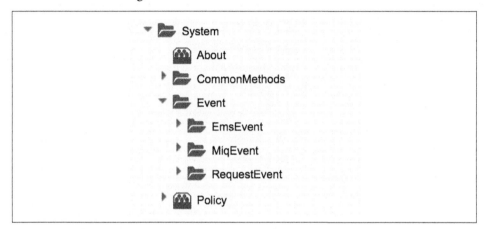

Figure 15-2. Event stream namespaces

Event stream source

Within each of the event stream namespaces are classes that define the *event stream source* instances. The selection of source class is made from the substitution of the `$ {/#event_stream.source}` part of the */System/Process/Event* `rel5` relationship. We can see that for the `EmsEvent` namespace, these represent the various external management systems (Amazon, OpenStack, etc.). See Figure 15-3.

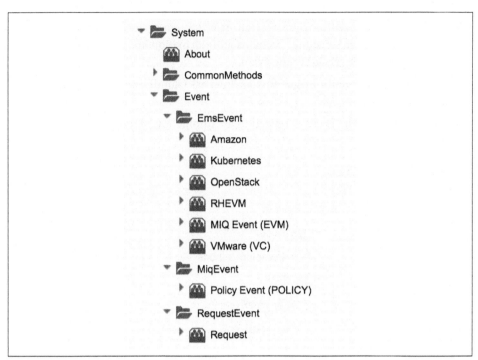

Figure 15-3. Event stream sources

Event type

Under the appropriate event stream source classes are instances that define the processing required for each *event type*. The selection of event type is made from the substitution of the ${/#event_type} part of the */System/Process/Event* rel5 relationship. We can see that these represent the various events that the EventCatcher::Runner workers detect from the provider message bus. Figure 15-4 shows the event types in the Amazon namespace.

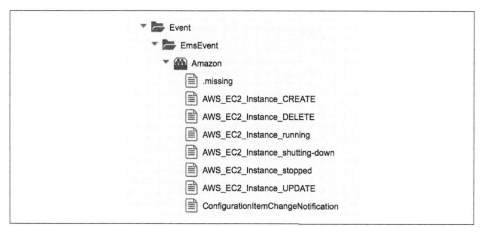

Figure 15-4. Event types for the Amazon event stream source

The event type instances contain one or more relationships to *event handlers* in the /
System/event_handlers namespace that define the actions to take for that event. For
example, the Amazon event `AWS_EC2_Instance_running` will call the *event_action_pol-
icy* handler to push a new `vm_start` policy event through the Switchboard. It also
calls the *event_action_refresh* handler to trigger a provider refresh so that the current
instance details can be retrieved (see Figure 15-5).

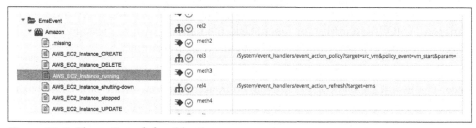

Figure 15-5. The actions defined by the event type instance

Event Handlers

Event handlers are instances and methods that perform the actual granular processing for each event. The methods are built in for execution efficiency; their code is not
visible in the Automate Explorer (see Figure 15-6).

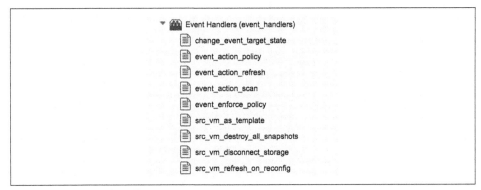

Figure 15-6. Event handler instances

Catching and Handling External Events

One of the CloudForms server roles that can be configured is *Event Monitor*. If we enable this role, we get two additional types of worker threads started on our appliance, to detect (*catch*) and process (*handle*) external provider events.

Event Catching

External (provider) events are monitored by *EventCatcher* workers, and these monitor the real-time message or event buses on the various providers: AWS:config for Amazon, AMQP/RabbitMQ for OpenStack, the native VMware message bus, or the RHEV-M events exposed through the RESTful API, for example.

There is a specific EventCatcher worker for each provider configured on an appliance. The EventCatcher workers are named in accordance with the new CloudForms 4.0 provider namespace format, so entries in *evm.log* appear as:

```
ManageIQ::Providers::Redhat::InfraManager::EventCatcher::Runner#process_event) \
     EMS [rhevm01] as [admin@internal] Caught event [USER_INITIATED_SHUTDOWN_VM]
ManageIQ::Providers::Redhat::InfraManager::EventCatcher::Runner#process_event) \
     EMS [rhevm01] as [admin@internal] Caught event [VM_DOWN]
...IQ::Providers::Openstack::CloudManager::EventCatcher::Runner#process_event) \
     EMS [rhosp-cont] as [admin] Caught event [compute.instance.power_on.start]
```

Event Processing

The EventCatcher workers queue the handling and processing of the specific event to one or more *EventHandler* workers. The arguments passed to the EventHandler include the provider-specific details for the event source.

We can trace the steps in the event processing workflow on an RHEV USER_RUN_VM event being caught.

Step 1

The first thing that we see in *evm.log* is the call to the EventHandler, along with arguments containing the RHEV API `ids` and `hrefs` describing the event source:

```
Args: [{:id=>"26790", \
    :href=>"/api/events/26790", \
    :cluster=>{
        :id=>"00000001-0001-0001-0001-000000000249", \
        :href=>"/api/clusters/00000001-0001-0001-0001-000000000249"}, \
    :data_center=>{
        :id=>"00000002-0002-0002-0002-000000000314", \
        :href=>"/api/datacenters/00000002-0002-0002-0002-000000000314"}, \
    :host=>{
        :id=>"b959325b-c667-4e3a-a52e-fd936c225a1a", \
        :href=>"/api/hosts/b959325b-c667-4e3a-a52e-fd936c225a1a"}, \
    :user=>{
        :id=>"fdfc627c-d875-11e0-90f0-83df133b58cc", \
         :href=>"/api/users/fdfc627c-d875-11e0-90f0-83df133b58cc"}, \
    :vm=>{
        :id=>"4e7b66b7-080d-4593-b670-3d6259e47a0f", \
        :href=>"/api/vms/4e7b66b7-080d-4593-b670-3d6259e47a0f"}, \
    :description=>"VM rhel7srv010 started on Host rhelh03.bit63.net", \
    :severity=>"normal", \
    :code=>32, \
    :time=>2016-01-31 15:53:29 UTC, \
    :name=>"USER_RUN_VM"}]
```

Step 2

The EventHandler worker feeds the event into the Event Switchboard by creating and passing an *EmsEvent* EventStream object into Automate in the form of a queued request (we discuss queued requests more in Chapter 45). The EventHandlers translate the provider-specific arguments (API `hrefs`) into CloudForms object IDs and include these as arguments to the Automate request:

```
Args: [{:object_type=>"EmsEvent", \
        :object_id=>1000000007999, \
        :attrs=>{:event_id=>1000000007999, \
                :event_stream_id=>1000000007999, \
                :event_type=>"USER_RUN_VM", \
                "VmOrTemplate::vm"=>1000000000023, \
                :vm_id=>1000000000023, \
                "Host::host"=>1000000000002, \
                :host_id=>1000000000002}, \
                :instance_name=>"Event", \
                :user_id=>1000000000001, \
                :miq_group_id=>1000000000002, \
                :tenant_id=>1000000000001, \
                :automate_message=>nil}]
```

Step 3

The request is dequeued and passed to the Automation Engine, which instantiates the *System/Process/Event* entry point to the Event Switchboard, along with the arguments passed by the EventHandler:

```
<AutomationEngine> Instantiating [/System/Process/Event?
                    EventStream%3A%3Aevent_stream=1000000007999& \
                    Host%3A%3Ahost=1000000000002& \
                    MiqServer%3A%3Amiq_server=1000000000001& \
                    User%3A%3Auser=1000000000001& \
                    VmOrTemplate%3A%3Avm=1000000000023& \
                    event_id=1000000007999& \
                    event_stream_id=1000000007999& \
                    event_type=USER_RUN_VM& \
                    host_id=1000000000002& \
                    object_name=Event& \
                    vm_id≈1000000000023& \
                    vmdb_object_type=event_stream]
```

Step 4

In the case of our RHEV `USER_RUN_VM` event, the Event Switchboard directs the processing to the *System/Event/EmsEvent/RHEVM/USER_RUN_VM* instance, which contains relationships to two Automation *event_handler* instances (see Figure 15-7).

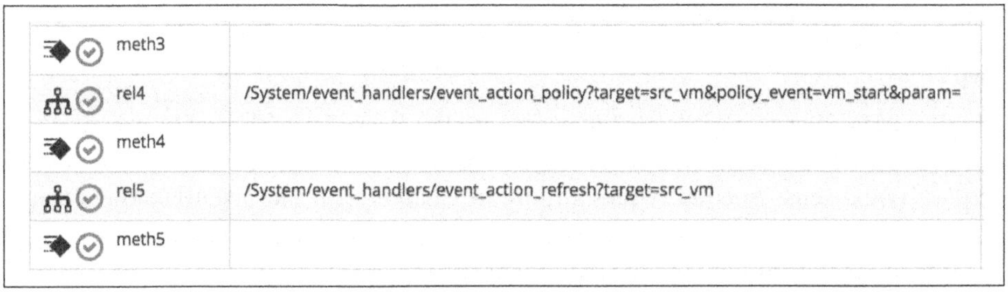

◈ ⊘	meth3	
🔗 ⊘	rel4	/System/event_handlers/event_action_policy?target=src_vm&policy_event=vm_start&param=
◈ ⊘	meth4	
🔗 ⊘	rel5	/System/event_handlers/event_action_refresh?target=src_vm
◈ ⊘	meth5	

Figure 15-7. Relationships to event_handler instances

Step 5

The `rel4` relationship of the *System/Event/EmsEvent/RHEVM/USER_RUN_VM* instance calls *System/event_handlers/event_action_policy* to initiate the creation of an internal generic `vm_start` event.

This completes the event processing workflow for the *external* `USER_RUN_VM` event.

Creating and Processing Internal Events

In addition to catching external events, CloudForms can raise its own events that can be processed by control policies or alerts. These are generated and handled by two internal (non-Automate) methods, build_evm_event and process_evm_event.

We saw in "Step 5" on page 124 that the rel4 relationship of the */System/Event/EmsEvent/RHEVM/USER_RUN_VM* instance initiates the creation of a generic vm_start event. We find that most of the provider-specific events (such as USER_RUN_VM for RHEV or AWS_EC2_Instance_running for Amazon) are reraised as their generic equivalent event (such as vm_start).

We can continue following the processing of the USER_RUN_VM into the internal vm_start event by examining *evm.log*.

Step 6

We see the */System/event_handlers/event_action_policy* event handler being invoked as requested in "Step 5" on page 124:

```
Invoking [builtin] method [/ManageIQ/System/event_handlers/event_action_policy] \
    with inputs [{"target"=>"src_vm", "policy_event"=>"vm_start", "param"=>""}]
```

This event handler calls the internal build_evm_event method to assemble the parameters for the creation of the new vm_start event:

```
<AutomationEngine> MiqAeEvent.build_evm_event >> event=<"vm_start">
    inputs=<{:"manageiq::providers::redhat::inframanager::vm"=>
                #<ManageIQ::Providers::Redhat::InfraManager::Vm
                id: 1000000000023,
                ...>,
            :ext_management_systems=>
                #<ManageIQ::Providers::Redhat::InfraManager
                id: 1000000000001,
                ...>,
            :ems_event=>
                #<EmsEvent
                id: 1000000007999,
                event_type: "USER_RUN_VM",
                message: "VM rhel7srv010 started on Host rhelh03.bit63.net",
                ...>,
            "MiqEvent::miq_event"=>1000000008000,
            :miq_event_id=>1000000008000,
            "EventStream::event_stream"=>1000000008000,
            :event_stream_id=>1000000008000}>
```

Step 7

The new event is queued for processing by the Automation Engine (much of the work of the Automate Engine involves queueing and dequeuing further Automate work tasks):

```
MIQ(MiqAeEngine.deliver) Delivering {:event_type=>"vm_start",
              :"manageiq::providers::redhat::inframanager::vm"=>
              #<ManageIQ::Providers::Redhat::InfraManager::Vm
              ...
              :event_stream_id=>1000000008000} for object \
                 [ManageIQ::Providers::Redhat::InfraManager::Vm.1000000000023] \
                 with state [] to Automate
```

Step 8

The Automation Engine dequeues the task and instantiates the */System/Process/Event* entry point into the Event Switchboard, along with the arguments assembled and passed by the build_evm_event internal method:

```
<AutomationEngine> Instantiating [/System/Process/Event?
  EventStream%3A%3Aevent_stream=1000000008000& \
  MiqEvent%3A%3Amiq_event=1000000008000& \
  MiqServer%3A%3Amiq_server=1000000000001& \
  User%3A%3Auser=1000000000001& \
  VmOrTemplate%3A%3Avm=1000000000023& \
  ems_event=1000000007999& \
  event_stream_id=1000000008000& \
  event_type=vm_start& \
  ext_management_systems=1000000000001&
  manageiq%3A%3Aproviders%3A%3Aredhat%3A%3Ainframanager%3A%3Avm=1000000000023& \
  miq_event_id=1000000008000& \
  object_name=Event& \
  vmdb_object_type=vm] \
```

Step 9

The Event Switchboard directs the processing to the */System/Event/MiqEvent/ POLICY/vm_start* instance, which does not exist by default (we could create one if we wished). The */System/Event/MiqEvent/POLICY/.missing* instance is run in its place:

```
Following Relationship [miqaedb:/System/Event/MiqEvent/POLICY/vm_start#create]

Instance [/ManageIQ/System/Event/MiqEvent/POLICY/vm_start] \
                           not found in MiqAeDatastore - trying [.missing]
```

The *.missing* instance contains a rel2 relationship to */System/event_handlers/ event_enforce_policy*, so we follow the relationship chain:

```
Invoking [builtin] method [/ManageIQ/System/event_handlers/ \
                           event_enforce_policy] with inputs [{}]
```

Step 10

The *event_enforce_policy* event handler initiates the processing of any control policies and alerts that may be associated with the event being handled.

This completes the event processing workflow for the *internal* vm_start event.

Event-Initiated Control Policy Processing

The next part of the event processing workflow handles any control policies that we might have associated with the event. This is where, for example, we would initiate a SmartState Analysis scan on a *VM Create Complete* policy event.

We can continue tracing the event processing from the previous sections, which started with an RHEV USER_RUN_VM event being caught. We saw "Step 10" on page 127 calling */System/event_handlers/event_enforce_policy*.

This method calls the internal process_evm_event method with a target argument corresponding to the VM object that raised the event:

```
MIQ(MiqEvent#process_evm_event) \
    target = [#<ManageIQ::Providers::Redhat::InfraManager::Vm \
                                          id: 1000000000023, ...>]
```

Step 11

The process_evm_event internal method raises the vm_start (VM Power On) policy event and processes any actions (i.e., control policies) associated with the triggering of this policy event:

```
MIQ(MiqEvent#process_evm_event) Event Raised [vm_start]
```

In our case we have a VM control policy that runs an Invoke a Custom Automation action when the VM Power On event is triggered. The custom automation instance runs */Stuff/Methods/ObjectWalker* (via */System/Request/Call_Instance*). See Figure 15-8.

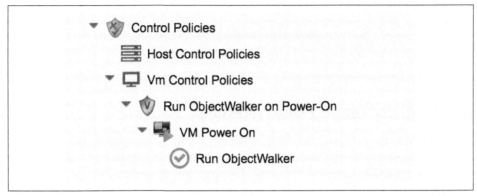

Figure 15-8. VM control policy that links a VM Power On event to Run ObjectWalker

Step 12

The automation request to run *Call_Instance* is queued for processing by the Automation Engine. This is subsequently dequeued and delivered to Automate:

```
MIQ(MiqAeEngine.deliver) Delivering \
                         {"namespace"=>"stuff", \
                         "class"=>"methods", \
                         "instance"=>"objectwalker", \
                         :request=>"call_instance", \
                         "MiqPolicy::miq_policy"=>1000000000001} \
        for object [VmOrTemplate.1000000000023] with state [] to Automate
```

We see *object_walker* running in the *automation.log* file.

Event-Initiated Alert Processing

The final part of the event processing workflow handles any alerts that we might have associated with the event.

Step 13

The internal `process_evm_event` method now raises the `vm_start` (VM Operation: VM Power On) alert and processes any actions associated with the triggering of this alert:

```
MIQ(MiqEvent#process_evm_event) Alert for Event [vm_start]
```

In our case we have an alert that sends a management event called *test* when the VM Operation: VM Power On alert is triggered (see Figure 15-9).

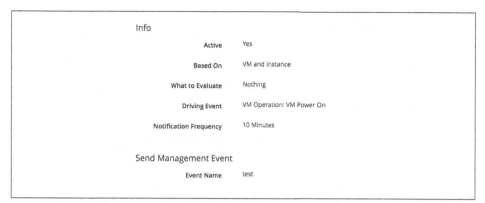

Info		
Active	Yes	
Based On	VM and Instance	
What to Evaluate	Nothing	
Driving Event	VM Operation: VM Power On	
Notification Frequency	10 Minutes	
Send Management Event		
Event Name	test	

Figure 15-9. An alert to send a test management event

Step 14

The alert is queued for processing by the internal `evaluate_alerts` method, and our *test* event is run:

```
MIQ(MiqAlert.evaluate_alerts) [vm_start] Target: \
    ManageIQ::Providers::Redhat::InfraManager::Vm Name: [rhel7srv010], \
    Id: [1000000000023] Queuing evaluation of Alert: [VM Powered On]
```

This completes the full event processing workflow that started when the USER_RUN_VM event was detected from the RHEV provider. We saw the workflow pass through four stages: the handling of the external event, the raising and processing of the corresponding internal event, and the subsequent control policy and alert processing that may have been been associated with the event type.

Event-Initiated Automation Request Workflows

Automation Engine workflows that involve separated requests and tasks (see Chapter 12) also use raised events to control the processing sequence.

We can take a detailed look at the Automation Engine's workflow by examining the steps involved in handling a RESTful API call to run the Automate */Stuff/Methods/Test* instance.

We know that this type of API call will be handled in *request* and *task* stages, where the "task" is the actual running of our automation script. We also know that requests must go through an approval workflow. We can follow the sequence of steps through the processing of the various events using *automation.log*, and the helpful "Following...Followed" messages that the Engine prints.

Step 1: The request_created Event

The first messages that we see after the API call has been made notify us of the request_created event happening. We're looking at CloudForms 4.0, so we see the new event stream information added to the event:

```
MIQ(AutomationRequest#call_automate_event) \
                Raising event [request_created] to Automate
MiqAeEvent.build_evm_event >> event=<"request_created"> \
                inputs=<{"EventStream::event_stream"=>1000000009327, \
                :event_stream_id=>1000000009327}>
MIQ(AutomationRequest#call_automate_event) \
                Raised  event [request_created] to Automate
Instantiating [/System/Process/Event? \
                AutomationRequest%3A%3Aautomation_request=1000000000029& \
                EventStream%3A%3Aevent_stream=1000000009340& \
                MiqRequest%3A%3Amiq_request=1000000000029& \
                MiqServer%3A%3Amiq_server=1000000000001& \
                User%3A3Auser=1000000000001& \
                event_stream_id=1000000009340& \
                event_type=request_created& \
                object_name=Event& \
                vmdb_object_type=automation_request]
```

Here we see the event being triggered, which takes us into the standard */System/ Process/Event* entry point instance. As we've seen, */System/Process/Event* directs us into the Event Switchboard:

```
/System/Event/${/#event_stream.event_namespace}/ \
                            ${/#event_stream.source}/${/#event_type}
```

Step 1.1

The variable substitutions are made from the EventStream object's attributes, and we follow the relationship chain through the Switchboard:

```
Following Relationship [miqaedb:/System/Event/RequestEvent/Request/\
                            request_created#create]
```

Step 1.2

The */System/Event/RequestEvent/Request/request_created* instance contains a single rel5 relationship to */System/Policy/request_created*. Once again we follow the relationship chain:

```
Following Relationship [miqaedb:/System/Policy/request_created#create]
```

Step 1.3

We are now in the */System/Policy* namespace, which is where the event-specific policies are defined—that is, what to do when this type of event happens. Instances in this namespace typically have several entries (see Figure 15-10).

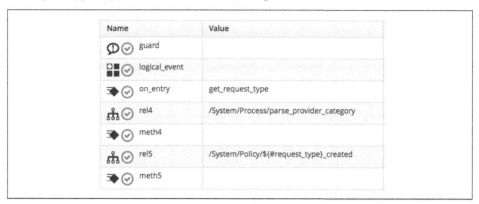

Name	Value
guard	
logical_event	
on_entry	get_request_type
rel4	/System/Process/parse_provider_category
meth4	
rel5	/System/Policy/${#request_type}_created
meth5	

Figure 15-10. The schema of the /System/Policy/request_created instance

A `request_created` event is raised for all types of request, so before any event-specific policy can be implemented, the type of request must be determined.

Step 1.4

The */System/Policy/request_created* instance first runs the *get_request_type* method to find out what type of request has been created:

```
Invoking [inline] method [/ManageIQ/System/Policy/get_request_type] \
                                                       with inputs [{}]
<AEMethod [/ManageIQ/System/Policy/get_request_type]> Starting
<AEMethod get_request_type> Request Type:<AutomationRequest>
<AEMethod [/ManageIQ/System/Policy/get_request_type]> Ending
```

The *get_request_type* method returns `Request Type:<AutomationRequest>`.

Step 1.5

The next entry in the */System/Policy/request_created* schema is the `rel4` relationship to */System/Process/parse_provider_category*, so we continue to follow the relationship chain:

```
Following Relationship [miqaedb:/System/Process/parse_provider_category#create]
```

Some event processing can be provider-specific; for example, we may wish to handle the same event in a different way, depending on whether it came from VMware or OpenStack. The `rel4` relationship from */System/Policy/request_created* takes us to the *parse_provider_category* instance to determine the provider.

The *parse_provider_category* instance runs the *parse_provider_category* method:

```
Invoking [inline] method [/ManageIQ/System/Process/parse_provider_category] \
                                                         with inputs [{}]
<AEMethod [/ManageIQ/System/Process/parse_provider_category]> Starting
<AEMethod parse_provider_category> Parse Provider Category Key: nil \
                                                         Value: unknown
<AEMethod [/ManageIQ/System/Process/parse_provider_category]> Ending
```

The *parse_provider_category* method returns a value of unknown, as this automation request does not involve any provider operations (as it would if we were provisioning a VM, for example).

Step 1.6

The final entry in the */System/Policy/request_created* schema is the rel5 relationship to */System/Policy/AutomationRequest_created* (AutomationRequest having been substituted for ${#request_type}).

This doesn't exist, so we see this warning message:

```
Instance [/ManageIQ/System/Policy/AutomationRequest_created] not found in \
                                 MiqAeDatastore - trying [.missing]
```

We can create a */System/Policy/AutomationRequest_created* instance if we choose, but in this case the *.missing* instance does nothing, so we end that event-initiated chain.

Step 2: The request_approved Event

The next event that we see is request_approved, which follows a very similar chain of relationships (we find that request_approved executes almost concurrently with request_created because we specified :auto_approve to be true in the automation request API call). Here we see the extract from *evm.log*:

```
MIQ(AutomationRequest#call_automate_event) \
    Raising event [request_approved] to Automate
MiqAeEvent.build_evm_event >> event=<"request_approved"> \
    inputs=<{"EventStream::event_stream"=>1000000009436,
    :event_stream_id=>1000000009436}>
MIQ(AutomationRequest#call_automate_event) \
    Raised  event [request_approved] to Automate
Instantiating [/System/Process/Event? \
    AutomationRequest%3A%3Aautomation_request=1000000000031& \
    EventStream%3A%3Aevent_stream=1000000009436& \
    MiqRequest%3A%3Amiq_request=1000000000031& \
    MiqServer%3A%3Amiq_server=1000000000001& \
    User%3A%3Auser=1000000000001& \
    event_stream_id=1000000009436& \
    event_type=request_approved& \
    object_name=Event& \
    vmdb_object_type=automation_request]
```

Step 2.1

```
Following Relationship [miqaedb:/System/Event/RequestEvent/Request/ \
                                              request_approved#create]
```

Step 2.2

```
Following Relationship [miqaedb:/System/Policy/request_approved#create]
```

Step 2.3

```
Following Relationship [miqaedb:/System/Process/ \
                                      parse_provider_category#create]
Invoking [inline] method [/ManageIQ/System/Process/ \
                             parse_provider_category] with inputs [{}]
<AEMethod [/ManageIQ/System/Process/parse_provider_category]> Starting
<AEMethod parse_provider_category> Parse Provider Category Key: nil \
                                                       Value: unknown
<AEMethod [/ManageIQ/System/Process/parse_provider_category]> Ending
```

Step 2.4

```
Following Relationship [miqaedb:/System/Policy/ \
                               AutomationRequest_Approved#create]
Instance [/ManageIQ/System/Policy/AutomationRequest_Approved] not found \
                             in MiqAeDatastore - trying [.missing]
```

The request_approved event processing doesn't call get_request_type, as there is no need for type-specific processing at this stage.

Once again we have no *AutomationRequest_Approved* method, so we terminate this event-initiated chain at this point.

Step 3: The request_starting Event

The third event that we see is request_starting. At this stage we're running within the context of an automation request; each of these log lines is preceded by the text Q-task_id([automation_request_1000000000031]).

```
MIQ(AutomationRequest#call_automate_event_sync) \
    Raising event [request_starting] to Automate synchronously
MiqAeEvent.build_evm_event >> event=<"request_starting"> \
    inputs=<{"EventStream::event_stream"=>1000000009437,
    :event_stream_id=>1000000009437}>

Instantiating [/System/Process/Event? \
    AutomationRequest%3A%3Aautomation_request=1000000000031& \
    EventStream%3A%3Aevent_stream=1000000009437& \
    MiqRequest%3A%3Amiq_request=1000000000031& \
    MiqServer%3A%3Amiq_server=1000000000001& \
    User%3A%3Auser=1000000000001& \
    event_stream_id=1000000009437& \
```

```
        event_type=request_starting& \
        object_name=Event& \
        vmdb_object_type=automation_request]
```

Step 3.1

```
Following Relationship [miqaedb:/System/Event/RequestEvent/Request/ \
                                              request_starting#create]
```

Step 3.2

```
Following Relationship [miqaedb:/System/Policy/request_starting#create]
Invoking [inline] method [/ManageIQ/System/Policy/get_request_type] \
                                                  with inputs [{}]
<AEMethod [/ManageIQ/System/Policy/get_request_type]> Starting
<AEMethod get_request_type> Request Type:<AutomationRequest>
<AEMethod [/ManageIQ/System/Policy/get_request_type]> Ending
```

Step 3.3

```
Following Relationship [miqaedb:/System/Process/ \
                                          parse_provider_category#create]
Invoking [inline] method [/ManageIQ/System/Process/ \
                                  parse_provider_category] with inputs [{}]
<AEMethod [/ManageIQ/System/Process/parse_provider_category]> Starting
<AEMethod parse_provider_category> Parse Provider Category Key: nil \
                                                        Value: unknown
<AEMethod [/ManageIQ/System/Process/parse_provider_category]> Ending
```

Step 3.4

```
Following Relationship [miqaedb:/System/Policy/ \
                                          AutomationRequest_starting#create]
Instance [/ManageIQ/System/Policy/AutomationRequest_starting] \
                              not found in MiqAeDatastore - trying [.missing]
```

Step 3.5

```
MIQ(AutomationRequest#call_automate_event_sync) \
                              Raised event [request_starting] to Automate
```

At the end of this chain we see the automation request queuing the automation task:

```
Q-task_id([automation_request_1000000000031]) \
    MIQ(AutomationTask#deliver_to_automate) \
        Queuing Automation Request: [Automation Task]...
Q-task_id([automation_request_1000000000031]) \
    MIQ(AutomationTask#execute_queue) \
        Queuing Automation Request: [Automation Task]...
```

Step 4: Automation Task Processing

Finally, we see the actual automation task running, which invokes our */Stuff/Methods/ Test* instance. At this stage, each of these log lines is preceded by the text Q-task_id([automation_task_1000000000034]) to indicate that we're running within the context of an automation task:

```
MIQ(AutomationTask#execute) Executing Automation Request request: \
                                                    [Automation Task]
MIQ(AutomationTask#execute) Automation Request initiated
Instantiating [/Stuff/Methods/Test? \
    AutomationTask%3A%3Aautomation_task=1000000000034& \
    MiqServer%3A%3Amiq_server=1000000000001& \
    User%3A%3Auser=1000000000001& \
    object_name=test& \
    userid=admin& \
    vmdb_object_type=automation_task]
Invoking [inline] method [/Stuff/Methods/Test] with inputs [{}]
<AEMethod [/Stuff/Methods/Test]> Starting
<AEMethod test> This is a test!
<AEMethod [/Stuff/Methods/Test]> Ending
Method exited with rc=MIQ_OK
```

Extending Automate Event Handling

The provider-specific event stream source classes and associated instances under */ System/Event/EmsEvent* do not necessarily handle every possible event that can be raised by the provider. Sometimes we need to extend event handling to process a nondefault event.

We can extend the out-of-the-box event handling by creating our own instances under */System/Event* (CloudForms 3.2) or */System/Event/EmsEvent/{Provider}* (CloudForms 4.0) to handle these nondefault events caught by the EventCatcher workers.

As an example, the compute.instance.power_on.end OpenStack event is not handled by default with CloudForms 4.0. If we look in *evm.log* we see:

```
Instance [/ManageIQ/System/Event/EmsEvent/OPENSTACK/ \
    compute.instance.power_on.end] not found in MiqAeDatastore - trying [.missing]
```

As a result, the Cloud instance's tile quadrant in the WebUI that shows power status doesn't always change to reflect the instance being powered on.

Adding a New Automation Instance to /System/Event/EmsEvent/

There is already a *ManageIQ/System/Event/EmsEvent/OpenStack/ compute.instance.power_off.end* instance to handle the `com pute.instance.power_off.end` event. This instance calls two `event_handlers` (see Figure 15-11).

Figure 15-11. Event handlers called by the compute.instance.power_off.end instance

We can copy this instance to our domain and rename it as */System/Event/EmsEvent/ OpenStack/compute.instance.power_on.end* (see Figure 15-12).

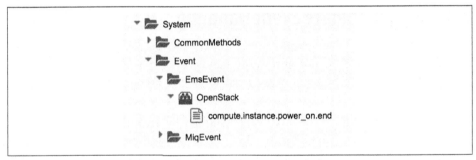

Figure 15-12. Creating a compute.instance.power_on.end instance

We change the second `event_handler` line to trigger a `vm_start` policy event (see Figure 15-13).

Figure 15-13. Editing the event handlers as required

Now when we power on an OpenStack instance, we see the instance's tile quadrant change correctly, and we see the raising and processing of the `vm_start` event:

```
Instantiating [/System/Process/Event? \
    EventStream%3A%3Aevent_stream= \
                            1000000009501&MiqEvent%3A%3Amiq_event=1000000009501& \
    MiqServer%3A%3Amiq_server=1000000000001& \
    User%3A%3Auser=1000000000001& \
    VmOrTemplate%3A%3Avm=1000000000035& \
    ems_event=1000000009500& \
    event_stream_id=1000000009501& \
    event_type=vm_start& \
    ext_management_systems= 1000000000002& \
    manageiq%3A%3Aproviders%3A%3Aopenstack%3A%3Acloudmanager%3A%3Avm= \
                                                    1000000000035& \
    miq_event_id=1000000009501& \
    object_name=Event& \
    vmdb_object_type=vm]
```

This will ensure that any control policies that are triggered by a VM Power On event will run correctly.

Summary

Phew! This has been a long theoretical chapter that has taken us on a detailed tour of how the Automation Engine handles events.

We have familiarized ourselves with the component parts of the new event handling mechanism in CloudForms 4.0. We have seen how external provider events are detected ("caught") and handled, and we have followed the event processing workflow from the detection of an RHEV provider event through the raising of the corresponding internal event and seen how related control policies and alerts are processed.

We have seen that Automate actions involving separated requests and tasks also use event-initiated workflows, and we have seen how to extend event handling to handle additional events.

Next Steps

This concludes Part I of the book. We now have enough knowledge of the Automate Datastore and the structures, concepts, and objects it comprises to be able to tackle most automation challenges.

In Part II we will put this knowledge to good use and start investigating the Automate operations involved in provisioning a virtual machine.

Provisioning Virtual Machines

Provisioning a virtual machine is probably the most complex operation that is performed by the out-of-the-box Automation Engine.

Part II introduces the steps and workflows involved in provisioning virtual machines and how we can customize these for our own purposes. It uses all of the automation features that we've discussed so far in the book.

## CHAPTER 16

Provisioning a Virtual Machine

One of the most common things that we do as cloud or virtualization administrators is to create new virtual machines or instances. We get used to the procedure: picking a template; selecting a target cluster, datastore, and network; and choosing a suitable name. These are generally manual steps, but CloudForms has an out-of-the-box virtual machine provisioning workflow that automates the process.

There are many steps involved in automatically provisioning a virtual machine. The CloudForms provisioning workflow has been designed to be extremely flexible, and it allows a great deal of customization based on tagging, the requesting user's group membership, and the destination provider type (e.g., RHEV, VMware, OpenStack, etc.).

The Provisioning Process

The virtual machine provisioning process starts with a user (the *requester*) selecting either Provision VMs from under the Infrastructure → Virtual Machines → Lifecycle button group, or Provision Instances from under the Cloud → Instances → Lifecycle button group (see Figure 16-1).

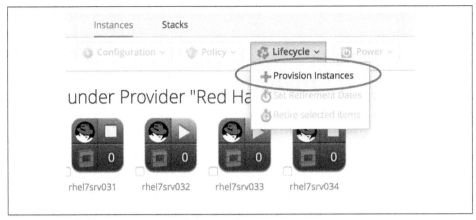

Figure 16-1. Initiating a provisioning operation

This takes us into a selection dialog where we pick an image or template to provision from and click the Continue button (see Figure 16-2).

Name ▲	Operating System	Platform	CPUs	Memory
Fedora 23		linux	0	0 Bytes
RHEL 7		linux	0	0 Bytes

Provision Instances based on the selected Image

Figure 16-2. Selecting the provisioning source template

Once we click Continue, we enter into the virtual machine provisioning workflow, starting with information retrieved from the *profile* and moving into the *state machine*.

Group-Specific Considerations, and Common Processing

Provisioning a virtual machine or instance involves many separate decisions, and steps that come together to form the VM provisioning workflow.

Some of these steps need to be performed or evaluated within the context of the requesting user's access-control group membership, such as the choice of provisioning dialog to present to the user in the WebUI. We may, for example, wish to customize the WebUI dialog to present a restricted set of options to certain groups of users (see also Chapter 25). We can decide to apply quotas to access-control groups, or create specific customizations such as group-specific virtual machine naming schemes. Group-specific processing is typically performed in the request context, before the tasks are created (see Chapter 12 for a description of requests and tasks).

Other steps in the virtual machine provisioning workflow are common to all virtual machine or instance provisioning operations. These typically include the allocation of an IP address, registration with a CMDB, or emailing the requester that the provision has completed, for example.

The group-specific *provisioning profile* contains the per-group attributes, instance names, and state machine names that are used in processing the provisioning request and in preparing the provisioning task(s).

The more generic sequence of common steps involved in provisioning a virtual machine or instance comes from the *VM provisioning state machine*. This is processed in the context of the provisioning task.

Summary

This short chapter has introduced the group-specific provisioning profile and the more generic VM provisioning state machine that combine to form the virtual machine provisioning workflow.

In the following chapters, we will examine these in more detail, starting with the provisioning profile.

## CHAPTER 17

The Provisioning Profile

As we have seen, some of the selections or choices involved in automating the provisioning process for virtual machines should be made within the context of the requesting user's access-control group. This allows our automation workflow to include group-specific processing logic. For example, we may wish to direct development and test virtual machines to a specific cluster, or automatically name some virtual machines according to our own group-specific naming convention.

The attributes, relationships, and method names that are used to determine these operations and decisions are stored in group-specific *provisioning profiles*. These include the selection of the appropriate provisioning dialog, checking the provisioning request against quota, an optional approval workflow for large VM requests, and the option to use group-specific VM naming and network allocation methods.

Location

The provisioning profiles are stored under */{Cloud,Infrastructure}/VM/Provisioning/ Profile*. There is one out-of-the-box group-specific profile for the EvmGroup-super_administrator group, but we can create new profiles for any user groups that we wish to provision from. If a user who is not a member of a listed group profile provisions a VM, the *.missing* profile will be used (see Figure 17-1).

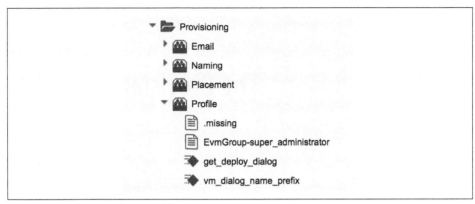

Figure 17-1. Provisioning profiles

Schema

The provisioning profile schema contains a number of attributes, relationships, and methods (see Figure 17-2).

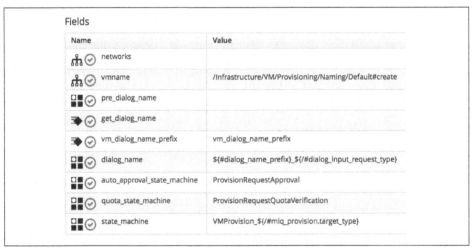

Figure 17-2. The Name and Value fields in the profile schema

Each of these is selected using a message and most use collect to propagate the attributes up to $evm.root in the provisioning operation (see Figure 17-3).

Fields		
Name	**Collect**	**Message**
networks	/networks = network	get_networks
vmname	/vmname = vmname	get_vmname
pre_dialog_name	/dialog_name = pre_dialog_name	get_pre_dialog_name
get_dialog_name		get_dialog_name
vm_dialog_name_prefix		get_dialog_name
dialog_name	/dialog_name = dialog_name	get_dialog_name
auto_approval_state_machine	/state_machine = auto_approval_state_machine	get_auto_approval_state_machine
quota_state_machine	/state_machine = quota_state_machine	get_quota_state_machine
state_machine	/state_machine = state_machine	get_state_machine

Figure 17-3. The Collect and Message fields in the profile schema

Customizing the Profile

The profile is designed to be user-customizable, and in fact we frequently add profiles for specific user groups or edit the *.missing* profile to account for updated VM naming methods or modified provisioning dialogs.

Profile Processing in Detail

Let's take a detailed look at how we use the group provisioning profile when provisioning a virtual machine.

The Provisioning Dialog

The first profile query is performed as soon as the requesting user selects a template to provision from and clicks the Continue button. The WebUI must launch the correct provisioning dialog for the target platform, operation type, and (optionally) the user group, and it determines this information from the profile.

The provisioning dialog presents the main set of tabs and elements that prompt us for all the information that we need to provision the VM: VM name, number of CPUs, VLAN, and so on (see Figure 17-4).

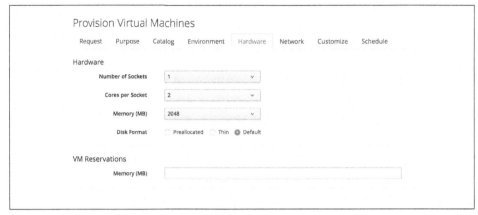

Figure 17-4. The provisioning dialog

To find the correct provisioning dialog to launch when we select a template and click the Continue button, the profile instance is launched using the messages get_pre_dialog_name and get_dialog_name. This action queries the pre_dia log_name and dialog_name attributes and runs the *vm_dialog_name_prefix* method. The dialog name to load is assembled from the runtime substitution of the variables in the string "${#dialog_name_prefix}_${/#dialog_input_request_type}".

> The profile querying at this stage is performed by the internal Rails class MiqRequestWorkflow, rather than by a method that we can see in the Automation Datastore.

We can see the output in *evm.log*:

```
...Querying Automate Profile for dialog name
...Invoking [inline] method [.../Profile/vm_dialog_name_prefix] with inputs [{}]
...vm_dialog_name_prefix> Detected Platform:<redhat>
...vm_dialog_name_prefix> Platform:<redhat> \
                          dialog_name_prefix:<miq_provision_redhat_dialogs>
...
...Loading dialogs <miq_provision_redhat_dialogs_template> for user <admin>
```

VM Name (Pass 1)

The profile is queried using the message get_vmname to retrieve the instance URI to be used to formulate the name of the VM to be provisioned. The VM name is saved as the collect variable vmname.

This VM name is then inserted into the text string that will form the request object's description attribute (miq_provision_request.description)—for example, "Provision from [rhel7-generic] to [rhel7srv004]".

If we are provisioning two or more VMs in a single request and letting Automate handle the VM auto–number-incrementing (e.g., rhel7srv005, rhel7srv006, etc.) then the request object description is more generic—for example, "Provision from [rhel7-generic] to [rhel7srvxxx]".

Approval

Once the request object is created, we begin a series of event-driven processing steps based on instances in */System/Policy* (see Figure 17-5).

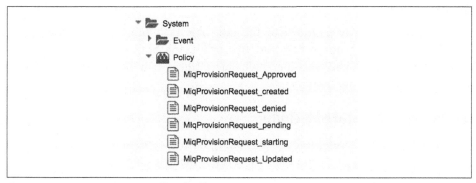

Figure 17-5. MiqProvision-related policy instances

The first of these to be triggered is *MiqProvisionRequest_created*. This contains two relationships, the first of which queries the profile using the message get_auto_approval_state_machine to retrieve the state machine name to be used to handle the auto-approval process. The second relationship runs the *Default* instance of this state machine.

Approved, pending, or denied

Depending on the outcome of the approval process (approved, pending, or denied), an email is sent to the requester by the corresponding event/policy instance.

Quota

The next event-driven policy instance to be triggered is *MiqProvisionRequest_starting*. On CloudForms 3.2 this contains two relationships. The first of these queries the profile using the message get_quota_state_machine to retrieve the state machine name to be used to handle the quota-checking process. The second relationship runs the *Default* instance of this state machine.

Quota handling has been rewritten for CloudForms 4.0, and so the *MiqProvisionRequest_starting* policy instance just contains a single relationship to the */System/CommonMethods/QuotaStateMachine/quota* state machine.

Once the quota has been checked and passed, the request continues processing, and the task objects are created.

VM Name (Pass 2)

The profile is again queried using the message `get_vmname` to retrieve the instance URI to be used to formulate the name of the VM to be provisioned. This second call is made while processing the provisioning request as part of the creation of the tasks that will handle the provisioning of each VM in the request. The VM name is saved as the collect variable `vmname`.

The derived VM name is added to the task object's options hash as `miq_provision.options[:vm_target_name]` and `miq_provision.options[:vm_target_host name]`. This is performed once per task object (there may be several task objects created for a single request object).

VM Provisioning State Machine

Finally, the profile is used by the provisioning task to determine the state machine instance to be used to provision the VM. A call is made to */Infrastructure/VM/Lifecycle/Provisioning#create*.

This instance contains two relationships. The first is */Infrastructure/VM/Provisioning/Profile/${/#user.normalized_ldap_group}#get_state_machine*. This queries the profile using the message `get_state_machine` to retrieve the state machine class name to be used to handle the provisioning of the VM. The state machine class name is saved as the collect variable `state_machine`.

The second relationship is */Infrastructure/VM/Provisioning/StateMachines/${/#state_machine}/${/#miq_provision.provision_type}*. This uses the `state_machine` variable retrieved from collect in the previous relationship and runs the instance of this state machine whose name corresponds to a variable substitution for `miq_provision.provision_type`. When we are performing a VM clone from a template (the most common VM provision operation), this will be *template*.

Summary

In this chapter we have seen how the access-control-group-specific selections are made as part of the virtual machine provisioning automation workflow. The provisioning profiles allow us considerable flexibility in customizing the workflow to take into account group-specific choices that we might wish to make.

The concept of using a group profile to hold group-specific options is not limited to virtual machine provisioning. It is also used for service provisioning, and we create a group profile to handle our automation request approval workflow in Chapter 43.

Further Reading

Provisioning Virtual Machines and Hosts—Provisioning Profiles (*http://red.ht/ 1sz08ZX*)

## CHAPTER 18

Approval

A newly provisioned virtual machine consumes resources in a virtual infrastructure and potentially costs money in a public cloud. To control the consumption of resources and keep cloud costs in check, an approval stage is built into the virtual machine and instance provisioning workflow. By default, requests for single small virtual machines are auto-approved, but attempts to provision larger or multiple VMs are redirected for administrative approval.

This chapter describes the approval process and shows how we can fine-tune the approval thresholds based on the number of VMs, number of CPUs, or amount of memory in the request.

Approval Workflow

The provision request approval workflows are triggered by the request_created and request_pending events (see Figure 18-1).

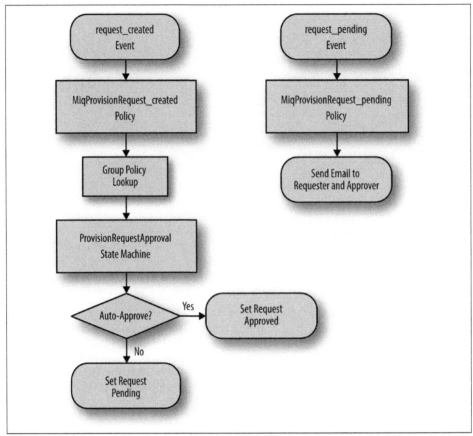

Figure 18-1. Event-triggered provision request approval workflows

Request Created Event

The approval workflow for a virtual machine provision request is entered as a result of the */System/Policy/MiqProvisionRequest_created* policy instance being run from a `request_created` event. This policy instance contains two relationships, `rel5` and `rel6`.

The `rel5` relationship performs a group profile lookup to read the value of the `auto_approval_state_machine` attribute, which by default is *ProvisionRequestApproval* for an infrastructure virtual machine or cloud instance provision request.

The `rel6` relationship runs the *Default* instance of this state machine (see Figure 18-2).

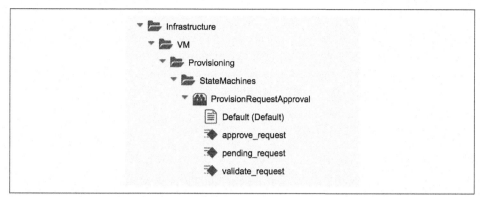

Figure 18-2. The ProvisionRequestApproval state machine instances and methods

The *Default* instance of the *ProvisionRequestApproval* state machine has the field values shown in Figure 18-3.

Name	Value	On Entry	On Error	Max Retries	Message
max_cpus					create
max_vms	1				create
max_memory					create
max_retirement_days					create
ValidateRequest		validate_request	pending_request	100	create
ApproveRequest		approve_request		100	create

Figure 18-3. The ProvisionRequestApproval/Default instance

This instance will auto-approve any VM provisioning request containing a single VM, but requests for more than this number will require explicit approval from an administrator or anyone in a group with the `EvmRole-approver` (or equivalent) role.

Methods

The *ProvisionRequestApproval* state machine uses three methods to perform the validation.

validate_request

The *validate_request* method is run from the On Entry field of the `ValidateRequest` state. It checks the provisioning request against the schema `max_` attributes, and if the request doesn't exceed these maxima, the method exits cleanly. If the request does exceed the maxima, the method sets `$evm.root['ae_result'] = 'error'` and a reason message before exiting.

pending_request

The *pending_request* method is run from the On Error field of the `ValidateRequest` state. This will be run if `validate_request` exits with `$evm.root['ae_result'] = 'error'`. The method is simple and merely raises a `request_pending` event to trigger the *MiqProvisionRequest_pending* policy instance:

```
# Raise automation event: request_pending
$evm.root["miq_request"].pending
```

approve_request

The *approve_request* method is run from the On Entry field of the `ApproveRequest` state. This will be run if *validate_request* exits cleanly. This is another very simple method that merely auto-approves the request:

```
# Auto-Approve request
$evm.log("info", "AUTO-APPROVING")
$evm.root["miq_request"].approve("admin", "Auto-Approved")
```

Request Pending Event

If the *ProvisionRequestApproval* state machine doesn't approve the request, it calls `$evm.root["miq_request"].pending`, which triggers a `request_pending` event. This is the trigger point into the second workflow through the *MiqProvisionRequest_pending* policy instance. This instance sends the emails to the requester and approver, notifying them that the provisioning request has not been auto-approved and needs manual approval.

Overriding the Defaults

We can copy the *Default* instance (including path) to our own domain and change or set any of the auto-approval schema attributes—that is, `max_cpus`, `max_vms`, `max_mem ory`, or `max_retirement_days`. Our new values will then be used when the next virtual machine is provisioned.

Template Tagging

We can also override the auto-approval `max_*` values stored in the *ProvisionRequestApproval* state machine on a per-template basis, by applying tags from one or more of the following tag categories to the template:

Tag category name	Tag category display name
prov_max_cpu	Auto Approve - Max CPU
prov_max_memory	Auto Approve - Max Memory
prov_max_retirement_days	Auto Approve - Max Retirement Days
prov_max_vm	Auto Approve - Max VM

If a template is tagged in such a way, then any VM provisioning request *from* that template will result in the template's tag value being used for auto-approval considerations, rather than the attribute value from the schema.

VM Provisioning–Related Email

There are four email instances with corresponding methods that are used to handle the sending of VM provisioning–related emails. The instances each have the attributes to_email_address, from_email_address, and signature, which we can (and should) customize, after copying the instances to our own domain.

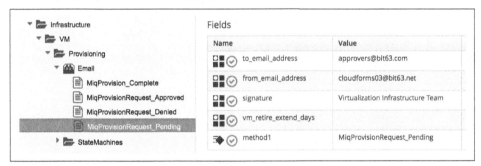

Figure 18-4. Copying and editing the approval email schema fields

Three of the instances are approval-related. The to_email_address value for the *MiqProvisionRequest_Pending* instance should contain the email address of a user (or mailing list) who is able to log in to the CloudForms appliance as an administrator or as a member of a group with the EvmRole-approver role or equivalent (see Figure 18-4).

Summary

This chapter has shown how the virtual machine provisioning workflow allows for the approval stage to filter requests for large virtual machines while auto-approving small requests. This simplifies our life as virtualization administrators considerably. It allows us to retain a degree of control over large resource requests, even allowing us to define our own concept of *large* by setting schema attributes accordingly. It also allows us to delegate responsibility for small virtual machine requests to our standard users. Automation allows us to intervene for the exceptional cases yet auto-approve the ordinary "business as usual" requests.

We have also seen how we can fine-tune these approval thresholds on a per-template basis, so that if some of our users have valid reasons to provision large virtual machines from specific templates, we can allow them to without interruption.

The approval state machine and methods are a good example of the utility of defining thesholds as schema attributes or by using tags. We can customize the approval process to our own requirements without the need to write or edit any Ruby code.

Further Reading

Provisioning Virtual Machines and Hosts Chapter 3—Working with Requests (*http:// red.ht/1tn9Zmv*)

## CHAPTER 19

Quota Management

In the last chapter we saw how every virtual machine or instance provisioning request involves an approval process, and that requests for larger VMs would normally require administrative approval. Even with auto-approval thresholds set at their low defaults, however, our users could still, over time, create a large number of small virtual machines, consume our virtual infrastructure resources, and increase cloud costs.

For this reason CloudForms also allows us to establish quotas on tenants or user groups. Quotas can be set for the number of virtual machines, number of CPUs, amount of memory, or quantity of storage *owned* by the tenant or group. If a virtual machine provisioning request would result in the quota being exceeded, the request is rejected and the requesting user is emailed.

Quotas are not enabled by default with CloudForms 4.0, but they are simple to turn on and configure.

Quotas in Cloudforms 4.0

Quota management has been completely rewritten for CloudForms 4.0. Prior to this release, quota management for cloud instance, infrastructure virtual machine, and service provisioning was handled in different places under the respective */Cloud*, */Infrastructure*, and */Service* namespaces. In CloudForms 4.0 these have been consolidated under */System/CommonMethods* in the Automate Datastore (see Figure 19-1).

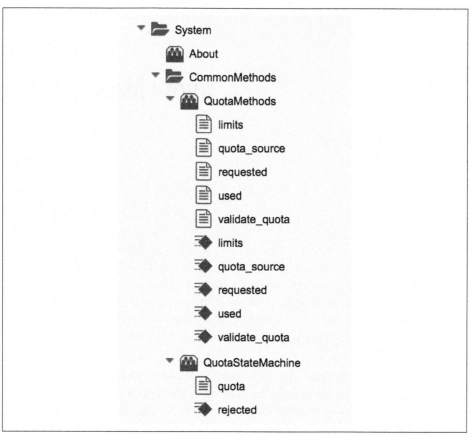

Figure 19-1. Quota classes, instances, and methods

The *ManageIQ/System/CommonMethods/QuotaStateMachine/quota* state machine instance has the field values shown in Figure 19-2.

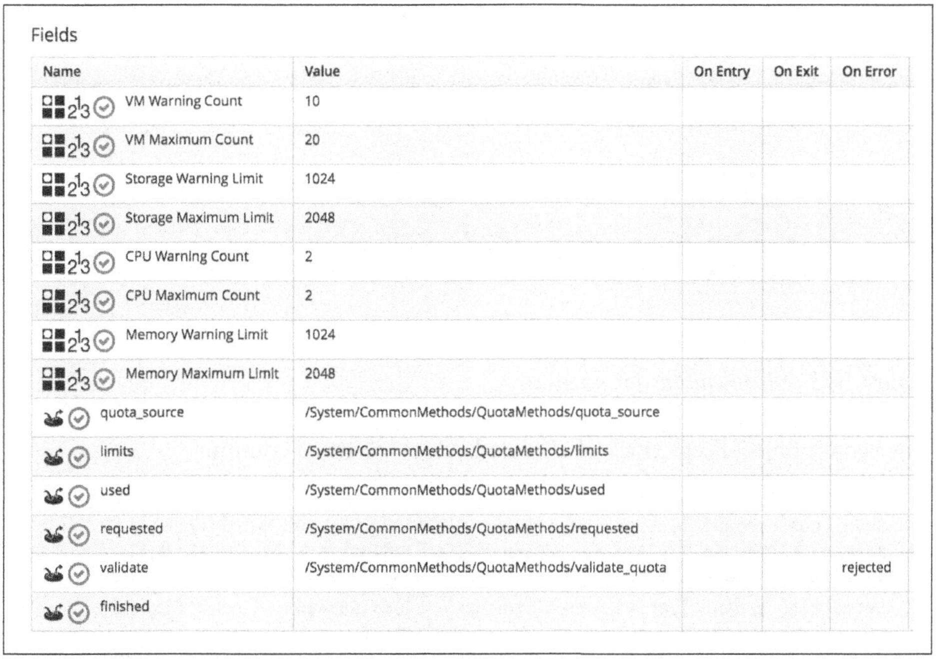

Fields				
Name	Value	On Entry	On Exit	On Error
VM Warning Count	10			
VM Maximum Count	20			
Storage Warning Limit	1024			
Storage Maximum Limit	2048			
CPU Warning Count	2			
CPU Maximum Count	2			
Memory Warning Limit	1024			
Memory Maximum Limit	2048			
quota_source	/System/CommonMethods/QuotaMethods/quota_source			
limits	/System/CommonMethods/QuotaMethods/limits			
used	/System/CommonMethods/QuotaMethods/used			
requested	/System/CommonMethods/QuotaMethods/requested			
validate	/System/CommonMethods/QuotaMethods/validate_quota			rejected
finished				

Figure 19-2. Schema of the quota state machine

We can see that quota processing follows a simple workflow of:

1. Determine the quota source.
2. Determine the quota limits assigned to that source.
3. Determine the resources currently used by that source.
4. Determine the new resources requested by the source.
5. Validate whether the new requested amount would exceed the quota.

Quota Source

A new concept with the reimplemented quota management mechanism is the *quota source*. This is the entity to which the quota is applied, and by default is a tenant. Tenant quotas can be edited in the WebUI under Configure → Configuration → Access Control → Tenants → *tenant* (see Figure 19-3).

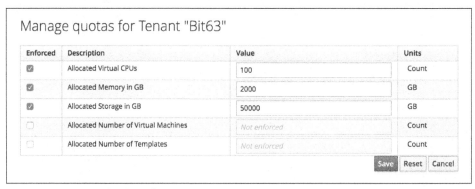

Figure 19-3. Setting quotas for a tenant

The tenant object keeps track of allocated values in virtual columns:

```
--- virtual columns follow ---
$evm.root['tenant'].allocated_memory = 48318382080    (type: Fixnum)
$evm.root['tenant'].allocated_storage = 498216206336   (type: Fixnum)
$evm.root['tenant'].allocated_vcpu = 23   (type: Fixnum)
$evm.root['tenant'].provisioned_storage = 546534588416   (type: Fixnum)
```

Alternative Quota Sources

If we wish to use an alternative quota source, we can copy the *quota_source* method to our own domain and edit it to define $evm.root['quota_source'] and $evm.root['quota_source_type'] as required. This commented-out example shows how to define a group as the quota source, in which case quota handling is done in the pre-Cloudforms 4.0 way:

```
# Sample code to enable group as the default quota source.
$evm.root['quota_source'] = @miq_request.requester.current_group
$evm.root['quota_source_type'] = 'group'
```

When we use an alternative quota source, we can set a quota in two ways.

Defining a quota in the state machines schema (the model)

We can set generic warn and max values for VM Count, Storage, CPU, and Memory by copying the *ManageIQ/System/CommonMethods/QuotaStateMachine/quota* instance into our domain and editing any of the eight schema attributes.

Quotas defined in the model in this way apply to all instances of the quota source (e.g., all groups).

Defining a quota using tags

We can override the default model attributes by applying tags from one or more of the tag categories listed in Table 19-1 to individual quota source entities (e.g., individual groups).

Table 19-1. Override tags

Tag category name	Tag category display name	Pre-exists
quota_warn_vms	Quota - Warn VMs	No; must be created
quota_max_vms	Quota - Max VMs	No; must be created
quota_warn_storage	Quota - Warn Storage	No; must be created
quota_max_storage	Quota - Max Storage	Yes
quota_warn_cpu	Quota - Warn CPUs	No; must be created
quota_max_cpu	Quota - Max CPUs	Yes
quota_warn_memory	Quota - Warn Memory	No; must be created
quota_max_memory	Quota - Max Memory	Yes

If a group is tagged in such a way, then any VM or service provisioning request from any group member is matched against the currently allocated CPUs, memory, or storage for the group.

If quotas are defined both in the model and with tags, the tagged value takes priority.

Quota Workflow

The quota-checking process for a virtual machine or instance provision request is triggered by a request_starting event (see Figure 19-4).

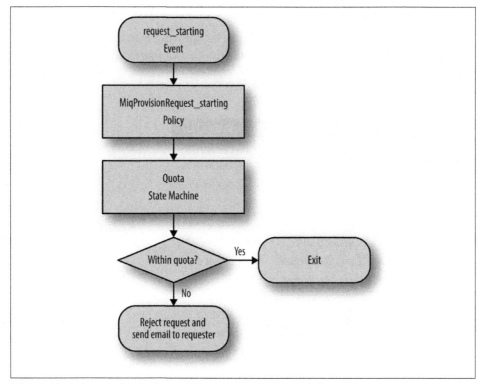

Figure 19-4. Event-triggered provision request quota workflow

This event policy is handled by the */System/Policy/MiqProvisionRequest_starting* policy instance, which has a single `rel5` relationship that calls the */System/CommonMethods/QuotaStateMachine/quota* state machine.

If the provisioning request would result in the quota being exceeded, then the request is rejected, and the requesting user is emailed through the */{Infrastructure,Cloud}/VM/Provisioning/Email/MiqProvisionRequest_Denied* email class.

If the request is within the quota, then the workflow simply exits.

Summary

Quotas allow us to maintain a degree of control over the depletion of our expensive virtualization resources while still empowering our users to create their own virtual machines or instances.

Quotas can be applied to access control groups or tenants. A quota allocated to a tenant can be further subdivided between any child tenants or tenant projects. For example, we might have a tenant representing our application development team, and they might have tenant projects representing applications currently under development. We can allocate the EvmRole-tenant_quota_administrator access-control role to a virtualization administrator, who can then further subdivide the development team's quota between projects as requested.

When we apply quotas to access-control groups, we can additionally tag the groups with warn and max threshold tags on a per-group basis to fine-tune the quota allocation.

Further Reading

Consolidated Service/VM quota validation (*https://github.com/ManageIQ/manageiq/pull/4338*)

## CHAPTER 20

The Options Hash

A user starts the virtual machine provisioning workflow by clicking on the Lifecycle → Provision VMs button in the Virtual Machines toolbar of the WebUI. After selecting a template to provision from, the requesting user completes the provisioning dialog and enters all of the details that are required to create the virtual machine—the number of CPUs, memory, network to connect to, and hard disk format, for example. Somehow this information collected from the WebUI must be added to the Automate provisioning workflow.

Provisioning a virtual machine or instance is a complex operation that, as we have just seen, involves an approval stage. We saw in Chapter 12 that an automation operation involving an approval stage is split into two parts, the request and the task. In the case of a virtual machine provisioning operation, the request is represented by an miq_provision_request object, and the task is represented by an miq_provision object.

The inputs and options selected from the provisioning dialog are added to the miq_provision_request object as key/value pairs in a data structure known as the *options hash*. When we write our custom Ruby methods to interact with the provisioning workflow, we frequently read from and write to the options hash.

If the provisioning request is approved, the options hash from the request object is propagated to the task object, but there are slight differences between the two hashes. We'll examine these next.

Request Object (miq_provision_request)

The contents of the request object's options hash varies slightly between provisioning targets (VMware, OpenStack, RHEV, etc.) and target VM operating system (Linux,

Windows, etc.), but a typical hash for a Linux virtual machine provision to an RHEV provider is:

```
request.options[:addr_mode] = ["static", "Static"]   (type: Array)
request.options[:cluster_filter] = [nil, nil]   (type: Array)
request.options[:cores_per_socket] = [1, "1"]   (type: Array)
request.options[:current_tab_key] = customize   (type: Symbol)
request.options[:customization_template_script] = nil
request.options[:customize_enabled] = ["disabled"]   (type: Array)
request.options[:delivered_on] = 2015-06-05 07:33:20 UTC   (type: Time)
request.options[:disk_format] = ["default", "Default"]   (type: Array)
request.options[:initial_pass] = true   (type: TrueClass)
request.options[:ip_addr] = nil
request.options[:linked_clone] = [nil, nil]   (type: Array)
request.options[:mac_address] = nil
request.options[:miqrequestdialog_name] = miq_provision_redhat_dialogs_template
request.options[:network_adapters] = [1, "1"]   (type: Array)
request.options[:number_of_sockets] = [1, "1"]   (type: Array)
request.options[:number_of_vms] = [1, "1"]   (type: Array)
request.options[:owner_email] = pemcg@bit63.com   (type: String)
request.options[:owner_first_name] = Peter   (type: String)
request.options[:owner_last_name] = McGowan   (type: String)
request.options[:pass] = 1   (type: Fixnum)
request.options[:placement_auto] = [false, 0]   (type: Array)
request.options[:placement_cluster_name] = [1000000000001, "Production"]
request.options[:placement_dc_name] = [1000000000002, "Default"]   (type: Array)
request.options[:placement_ds_name] = [1000000000001, "Data"]   (type: Array)
request.options[:placement_host_name] = [1000000000001, "rhevh12.bit63.net"]
request.options[:provision_type] = ["native_clone", "Native Clone"]
request.options[:retirement] = [0, "Indefinite"]   (type: Array)
request.options[:retirement_warn] = [604800, "1 Week"]   (type: Array)
request.options[:root_password] = nil
request.options[:schedule_time] = 2015-06-06 00:00:00 UTC   (type: Time)
request.options[:schedule_type] = ["immediately", "Immediately on Approval"]
request.options[:src_ems_id] = [1000000000001, "RHEV"]   (type: Array)
request.options[:src_vm_id] = [1000000000004, "rhel7-generic"]   (type: Array)
request.options[:start_date] = 6/6/2015   (type: String)
request.options[:start_hour] = 00   (type: String)
request.options[:start_min] = 00   (type: String)
request.options[:stateless] = [false, 0]   (type: Array)
request.options[:subnet_mask] = nil
request.options[:vlan] = ["public", "public"]   (type: Array)
request.options[:vm_auto_start] = [false, 0]   (type: Array)
request.options[:vm_description] = nil
request.options[:vm_memory] = ["2048", "2048"]   (type: Array)
request.options[:vm_name] = rhel7srv002   (type: String)
request.options[:vm_prefix] = nil
request.options[:vm_tags] = []   (type: Array)
```

When we work with our own methods that interact with the VM provisioning process, we can read any of the options hash keys using the miq_provi sion_request.get_option method, like so:

```
memory_in_request = miq_provision_request.get_option(:vm_memory).to_i
```

We can also set most options using the miq_provision_request.set_option method, as follows:

```
miq_provision_request.set_option(:subnet_mask,'255.255.254.0')
```

Several options hash keys have their own set method, listed in Table 20-1, which we should use in place of request.set_option.

Table 20-1. Options hash keys set methods

Options hash key	set method
:vm_notes	request.set_vm_notes
:vlan	request.set_vlan
:dvs	request.set_dvs
:addr_mode	request.set_network_address_mode
:placement_host_name	request.set_host
:placement_ds_name	request.set_storage
:placement_cluster_name	request.set_cluster
:placement_rp_name	request.set_resource_pool
:placement_folder_name	request.set_folder
:pxe_server_id	request.set_pxe_server
:pxe_image_id (Linux server provision)	request.set_pxe_image
:pxe_image_id (Windows server provision)	request.set_windows_image
:customization_template_id	request.set_customization_template
:iso_image_id	request.set_iso_image
:placement_availability_zone	request.set_availability_zone
:cloud_tenant	request.set_cloud_tenant
:cloud_network	request.set_cloud_network
:cloud_subnet	request.set_cloud_subnet
:security_groups	request.set_security_group
:floating_ip_address	request.set_floating_ip_address
:instance_type	request.set_instance_type
:guest_access_key_pair	request.set_guest_access_key_pair

All but the first four of the set methods just listed perform a validity check to verify that the value we're setting is an eligible resource for the provisioning instance. They also take an object as an argument, rather than a text string—for example:

```
cloud_network = $evm.vmdb('CloudNetwork', '1000000000012')
prov.set_cloud_network(cloud_network)
```

Use one of the techniques discussed in Chapter 10 to find out what key/value pairs are in the options hash to manipulate.

Task Object (miq_provision)

The options hash from the request object is propagated to each task object, where it is subsequently extended by task-specific methods such as those handling VM naming and placement:

```
miq_provision.options[:dest_cluster] = [1000000000001, "Default"]
miq_provision.options[:dest_host] = [1000000000001, "rhelh03.bit63.net"]
miq_provision.options[:dest_storage] = [1000000000001, "Data"]
miq_provision.options[:vm_target_hostname] = rhel7srv002
miq_provision.options[:vm_target_name] = rhel7srv002
```

Some options hash keys, such as :number_of_vms, have no effect if changed in the task object; they are relevant only for the request.

Adding Network Adapters

There are two additional methods that we can call on an miq_provision object, to add further network adapters. These are .set_nic_settings and .set_network_adapter:

```
idx = 1
miq_provision.set_network_adapter(idx,
                    {
                      :network => 'VM Network',
                      :devicetype => 'VirtualVmxnet3',
                      :is_dvs => false
                    })

miq_provision.set_nic_settings(idx,
                    {
                      :ip_addr => '10.2.1.23',
                      :subnet_mask => '255.255.255.0',
                      :addr_mode => ['static', 'Static']
                    })
```

Correlation with the Provisioning Dialog

The key/value pairs that make up the options hash initially come from the provisioning dialog. If we look at an extract from one of the provisioning dialog YAML files, we see the dialog definitions for the number_of_sockets and cores_per_socket options:

```
:number_of_sockets:
  :values:
    1: '1'
    2: '2'
    4: '4'
    8: '8'
  :description: Number of Sockets
  :required: false
  :display: :edit
  :default: 1
  :data_type: :integer
:cores_per_socket:
  :values:
    1: '1'
    2: '2'
    4: '4'
    8: '8'
  :description: Cores per Socket
  :required: false
  :display: :edit
  :default: 1
  :data_type: :integer
```

These correspond to:

```
miq_provision_request.options[:cores_per_socket]
miq_provision_request.options[:number_of_sockets]
```

Adding Our Own Options: The ws_values Hash

Sometimes we wish to add our own custom key/value pairs to the request or task object, so that they can be used in a subsequent stage in the VM provision state machine for custom processing. An example might be the size and mount point for a secondary disk to be added as part of the provisioning workflow. Although we could add our own key/value pairs directly to the option hash, we risk overwriting a key defined in the core provisioning code (or one added in a later release of Cloud-Forms).

There is an existing options hash key that is intended to be used for this, called ws_values. The value of this key is itself a hash, containing our key/value pairs that we wish to save:

```
miq_provision.options[:ws_values] = {:disk_dize_gb=>100, :mountpoint=>"/opt"}
```

The ws_values hash is also used to store custom values that we might supply if we provision a VM programmatically from either the RESTful API or from create_pro vision_request. One of the arguments for a programmatic call to create a VM is a set of key/value pairs called additional_values (it was originally called additional

Values in the SOAP call). Any key/value pairs supplied with this argument for the automation call will automatically be added to the ws_options hash.

By using the ws_options hash to store our own custom key/value pairs, we make our code compatible with the VM provision request being called programmatically.

Summary

The options hashes in the miq_provision_request and miq_provision objects are some of the most important data structures that we work with. They contain all of the information required to create the new virtual machine or instance, and by setting their key values programmatically we can influence the outcome of the provisioning operation.

As discussed in Chapter 12, the challenge is sometimes knowing whether we should access the options hash in the miq_provision_request or miq_provision objects, particularly when setting values. We need to apply our knowledge of requests and tasks to determine which context we're working in.

We also need to be aware of which options hash keys have their own set method, as these keys typically require an array formatted in a particular way.

## CHAPTER 21

The Provisioning State Machine

So far in Part II we have studied the access-control-group-specific processing related to provisioning a virtual machine. We have seen how approval and quotas are handled, and how the entries from the WebUI provisioning dialog are added to the provisioning request and task objects in the options hash.

The common workflow for provisioning virtual machines is handled by the VM provision state machine.

The virtual machine and instance provisoning workflows are each controlled by a VM provision state machine in their respective */Infrastructure* and */Cloud* namespaces. These state machines define the steps in the virtual machine provisioning workflow and contain flexible preprovision and postprovision processing options. Instances run as part of this state machine have access to the provisioning task object via $evm.root['miq_provision'].

State Machine Schema

The VM provision state machine (*{Cloud/Infrastructure}/VM/Provisioning/StateMachines/VMProvision_VM*) class schema contains a number of states (see Figure 21-1).

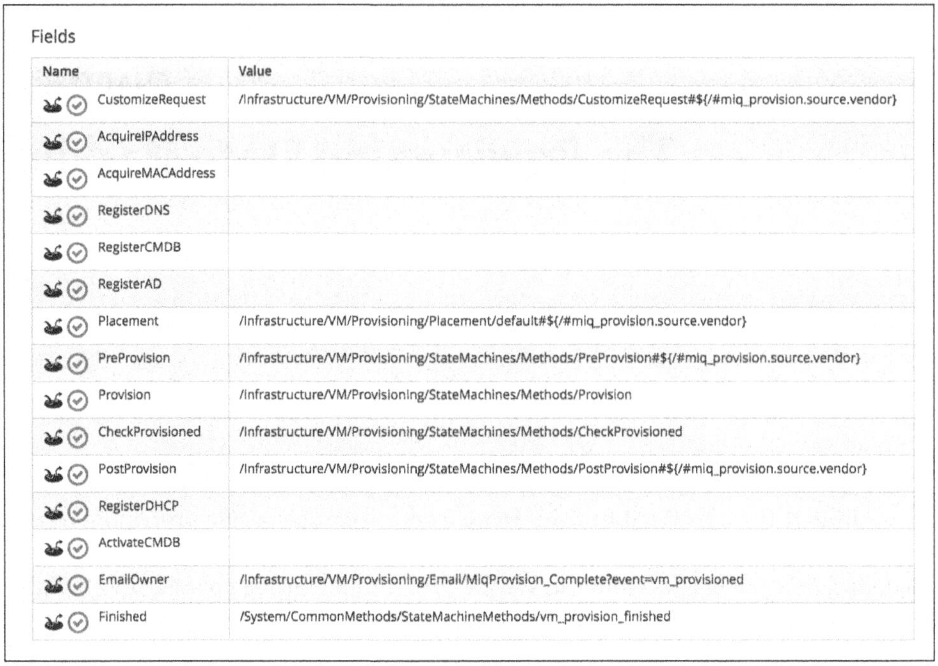

Fields	

Name	Value
🦢✅ CustomizeRequest	/Infrastructure/VM/Provisioning/StateMachines/Methods/CustomizeRequest#${/#miq_provision.source.vendor}
🦢✅ AcquireIPAddress	
🦢✅ AcquireMACAddress	
🦢✅ RegisterDNS	
🦢✅ RegisterCMDB	
🦢✅ RegisterAD	
🦢✅ Placement	/Infrastructure/VM/Provisioning/Placement/default#${/#miq_provision.source.vendor}
🦢✅ PreProvision	/Infrastructure/VM/Provisioning/StateMachines/Methods/PreProvision#${/#miq_provision.source.vendor}
🦢✅ Provision	/Infrastructure/VM/Provisioning/StateMachines/Methods/Provision
🦢✅ CheckProvisioned	/Infrastructure/VM/Provisioning/StateMachines/Methods/CheckProvisioned
🦢✅ PostProvision	/Infrastructure/VM/Provisioning/StateMachines/Methods/PostProvision#${/#miq_provision.source.vendor}
🦢✅ RegisterDHCP	
🦢✅ ActivateCMDB	
🦢✅ EmailOwner	/Infrastructure/VM/Provisioning/Email/MiqProvision_Complete?event=vm_provisioned
🦢✅ Finished	/System/CommonMethods/StateMachineMethods/vm_provision_finished

Figure 21-1. The VMProvision_VM state machine

Several of these states (such as `RegisterCMDB` or `RegisterAD`) contain no out-of-the-box values but are there as placeholders should we wish to add the functionality to our own customized instance.

Some states (such as `PreProvision`) have values that include an appended message—for example:

```
...StateMachines/Methods/PreProvision#${/#miq_provision.source.vendor}
```

The message is selected at runtime from a variable substitution for `#${/#miq_provision.source.vendor}` and allows for the dynamic selection of provider-specific processing options (in this case allowing for alternative preprovisioning options for VMware, RedHat, Microsoft, Amazon, or OpenStack).

Filling in the Blanks

We can copy the VM provision state machine into our own domain and add instance URIs to any of the blank states as required, or extend the state machine by inserting new states. A common addition is to add a method at the `AcquireIPAddress` step to retrieve an IP address from a corporate IPAM solution such as an Infoblox appliance. Once retrieved, the IP address is inserted into the task's options hash using the `set_option` method, like so:

```
$evm.root['miq_provision'].set_option(:ip_addr, allocated_ip_address)
```

Summary

The VM provisioning state machine is one of the most complex that we find in CloudForms. There are versions of this state machine in both the */Infrastructure* and */Cloud* namespaces, and they orchestrate the provisioning steps into their respective providers.

The state machines are designed to be extensible, however, and we'll develop this concept in the next chapter, where we'll copy the state machine to our own domain and extend it to add a second disk as part of the provisioning process.

## CHAPTER 22

Customizing Virtual Machine Provisioning

In Chapter 21 we saw how the VM provision state machine was designed to be customizable. In this chapter we'll go through the steps involved in copying and extending the state machine to add a second hard disk to the virtual machine. This is a simple example but a typical real-world requirement.

Scenario

We are using an RHEV provider with our CloudForms installation, and we can successfully provision virtual machines using the Native Clone provision type from fully configured RHEV templates. The templates all have a single 30 GB thin-provisioned hard drive.

Task

We would like all virtual machines provisioned from these templates to have a second 30 GB hard drive added automatically during provisioning. The second drive should be created in the same RHEV storage domain as the first drive (i.e., not hardcoded to a storage domain).

Methodology

Edit the *VMProvision_VM* state machine to add two new states to perform the task. We'll add the second disk using the RHEV RESTful API, using credentials stored for the provider. We can achieve this in a series of steps.

Step 1: Extend the State Machine

We're going to extend the VM provisioning state machine by adding states, but we cannot do this to the state machine in the locked *ManageIQ* domain.

Copy the state machine

The first thing that we must do is copy the *ManageIQ/Infrastructure/VM/Provisioning/StateMachines/VMProvision_VM/Provision VM from Template (template)* state machine instance into our own *ACME* domain so that we can edit the schema.

Edit the schema

Now we edit the schema of the copied class (see Figure 22-1).

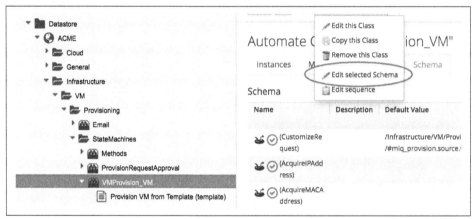

Figure 22-1. Editing the schema of the copied class

Add the new states

We add two more steps, `AddDisk` and `StartVM`, to the bottom of the schema (see Figure 22-2).

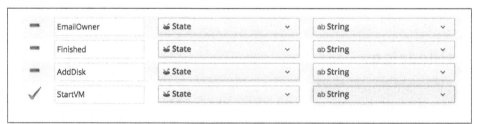

Figure 22-2. Adding two further states

Adjust the sequence

Now we adjust the class schema sequence so that our new states come after `PostPro` `vision` (see Figure 22-3).

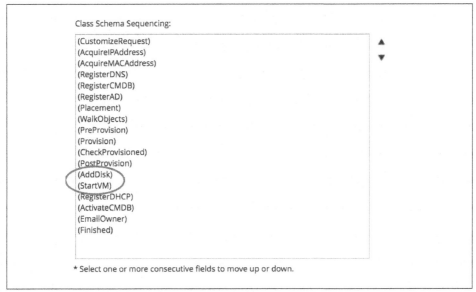

Figure 22-3. Adjusting the class schema sequence

Step 2: Disable Auto-Power-On

We're going to override the default behavior of the VM provisioning workflow, which is to autostart a VM after provisioning. We do this because we want to add our new disk with the VM powered off, and then power on the VM ourselves afterward.

Copy the method

We copy the */Infrastructure/VM/Provisioning/StateMachines/Methods/ redhat_CustomizeRequest* method from the *RedHat* domain into ours (see Figure 22-4).

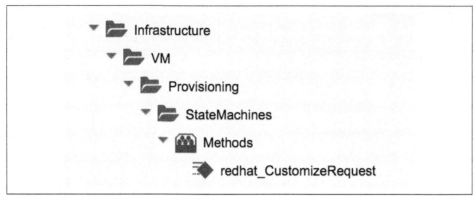

Figure 22-4. The redhat_CustomizeRequest method

 The *RedHat* domain contains an enhanced version of *redhat_Cus‐tomizeRequest*. Make sure you copy and extend the RedHat version rather than the *ManageIQ* domain version.

Edit the method

We edit *redhat_CustomizeRequest* to set the options hash key :vm_auto_start to be false. We must do this after the line:

```
prov = $evm.root["miq_provision"]
```

The additional lines are as follows:

```
# Get provisioning object
prov = $evm.root["miq_provision"]

####  Add the following lines
# Set the autostart parameter to false so that RHEV won't start the VM directly
$evm.log(:info, "Setting vm_auto_start to false")
prov.set_option(:vm_auto_start, [false, 0])
####  End of additional lines
```

Step 3: Create Our New Instances and Methods

We'll create a new namespace, *Integration/RedHat*, in our own domain, and create a simple one-field *Methods* class as we did in Chapter 3. We add two new instances, *AddDisk* and *StartVM*, and two new methods, *add_disk* and *start_vm*, to this class (see Figure 22-5).

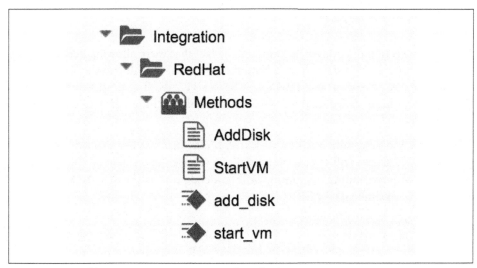

Figure 22-5. Adding two new instances and methods

Next we'll examine the interesting parts of the code in each of the methods.

add_disk

add_disk defines its own method, *call_rhev*, that handles the REST communication with the Red Hat Enterprise Virtualizaton Manager:

```
def call_rhev(servername, username, password, action,
              ref=nil, body_type=:xml, body=nil)
  #
  # If ref is a url then use that one instead
  #
  unless ref.nil?
    url = ref if ref.include?('http')
  end
  url ||= "https://#{servername}#{ref}"

  params = {
    :method => action,
    :url => url,
    :user => username,
    :password => password,
    :headers => { :content_type=>body_type, :accept=>:xml },
    :verify_ssl => false
  }
  params[:payload] = body if body
  rest_response = RestClient::Request.new(params).execute
  #
  # RestClient raises an exception for us on any non-200 error
  #
```

```
      return rest_response
    end
```

In the main section of code we account for the fact that we're allowing *add_disk* to be callable in either of two ways: from a button on a virtual machine in the WebUI, or as part of the VM provision workflow (see Chapter 11). We first need to find out how *add_disk* has been called and retrieve the virtual machine service model object accordingly.

We also need to determine the new disk size. If *add_disk* has been called from a button, the new disk size will have been passed as a service dialog element. If it's called as part of a VM provisioning operation, we'll hardcode this as the NEW_DISK_SIZE constant (for this example it's 30 GB):

```
case $evm.root['vmdb_object_type']
when 'miq_provision'                   # called from a VM provision workflow
  vm = $evm.root['miq_provision'].destination
  disk_size_bytes = NEW_DISK_SIZE * 1024**3
when 'vm'
  vm = $evm.root['vm']                 # called from a button
  disk_size_bytes = $evm.root['dialog_disk_size_gb'].to_i * 1024**3
end
```

We're going to create the new disk on the same storage domain as the existing first disk, so we need to find the existing storage domain details:

```
storage_id = vm.storage_id rescue nil
#
# Extract the RHEV-specific Storage Domain ID
#
unless storage_id.nil? || storage_id.blank?
  storage = $evm.vmdb('storage').find_by_id(storage_id)
  storage_domain_id = storage.ems_ref.match(/.*\/(\w.*)$/)[1]
end
```

Next we extract the credentials of the RHEV Manager (from the ext_manage ment_system object), as we'll need to use these when we make the REST call. We also build our XML payload using the Nokogiri gem:

```
unless storage_domain_id.nil?
  #
  # Extract the IP address and credentials for the RHEV provider
  #
  servername = vm.ext_management_system.ipaddress ||
                             vm.ext_management_system.hostname
  username = vm.ext_management_system.authentication_userid
  password = vm.ext_management_system.authentication_password

  builder = Nokogiri::XML::Builder.new do |xml|
    xml.disk {
      xml.storage_domains {
        xml.storage_domain :id => storage_domain_id
```

```
      }
      xml.size disk_size_bytes
      xml.type 'system'
      xml.interface 'virtio'
      xml.format 'cow'
      xml.bootable 'false'
    }
  end

  body = builder.to_xml
```

We make the REST call to the RHEV Manager and parse the response:

```
$evm.log(:info,
         "Adding #{disk_size_bytes / 1024**3} GByte disk to VM: #{vm.name}")
response = call_rhev(servername, username, password, :post, \
                                  "#{vm.ems_ref}/disks", :xml, body)
#
# Parse the response body XML
#
doc = Nokogiri::XML.parse(response.body)
```

The initial response back from the API contains some hrefs that we need to use, so we extract those:

```
#
# Pull out some reusable hrefs from the initial response
#
disk_href = doc.at_xpath("/disk")['href']
creation_status_href = \
                 doc.at_xpath("/disk/link[@rel='creation_status']")['href']
activate_href = doc.at_xpath("/disk/actions/link[@rel='activate']")['href']
```

We poll the API for the completion status:

 It's not good practice to sleep in an Automate method. For simplicity in this example, we're handling the sleep → retry counter logic ourselves to avoid the possibility of sleeping forever. In a production environment we'd use the built-in state machine retry logic to handle this for us.

```
#
# Validate the creation_status (wait for up to a minute)
#
creation_status = doc.at_xpath("/disk/creation_status/state").text
counter = 13
while creation_status != "complete"
  counter -= 1
  if counter == 0
    raise "Timeout waiting for new disk creation_status to reach \
                          \"complete\": Creation Status = #{creation_status}"
  else
```

```
    sleep 5
    response = call_rhev(servername, username, password, :get,
                                          creation_status_href, :xml, nil)
    doc = Nokogiri::XML.parse(response.body)
    creation_status = doc.at_xpath("/creation/status/state").text
  end
end
```

If the disk has been attached to a powered-on VM (as it may have been if the method is called from a button), we would need to activate the disk in RHEV. If the VM is powered off when the disk is added, this stage is unnecessary:

```
#
# Disk has been created successfully,
# now check its activation status and if necessary activate it
#
response = call_rhev(servername, username, password, :get,
                                          disk_href, :xml, nil)
doc = Nokogiri::XML.parse(response.body)
if doc.at_xpath("/disk/active").text != "true"
  $evm.log(:info, "Activating disk")
  body = "<action/>"
  response = call_rhev(servername, username, password, :post,
                                          activate_href, :xml, body)
else
  $evm.log(:info, "New disk already active")
end
end
#
# Exit method
#
$evm.root['ae_result'] = 'ok'
exit MIQ_OK
```

start_vm

The code for *start_vm* is as follows:

```
begin
  vm = $evm.root['miq_provision'].destination
  $evm.log(:info, "Current VM power state = #{vm.power_state}")
  unless vm.power_state == 'on'
    vm.start
    vm.refresh
    $evm.root['ae_result'] = 'retry'
    $evm.root['ae_retry_interval'] = '30.seconds'
  else
    $evm.root['ae_result'] = 'ok'
  end

rescue => err
  $evm.log(:error, "[#{err}]\n#{err.backtrace.join("\n")}")
```

```
    $evm.root['ae_result'] = 'error'
end
```

The full scripts are also available from GitHub (*http://bit.ly/1VOFeSa*).

Step 4: Add Our New Instances to the Copied State Machine

Now we edit our copied `Provision VM from Template` state machine instance to add the *AddDisk* and *StartVM* instance URIs to the appropriate steps (see Figure 22-6).

⚙️✓	Provision	/Infrastructure/VM/Provisioning/StateMachines/Methods/Provision
⚙️✓	CheckProvisioned	/Infrastructure/VM/Provisioning/StateMachines/Methods/CheckProvisioned
⚙️✓	PostProvision	/Infrastructure/VM/Provisioning/StateMachines/Methods/PostProvision#${/#miq_provision.source.vendor}
⚙️✓	AddDisk	/Integration/RedHat/Methods/AddDisk
⚙️✓	StartVM	/Integration/RedHat/Methods/StartVM

Figure 22-6. Adding the instance URIs to the provisioning state machine

Step 5: Provision a Virtual Machine

We'll provision a VM to test this. We should see that the VM is not immediately started after creation, and suitable messages in *automation.log* show that our additional methods are working:

```
...<AEMethod add_disk> Adding 30GB disk to VM: rhel7srv006
...<AEMethod add_disk> Creation Status: pending
...<AEMethod add_disk> Creation Status: complete
...<AEMethod add_disk> New disk already active
...
...<AEMethod start_vm> Current VM power state = off
...<AEMethod start_vm> Current VM power state = unknown
...<AEMethod start_vm> Current VM power state = on
```

We can take a look at the number of disks in the virtual machine details page in the CloudForms WebUI (see Figure 22-7).

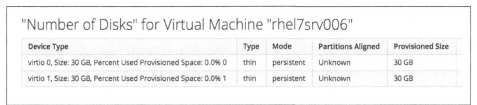

"Number of Disks" for Virtual Machine "rhel7srv006"

Device Type	Type	Mode	Partitions Aligned	Provisioned Size
virtio 0, Size: 30 GB, Percent Used Provisioned Space: 0.0% 0	thin	persistent	Unknown	30 GB
virtio 1, Size: 30 GB, Percent Used Provisioned Space: 0.0% 1	thin	persistent	Unknown	30 GB

Figure 22-7. VM details pane showing additional disk

Here we see the second disk attached to the virtual machine. Our modified VM provisioning workflow has been successful.

Summary

This chapter has shown how we can extend the provisioning state machine to add our own workflow stages. Although this has been a simple example, some kind of provisioning workflow extension is very common in practice. We see another example in Chapter 28 where we extend the workflow to register our newly provisioned virtual machine with a Satellite 6 server.

The example has also shown the integration functionality of CloudForms, and how we can use API calls—in this case, using the REST client—to extend our workflows into the wider enterprise.

Further Reading

Red Hat Enterprise Virtualization 3.6 REST API Guide (*http://red.ht/21d36hT*)

REST Client Gem (*http://www.rubydoc.info/github/rest-client/rest-client*)

Nokogiri Gem (*http://www.rubydoc.info/github/sparklemotion/nokogiri*)

## CHAPTER 23

Virtual Machine Naming During Provisioning

When we provision a virtual machine using the native provider manager—VMware vSphere or the Red Hat Enterprise Virtualization Manager, for example—we must provide the name of the new virtual machine to be created. One of the benefits of a cloud management platform like CloudForms is that we can partially or fully automate the creation of virtual machine names as part of the provisioning workflow.

CloudForms has a very flexible way of letting us assign names to virtual machines at provisioning time, in a process known as *naming*. It allows us to explicitly name the VM (fine for single-VM provisioning operations) or to auto-append a zero-padded number for multi-VM provisioning requests. It also allows us to use or create a custom naming policy whereby CloudForms autogenerates VM names based on a number of factors, including a common prefix, tags, or group membership, for example.

VM Name-Related Provisioning Options

The naming process has several inputs and usually two outputs. The *inputs* to the naming process are a number of variables and symbols that are set (and we can customize) during the provisioning dialog, or defined in the *Naming* class schema. The *outputs* from the naming process are the VM name and optionally the hostname (i.e., fully qualified domain name [FQDN] first part) to be applied to the VM's operating system.

Inputs to the Naming Process

The following subsections detail the variables and symbols used as inputs to the VM naming logic.

vm_name

vm_name is given the value from the VM Name box in Provision Virtual Machines →
Catalog (see Figure 23-1).

```
Naming

VM Name *              websrv033

VM Description ( 0 / 100)
```

Figure 23-1. Prompting for the VM name during provisioning

The symbol is added to the request options hash as:

```
miq_provision_request.options[:vm_name]
```

vm_prefix

vm_prefix can be used to build a custom VM name and is read from the vm_prefix
variable in the naming instance schema; the default is cfme, but we can define our
own if required (see Figure 23-2).

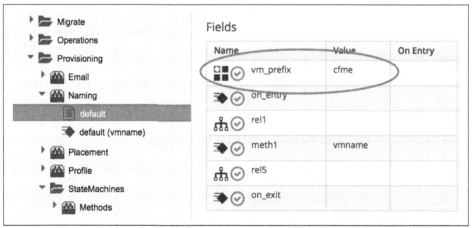

Figure 23-2. Defining the vm_prefix value in the default naming instance

Alternatively, we can set a value in the request options hash:

```
miq_provision_request.options[:vm_prefix]
```

hostname

hostname is given the value of the Host Name box in Provision Virtual Machines →
Customize (see Figure 23-3).

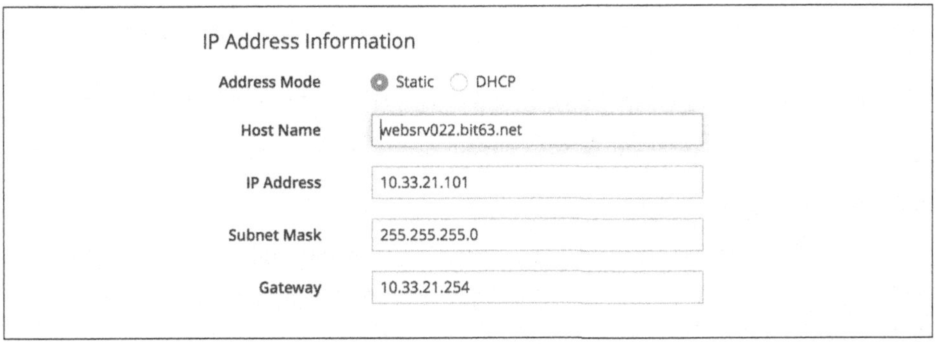

IP Address Information	
Address Mode	● Static ○ DHCP
Host Name	websrv022.bit63.net
IP Address	10.33.21.101
Subnet Mask	255.255.255.0
Gateway	10.33.21.254

Figure 23-3. Prompting for the VM hostname during provisioning

The symbol is added to the request options hash as:

```
miq_provision_request.options[:hostname]
```

linux_host_name

If a VMware customization specification for Linux is used, linux_host_name is the
specific name extracted from the template. The naming logic uses it to set the operating system hostname.

The symbol is added to the request options hash as:

```
miq_provision_request.options[:linux_host_name]
```

sysprep_computer_name

If a VMware customization specification for Windows is used, sysprep_com
puter_name is the *specific name* extracted from the template. CloudForms naming
uses it as input to the sysprep process to set the NetBIOS name.

The symbol is added to the request options hash as:

```
miq_provision_request.options[:sysprep_computer_name]
```

miq_force_unique_name

miq_force_unique_name is used internally when we provision VMs from a service
catalog. When the miq_provision task is created for the VM provision catalog item,
its options hash key is set as:

```
miq_provision.options[:miq_force_unique_name] = [true, 1]
```

Outputs from the Naming Process

The symbols discussed in the folliowing subsections are derived by the VM naming method and added to the task options hash.

vm_target_name

vm_target_name represents the new VM name. It is added to the task options hash as:

```
miq_provision.options[:vm_target_name]
```

vm_target_hostname

vm_target_hostname is the VM $(hostname) assigned from the output of the VM naming logic (15 characters for Windows, 63 characters for Linux). It is added to the task options hash as:

```
miq_provision.options[:vm_target_hostname]
```

Name Processing

Much of the VM naming logic happens in the Rails code that is not exposed to the Automation Engine. This code does, however, call the naming instance/method defined in the provisioning group profile (the vmname field), and we can use this to add our own customizations. The profile-defined naming method writes its suggested name into $evm.object['vmname'], which is propagated back to the internal Rails method via a collect.

If the profile-defined naming method suggests a name that should be numerically suffixed (e.g., #{vm_name}$n{3}), then the backend Rails code will allocate the next free number in the sequence and form the VM name accordingly.

The default profile-defined naming method for infrastructure VMs in CloudForms 4.0 is *Infrastructure/VM/Provisioning/Naming/vmname*. It is a relatively simple method, as follows:

```
#
# Description: This is the default vmnaming method
# 1. If VM name was not chosen during dialog processing then use vm_prefix
#    from dialog; else use model and [:environment] tag to generate name
# 2. Else use VM name chosen in dialog
# 3. Then add 3-digit suffix to vm_name
# 4. Added support for dynamic service naming
#

$evm.log("info", "Detected vmdb_object_type:<#{$evm.root['vmdb_object_type']}>")

prov = $evm.root['miq_provision_request'] || \
       $evm.root['miq_provision'] || \
```

```
            $evm.root['miq_provision_request_template']

vm_name = prov.get_option(:vm_name).to_s.strip
number_of_vms_being_provisioned = prov.get_option(:number_of_vms)
diamethod = prov.get_option(:vm_prefix).to_s.strip

# If no VM name was chosen during dialog
if vm_name.blank? || vm_name == 'changeme'
  vm_prefix = nil
  vm_prefix ||= $evm.object['vm_prefix']
  $evm.log("info", "vm_name from dialog:<#{vm_name.inspect}> \
        vm_prefix from dialog:<#{diamethod.inspect}> \
        vm_prefix from model:<#{vm_prefix.inspect}>")

  # Get provisioning tags for VM name
  tags = prov.get_tags
  $evm.log("info", "Provisioning Object Tags: #{tags.inspect}")

  # Set a prefix for VM naming
  if diamethod.blank?
    vm_name = vm_prefix
  else
    vm_name = diamethod
  end
  $evm.log("info", "VM Naming Prefix: <#{vm_name}>")

  # Check :environment tag
  env = tags[:environment]

  # If environment tag is not nil
  unless env.nil?
    $evm.log("info", "Environment Tag: <#{env}> detected")
    # Get the first 3 characters of the :environment tag
    env_first = env[0, 3]

    vm_name =  "#{vm_name}#{env_first}"
    $evm.log("info", "Updating VM Name: <#{vm_name}>")
  end
  derived_name = "#{vm_name}$n{3}"
else
  if number_of_vms_being_provisioned == 1
    derived_name = "#{vm_name}"
  else
    derived_name = "#{vm_name}$n{3}"
  end
end

$evm.object['vmname'] = derived_name
$evm.log("info", "VM Name: <#{derived_name}>")
```

If we examine this code we can start to see the logic that the virtual machine naming methods use to determine names. There are two main conditions, as follows.

Provisioning a Single VM or Instance

Provisioning a single VM from either Infrastructure → Virtual Machines → Lifecycle → Provision VMs or from a service catalog will result in the VM being given the value of :vm_name, unless :vm_name is blank or has the value changeme. If :vm_name is blank or changeme, then we loop through the logic in the Automation Engine naming method, which assembles a VM name by combining the value of :vm_prefix with the first three characters of the :environment tag (if it exists) and appending three zero-padded digits.

Provisioning Multiple VMs or Instances in a Single Request

Provisioning multiple servers from a service catalog will result in the :miq_force_unique_name symbol being set to true for each task. If :vm_name is not blank or changeme, then the servers will be named as :vm_name with _n{4} appended—for example, server_0001, server_0002, and so on—according to the logic in the internal Rails class MiqProvision::Naming. In this scenario the profile-defined naming method is not used.

Provisioning multiple servers from Infrastructure → Virtual Machines → Lifecycle → Provision VMs will not result in :miq_force_unique_name being set to true, and the VM naming logic in the profile-defined naming method will apply. The servers will be given the value of :vm_name, appended by three zero-padded digits—for example, server001, server002, and so on.

Customizing the Naming Process

We often wish to customize the naming process to our own requirements. For example, we might wish to name all servers using a fixed prefix (:vm_prefix), followed by the value of the server_role tag, followed by a zero-padded digit extension. We can do this using a slight modification of the profile-defined naming method, in conjunction with tagging the servers that we wish to special-case:

```
...
prefix = prov.get_option(:vm_prefix).to_s.strip
#
# Special-case the any servers tagged with "server_role" - pemcg
#
# Get provisioning tags for VM name
tags = prov.get_tags
#
# Check :server_role tag
#
server_role = tags[:server_role]
unless server_role.nil?
  derived_name = "#{prefix}#{server_role}$n{2}"
```

```
    $evm.object['vmname'] = derived_name
    $evm.log("info", "#{@method} - VM Name: <#{derived_name}>") if @debug
    #
    # Exit method
    #
    $evm.log("info", "#{@method} - EVM Automate Method Ended")
    exit MIQ_OK
end
#
# End of special case for servers tagged with "server_role"
#
...
```

We copy the */Infrastructure/VM/Provisioning/Naming/default* instance and */Infra-structure/VM/Provisioning/Naming/vmname* method into our own domain and edit-ing the schema or method accordingly.

Summary

As we have seen, the naming process for virtual machines is very flexible and allows us to create a custom naming scheme for our cloud or virtual infrastructure. The naming logic is called during the processing of the group profile during provisioning, so different user groups can have entirely different VM naming schemes if we wish.

We have also seen that the naming process generates operating system *hostnames* as well as the virtual machine names. Setting a hostname is an operating system (rather than virtual machine container) function, so we must pass this value to some other process for it to be set.

If we are PXE-booting our new Red Hat virtual machines and performing a kickstart installation, then we can inject the hostname value into the kickstart script at run-time. If we are provisioning from fully configured templates, then we need to use a VMware *customization specification* or cloud-init script to perform the hostname injection.

Further Reading

Red Hat CloudForms Management Engine PXE and ISO Provisioning with RHEV (*https://access.redhat.com/articles/349393*)

Complying with Name Restrictions for Hosts and Domains (*http://bit.ly/1UaNf1k*)

Picking server hostnames (*http://bit.ly/1Xey36F*)

## CHAPTER 24

Virtual Machine Placement During Provisioning

The process of deciding where in our virtual infrastructure to position a new virtual machine—the hypervisor or cluster, and datastore—is another step that can be automated as part of the VM provisioning workflow. We might wish to locate VMs on the cluster with the lightest current load, for example, or restrict visibility of selected datastores to some of our users.

CloudForms refers to this process as *placement*, and there is a corresponding Placement stage in the *VMProvision_VM* state machine.

In this chapter we'll look at the various options for automating placement, and how we can create customized placement algorithms to suit our own requirements.

Placement Methods

There are several alternative placement methods that we can use out-of-the-box to determine where to place our new virtual machines. For example, there are three in the *ManageIQ* domain (see Figure 24-1).

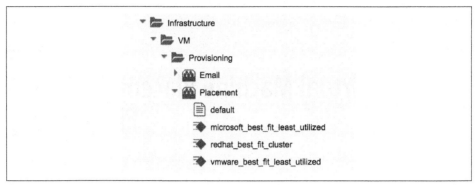

Figure 24-1. Placement methods in the ManageIQ domain

The default value for the `Placement` stage in the *VMProvision_VM/template* state machine is as follows:

```
/Infra.../VM/Provisioning/Placement/default#${/#miq_provision.source.vendor}
```

We can see that this URI includes a *message* component at the end, which corresponds to the runtime value of the `${/#miq_provision.source.vendor}` attribute. This is the string value for the provider type that we are provisioning into.

If we look at the schema fields in the */Infrastructure/VM/Provisioning/Placement/ default* placement instance, we see that the messages correspond to the same provider type string: `redhat`, `vmware`, or `microsoft` (see Figure 24-2).

Fields

Name	Value	Message
redhat	redhat_best_fit_cluster	redhat
vmware	vmware_best_fit_least_utilized	vmware
microsoft	microsoft_best_fit_least_utilized	microsoft

Figure 24-2. The schema fields of the default placement instance

This is a neat way of handling provider-specific placement requirements in an automated manner. The message is dynamically translated for each provisioning operation, and this selects the correct placement method.

Method Description

The *redhat_best_fit_cluster* method just places the new VM into the same cluster as the source template. The other two methods select the host with the least running VMs and most available datastore space.

Customising Placement

As part of the added value that CloudForms brings over ManageIQ, the *RedHat* domain includes improved placement methods that we can optionally use (see Figure 24-3).

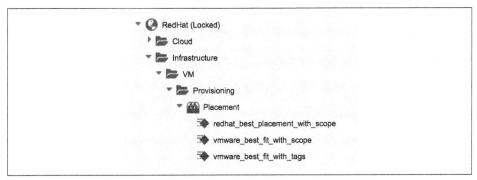

Figure 24-3. Placement methods in the RedHat domain

The *_with_scope* methods allow us to apply a tag from the `prov_scope` (provisioning scope) tag category to selected hosts and datastores. This tag indicates whether or not they should be included for consideration for automatic VM placement. The `prov_scope` tag should be `all`, or the name of a CloudForms user group. By tagging with a group name, we can direct selected workloads (such as developer VMs) to specific hosts and datastores.

The *vmware_best_fit_with_tags* method considers any host or datastore tagged with the same tag as the provisioning request—that is, selected from the Purpose tab of the provisioning dialog.

All three *RedHat* domain methods also allow us to set thresholds for datastore usage in terms of utilization percentage and number of existing VMs when considering datastores for placement.

Using Alternative Placement Methods

To use the *RedHat* domain placement methods (or any others that we choose to write), we copy the *ManageIQ/Infrastructure/VM/Provisioning/Placement/default* instance into our own domain and edit the value for the `redhat`, `vmware`, or `micro soft` schema fields as appropriate to specify the name of our preferred method.

For example, if we wished to use the RHEV placement method from the *RedHat* domain we would set the `redhat` schema field value to be `redhat_best_place ment_with_scope`.

Summary

We can see that we have a lot of control of the placement options available to us when we provision a virtual machine. We also start to see some of the added value that the CloudForms product brings over the ManageIQ project, with the inclusion of placement methods that enable us to use Smart Management tags to control where our virtual machines are positioned.

When we start working with custom placement methods, we also need to take into account the infrastructure components that users can see from their role-based access-control filters. When we configure CloudForms access control for groups, we can set optional *assigned filters* to selected hosts and clusters. We can also restrict a group's visibility of infrastructure components to those tagged with specific tags. If we use assigned filters in this way, we need to ensure that our placement logic doesn't select a host, cluster, or datastore that the user doesn't have RBAC permission to see; otherwise, the provisioning operation will fail.

Further Reading

Placement Profile—Best Fit Cluster using Tags (*http://red.ht/1PkyS6g*)

## CHAPTER 25

The Provisioning Dialog

So far in Part II we have looked at several ways in which the virtual machine provisioning *process* can be customized. We have seen how we can automate the selection of the virtual machine name, decide where to place the virtual machine, and expand the state machine to insert our own provisioning workflow steps.

This chapter will look at how the initial dialog that launched the provisioning process can also be customized. We might want to do this to expand the options available to us, or to preconfigure and hide other dialog elements for certain groups of users.

The specification for the new virtual machine or instance is entered into the *provisioning dialog* that is displayed to the user in the WebUI. This dialog prompts for all of the parameters and characteristics that will make up the new VM, such as the name, number of CPUs, and IP address.

Tabs and Input Fields

The provisioning dialog contains a number of tabs (Request, Purpose, Catalog, Environment, etc.), and a number of input fields per tab (see Figure 25-1).

Figure 25-1. The Hardware tab of the VM provisioning dialog

The provisioning dialog is context-sensitive, so a different set of input field options will be displayed when we're provisioning into VMware or OpenStack, for example.

Dialog YAML

Each provisioning dialog is formatted from a large (900+ lines) YAML file, specifying the main tabs, dialogs, and fields to be displayed—for example:

```
---
:buttons:
- :submit
- :cancel
:dialogs:
  :requester:
    :description: Request
    :fields:
      :owner_phone:
        :description: Phone
        :required: false
        :display: :hide
        :data_type: :string
...
      :owner_email:
        :description: E-Mail
        :required: true
        :display: :edit
        :data_type: :string
...
    :purpose:
    :description: Purpose
    :fields:
      :vm_tags:
        :required_method: :validate_tags
        :description: Tags
```

```
      :required: false
      :options:
        :include: []
  ...

      :display: :edit
      :required_tags: []
      :data_type: :integer
    :display: :hide
    :field_order:

  ...
  :dialog_order:
- :requester
- :purpose
```

Dialog tabs and fields have four useful attributes that can be set:

- Hidden (:display: :hide)

- Visible (:display: :show)

- Editable (:display: :edit)

- Mandatory (:required: true)

Selection of VM Provisioning Dialog

There are a number of VM provisioning dialogs supplied out-of-the-box with Cloud-Forms, each of which provides the context sensitivity for the particular provisioning operation (see Table 25-1). They are found under the Automate → Customization menu, in the Provisioning Dialogs accordion.

Table 25-1. VM provisioning dialogs for provisioning operations

Name	Description
miq_provision_amazon_dialogs_template	Sample Amazon instance provisioning dialog
miq_provision_microsoft_dialogs_template	Sample Microsoft VM provisioning dialog
miq_provision_openstack_dialogs_template	Sample OpenStack instance provisioning dialog
miq_provision_redhat_dialogs_clone_to_vm	Sample RedHat VM clone to VM dialog
miq_provision_redhat_dialogs_template	Sample RedHat VM provisioning dialog
miq_provision_dialogs_clone_to_template	Sample VM clone to template dialog
miq_provision_dialogs_clone_to_vm	Sample VM clone to VM dialog
miq_provision_dialogs_pre_sample	Sample VM preprovisioning dialog
miq_provision_dialogs	Sample VM provisioning dialog
miq_provision_dialogs_template	Sample VM provisioning dialog (template)
miq_provision_dialogs-user	Sample VM provisioning dialog for user

The various dialogs contain values that are relevant to their target provider type (Amazon, OpenStack, Microsoft, VMware, or Red Hat), and also to the operation type (clone from template, clone to template, or clone to vm).

The selection of VM provisioning dialog to display to a user depends on the dia log_name attribute in the provisioning group profile. The default dialog_name value for the *.missing* and *EvmGroup-super_administrator* profiles is:

```
${#dialog_name_prefix}_${/#dialog_input_request_type}
```

The two variables are substituted at runtime and provide the context sensitivity. The dialog_name_prefix value is determined by the *vm_dialog_name_prefix* method, which contains the lines:

```
dialog_name_prefix = "miq_provision_#{platform}_dialogs"
dialog_name_prefix = "miq_provision_dialogs" if platform == "vmware"
```

The dialog_input_request_type value is translated by the Rails class MiqRequest Workflow to be the instance name of the VM provisioning state machine that we are using—that is, template, clone_to_vm, or clone_to_template.

So for a VM provision request from template into an RHEV provider, the dia log_name value will be substituted as follows:

```
miq_provision_redhat_dialogs_template
```

Group-Specific Dialogs

We can set separate provisioning dialogs for individual groups if we wish. As an example, the VMware-specific miq_provision_dialogs-user dialog presents a reduced set of tabs, dialogs, and input fields. The hidden tabs have been given default values, and automatic placement has been set to true:

```
:placement_auto:
  :values:
    false: 0
    true: 1
  :description: Choose Automatically
  :required: false
  :display: :edit
  :default: true
  :data_type: :boolean
```

We can create per-group dialogs as we wish, customizing the values that are hidden or set as default.

Example: Expanding the Dialog

In some cases it's useful to be able to expand the range of options presented by the dialog. For example, the standard dialogs only allow us to specify VM memory in units of 1 GB, 2 GB, or 4 GB (see Figure 25-2).

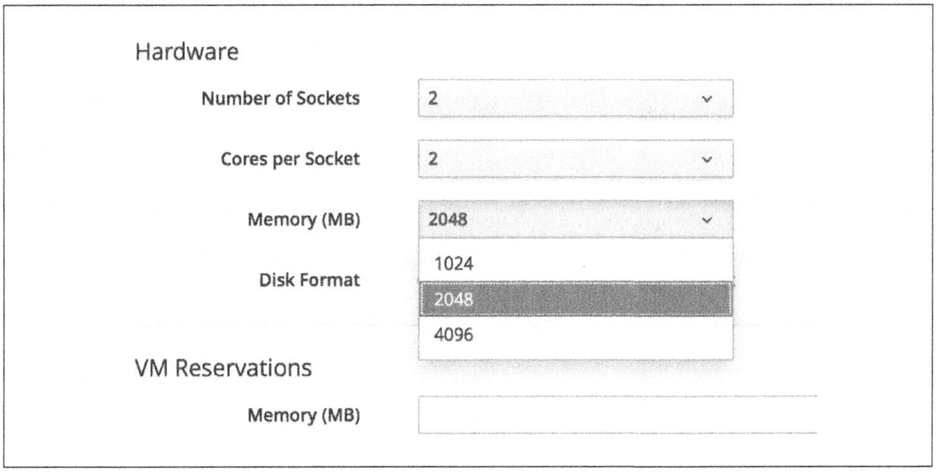

Figure 25-2. Default memory size options

These options come from the `:vm_memory` dialog section:

```
:vm_memory:
  :values:
    '2048': '2048'
    '4096': '4096'
    '1024': '1024'
  :description: Memory (MB)
  :required: false
  :display: :edit
  :default: '1024'
  :data_type: :string
```

We sometimes need to be able to provision larger VMs, but fortunately we can customize the dialog to our own needs.

Copy the existing dialog

If we identify the dialog that is being used (in this example case, it is `miq_provision_redhat_dialogs_template` as we're provisioning into RHEV using native clone), we can copy the dialog to make it editable (we'll call the new version `bit63_miq_provision_redhat_dialogs_template`).

We can then expand the `:vm_memory` section to match our requirements:

```
:vm_memory:
  :values:
    '1024': '1024'
    '2048': '2048'
    '4096': '4096'
    '8192': '8192'
    '16384': '16384'
  :description: Memory (MB)
  :required: false
  :display: :edit
  :default: '1024'
  :data_type: :string
```

Create a group profile

Now we copy the */Infrastructure/VM/Provisioning/Profile* class into our own domain and create a profile instance for the group that we wish to assign the new dialog to, in this case *Bit63Group-user* (see Figure 25-3).

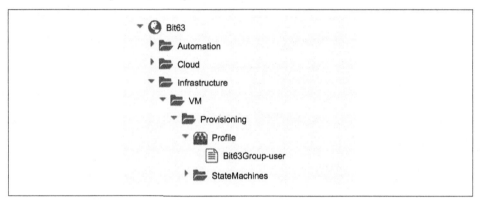

Figure 25-3. Creating a new profile instance

The dialog_name field in the new profile should contain the name of our new dialog (see Figure 25-4).

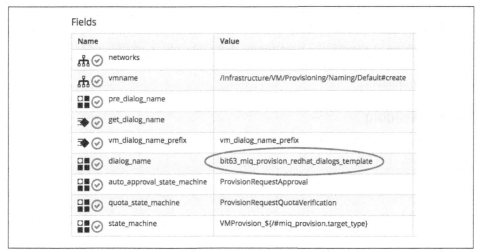

Figure 25-4. *The dialog_name schema field value changed to the new profile name*

Testing the provisioning dialog

To test this we log in as a user who is a member of the Bit63Group-user group and provision a virtual machine. If we navigate to the Hardware tab of the provisioning dialog, we should see the expanded range of memory options (see Figure 25-5).

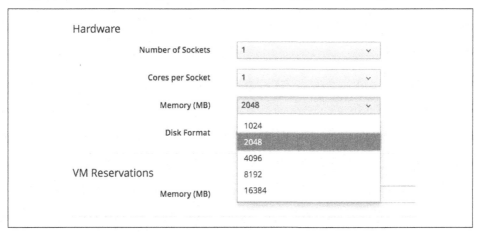

Figure 25-5. *Expanded range of memory sizes*

Summary

In this chapter we've seen how the virtual machine provisioning dialog is used and how it can be customized.

We often create group-specific dialogs that contain a default set of provisioning options, and we can take advantage of this when we make an API call to provision a virtual machine as a particular user, for example. The user's group profile will provide default values for the virtual machine, so we need only specify override values in our API call parameters.

Further Reading

Provisioning Virtual Machines and Hosts—Customizing Provisioning Dialogs (*http://red.ht/1UHEDz3*)

## CHAPTER 26

Virtual Machine Provisioning Objects

When we write our own automation scripts to interact with the virtual machine provisioning workflow, we need to know how to locate the useful service model objects that are involved in the process. We might, for example, wish to determine the virtual machine operating system being provisioned, so that we can decide whether or not to register the new VM with a Red Hat Satellite server. Our experience up to now tells us that this is likely to be a service model attribute, but which one?

This chapter will examine the main service model objects that are involved in the virtual machine provisioning workflow, and how and why we access them.

Object Overview

There are several service model objects involved in the virtual machine or instance provisioning process, but we generally only work with four of them when we write our own Automate methods to interact with the provisioning workflow (see Figure 26-1).

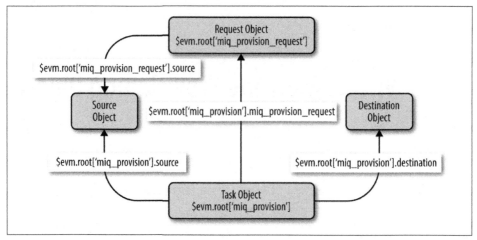

Figure 26-1. VM provisioning objects

The Provision Request Object

We've discussed the provision request object in detail already. It is the object that contains all of the information relating to the virtual machine provisioning request.

Request Context

When working at the request stage of the provisioning process (i.e., prior to approval), we can access the provision request object directly from our workspace:

```
$evm.root['miq_provision_request']
```

There are a number of useful attributes that we can read from the provision request object, including the requester (person) details, and we can set key/value pairs in the options hash to control the virtual machine provisioning process itself.

The provision request object has a number of useful methods that we can use, such as:

```
miq_provision_request.add_tag
miq_provision_request.approve
miq_provision_request.authorized?
miq_provision_request.check_quota
miq_provision_request.ci_type
miq_provision_request.clear_tag
miq_provision_request.deny
miq_provision_request.description=
miq_provision_request.eligible_resources
miq_provision_request.get_classification
miq_provision_request.get_classifications
miq_provision_request.get_folder_paths
miq_provision_request.get_option
```

```
miq_provision_request.get_option_last
miq_provision_request.get_retirement_days
miq_provision_request.get_tag
miq_provision_request.get_tags
miq_provision_request.pending
miq_provision_request.register_automate_callback
miq_provision_request.set_cluster
miq_provision_request.set_customization_template
miq_provision_request.set_dvs
miq_provision_request.set_folder
miq_provision_request.set_host
miq_provision_request.set_iso_image
miq_provision_request.set_message
miq_provision_request.set_network_adapter
miq_provision_request.set_network_address_mode
miq_provision_request.set_nic_settings
miq_provision_request.set_option
miq_provision_request.set_pxe_image
miq_provision_request.set_pxe_server
miq_provision_request.set_resource
miq_provision_request.set_resource_pool
miq_provision_request.set_storage
miq_provision_request.set_vlan
miq_provision_request.set_vm_notes
miq_provision_request.set_windows_image
miq_provision_request.src_vm_id
miq_provision_request.target_type
```

In particular, notice the various set methods that are available to define values for some options hash keys (see Chapter 20 for more details on these methods).

Task Context

When working at the provision task stage we have a different workspace ($evm), and here $evm.root does not link directly to miq_provision_request. We can, however, still get to the provision request object via an association from the miq_provision task object:

```
$evm.root['miq_provision'].miq_provision_request
```

 By the time we're in the provision task, setting options in the provision request object will have no effect. It's still useful, however, to be able to read values from the provision request object when at the provision task stage of the virtual machine provisioning process.

The Provision Task Object

The *provision task object* is created once the virtual machine provisioning request has been approved. Most of the information in the provision request object—most important, the options hash—is propagated into the provision task object.

The provision task object has a similar set of methods to the request object:

```
miq_provision.add_tag
miq_provision.check_quota
miq_provision.clear_tag
miq_provision.eligible_resources
miq_provision.execute
miq_provision.finished
miq_provision.get_classification
miq_provision.get_classifications
miq_provision.get_domain_details
miq_provision.get_domain_name
miq_provision.get_folder_paths
miq_provision.get_network_details
miq_provision.get_network_scope
miq_provision.get_option
miq_provision.get_option_last
miq_provision.get_tag
miq_provision.get_tags
miq_provision.message=
miq_provision.register_automate_callback
miq_provision.set_cluster
miq_provision.set_customization_spec
miq_provision.set_customization_template
miq_provision.set_dvs
miq_provision.set_folder
miq_provision.set_host
miq_provision.set_iso_image
miq_provision.set_network_adapter
miq_provision.set_network_address_mode
miq_provision.set_nic_settings
miq_provision.set_option
miq_provision.set_pxe_image
miq_provision.set_pxe_server
miq_provision.set_resource
miq_provision.set_resource_pool
miq_provision.set_storage
miq_provision.set_vlan
miq_provision.set_vm_notes
miq_provision.set_windows_image
miq_provision.statemachine_task_status
miq_provision.target_type
miq_provision.user_message=
```

The most important of these is `execute`, which launches the *internal* virtual machine provisioning state machine.[1]

The Source Object

When provisioning a virtual machine from a template, we need an object to represent the source template itself; this is the *source object.*

The source object is accessible via either of two associations from a request or task object:

```
$evm.root['miq_provision_request'].source
$evm.root['miq_provision_request'].vm_template
```

or:

```
$evm.root['miq_provision'].source
$evm.root['miq_provision'].vm_template
```

We can therefore access the source object when working in either the request or task context.

The source object contains a very useful attribute:

```
source.vendor
```

This has the value of either `RedHat`, `VMware`, or `Microsoft` if we're provisioning to an infrastructure provider. We can use this to determine the provider type for this provisioning operation and make workflow decisions accordingly. This attribute is used in several places in the out-of-the-box *VMProvision_VM* state machine to select the appropriate instance to handle vendor-specific tasks such as virtual machine placement:

```
/Infra.../VM/Provisioning/Placement/default#${/#miq_provision.source.vendor}
```

There is also an equally useful virtual column:

```
source.platform
```

This has the value of either `linux` or `windows`, and we can similarly use it to make provisioning workflow decisions. We would typically use it to decide whether or not to register a new virtual machine in Foreman/Satellite 6 as part of the provisioning process, for example.

---

1 This *internal* state machine performs the granular provider-specific steps to create the new virtual machine. It is implemented in the Rails `MiqProvision::StateMachine` module and is not customizable from Automate.

All of the source object classes extend from `MiqAeServiceVmOrTemplate` and so have the same methods as a generic virtual machine. In practice we rarely need to run a source method.

The Destination Object

Once the virtual machine has been created (i.e., after the Provision state of the *VMProvision_VM* state machine), we have an object that represents the newly created VM. This is the *destination object*.

The destination object is accessible as an association from the task object:

```
$evm.root['miq_provision'].destination
```

If we wish to make any customizations to the virtual machine as part of the provisioning workflow—such as add a disk or NIC, change VLAN, and so on—we make the changes to the destination object.

The destination object is a subclass of `MiqAeServiceVmOrTemplate`, so it has the standard set of VM-related methods:

```
destination.add_to_service
destination.changed_vm_value?
destination.collect_running_processes
destination.create_snapshot
destination.custom_get
destination.custom_keys
destination.custom_set
destination.ems_custom_get
destination.ems_custom_keys
destination.ems_custom_set
destination.ems_ref_string
destination.error_retiring?
destination.event_log_threshold?
destination.event_threshold?
destination.finish_retirement
destination.group=
destination.migrate
destination.owner=
destination.performances_maintains_value_for_duration?
destination.reboot_guest
destination.reconfigured_hardware_value?
destination.refresh
destination.registered?
destination.remove_all_snapshots
destination.remove_from_disk
destination.remove_from_service
destination.remove_from_vmdb
destination.remove_snapshot
destination.retire_now
destination.retired?
```

```
destination.retirement_state=
destination.retirement_warn=
destination.retires_on=
destination.retiring?
destination.revert_to_snapshot
destination.scan
destination.shutdown_guest
destination.snapshot_operation
destination.standby_guest
destination.start
destination.start_retirement
destination.stop
destination.suspend
destination.sync_or_async_ems_operation
destination.unlink_storage
destination.unregister
```

In the case of provisioning a virtual machine, the same destination object is also available via the vm association:

```
$evm.root['miq_provision'].vm
```

We often find that objects are accessible via multiple association names.

Summary

This chapter has discussed the four main service model objects that we work with when we interact with the virtual machine or instance provisioning workflow, and we've seen the methods that are available to call on each object.

The virtual machine provisioning workflow is the same for all VMs that we provision into the same provider category: *Infrastructure* or *Cloud*. Our provisioning state machine is used to provision virtual machines into all providers within that category (both VMware and RHEV, for example), all provisioning methods (such as PXE boot or clone from *fat* template), and regardless of the operating system being provisioned. We must frequently make choices within our workflow based on some of these criteria, particularly the destination provider vendor and the operating system being provisioned. Using the various properties of the source and request objects, we can ascertain exactly the flavor of virtual machine being provisioned, the provisioning type being used, and the provider being targeted.

We also have several options to fine-tune the characteristics of the final virtual machine by calling methods on the destination object. We might want to explictly set the owning group and perhaps set a custom attribute. We could call destina tion.group= and destination.custom_set toward the end of the provisioning workflow to achieve this.

## CHAPTER 27

Creating Provisioning Requests Programmatically

As we've seen, the most common way to provision a virtual machine is via the Cloud-Forms WebUI (see Chapter 16). We click on Lifecycle → Provision VMs, complete the provisioning dialog, and a few minutes later our new virtual machine is ready.

There are times, however, when it is useful to be able to start the virtual machine provisioning process from an automation script, with no manual interaction. This then allows us to autoscale our virtual infrastructure, based on real-time or anticipated performance criteria. Perhaps we are an online retailer selling barbeques, for example. We could automatically monitor the short-range weather forecast via the API of a well-known weather website and scale out our online store servers if a period of fine weather is anticipated.

Making the Call

We can initiate the provisioning process programmatically by calling `$evm.execute` to run the method `create_provision_request` (see Chapter 7 for more information on these methods).

The `create_provision_request` method takes a number of arguments, which correspond to the argument list for the original `EVMProvisionRequestEx` SOAP API call. A typical call to provision a VM into RHEV might be:

```
# arg1 = version
args = ['1.1']

# arg2 = templateFields
args << {'name'         => 'rhel7-generic',
         'request_type' => 'template'}

# arg3 = vmFields
args << {'vm_name'   => 'rhel7srv010',
         'vlan'      => 'public',
         'vm_memory' => '1024'}

# arg4 = requester
args << {'owner_email'      => 'pemcg@bit63.com',
         'owner_first_name' => 'Peter',
         'owner_last_name'  => 'McGowan'}

# arg5 = tags
args << nil

# arg6 = additionalValues (ws_values)
args << {'disk_size_gb' => '50',
         'mountpoint'   => '/opt'}

# arg7 = emsCustomAttributes
args << nil

# arg8 = miqCustomAttributes
args << nil

request_id = $evm.execute('create_provision_request', *args)
```

Argument List

The arguments to the create_provision_request call are described next. The arguments match the fields in the provisioning dialog (and the values from the corresponding YAML template), and any arguments that are set to required: true in the dialog YAML, but don't have a :default: value, should be specified. The exception for this is for subdependencies of other options; for example, if :provision_type: is pxe, then the suboption :pxe_image_id: is mandatory. If the :provision_type: value is anything else, then :pxe_image_id: is not relevant.

In CloudForms versions prior to 4.0, the arguments were specified as a string, with each value separated by a pipe (|) symbol, like so:

```
"vm_name=rhel7srv010|vlan=public|vm_memory=1024"
```

With CloudForms 4.0, however, this syntax has been deprecated, and the options within each argument type should be defined as a hash as shown in the preceding example. This is more compatible with the equivalent RESTful API call to create a provisioning request.

The *value* for each hashed argument pair should always be a string; for example:

```
{'number_of_vms' => '4'}
```

rather than:

```
{'number_of_vms' => 4}
```

version

The version argument refers to the interface version. It should be set to 1.1.

templateFields

The templateFields argument denotes fields specifying the VM or template to use as the source for the provisioning operation. We supply a guid or ems_guid to protect against matching same-named templates on different providers within CloudForms Management Engine. The request_type field should be set to one of: template, clone_to_template, or clone_to_vm as appropriate. A normal VM provision from template is specified as:

```
'request_type' => 'template'
```

vmFields

vmFields allows for the setting of properties from the Catalog, Hardware, Network, Customize, and Schedule tabs in the provisioning dialog. Some of these are provider-specific, so when provisioning an OpenStack instance, for example, we need to specify the instance_type, as follows:

```
# arg2 = vmFields
arg2 = {'number_of_vms'  => '3',
        'instance_type'   => '1000000000007', # m1.small
        'vm_name'         => "#{$instance_name}",
        'retirement_warn' => "#{2.weeks}"}
args << arg2
```

requester

The requester argument allows for the setting of properties from the Request tab in the provisioning dialog. owner_email, owner_first_name, and owner_last_name are required fields.

tags

The `tags` argument refers to tags to apply to the newly created VM—for example:

```
{'server_role' => 'web_server',
 'cost_center' => '0011'}
```

additionalValues (aka ws_values)

Additional values, also known as `ws_values`, are name/value pairs stored with a provision request, but not used by the core provisioning code. These values are usually referenced from Automate methods for custom processing. They are added into the request options hash and can be retrieved as a hash from:

```
$evm.root['miq_provision'].options[:ws_values]
```

emsCustomAttributes

`emsCustomAttributes` are custom attributes applied to the virtual machine through the provider as part of provisioning. Not all providers support this, although VMware does support native vCenter custom attributes, which if set are visible both in Cloud-Forms and in the vSphere/vCenter UI.

miqCustomAttributes

`miqCustomAttributes` are custom attributes applied to the virtual machine and stored in the CloudForms Management Engine database as part of provisioning. These VMDB-specific custom attributes are displayed on the VM details page (see Chapter 5 for an example of setting a custom attribute from a script).

Setting Placement Options

The Rails code that implements the `create_provision_request` call makes the assumption that any noninteractive provision request will use automatic placement, and it sets `options[:placement_auto] = [true, 1]` as a request option. This also means, however, that it disregards any `vmFields` options that we may set that are normally found under the Environment tab of an interactive provision request, such as `cloud_tenant` or `cloud_network` (these are hidden in the WebUI if we select Choose Automatically; see Figure 27-1).

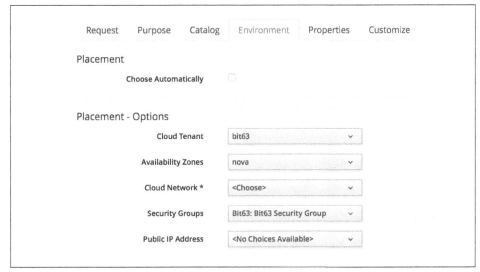

Figure 27-1. Setting the environment placement options for a cloud instance

If we try adding one of these (such as `cloud_network`), we see in *evm.log*:

```
Unprocessed key <cloud_network> with value <"1000000000007">
```

The only way that we can set any of these placement options is to add them to the *additionalValues/ws_values (arg6)* argument list and then handle them ourselves in the `CustomizeRequest` stage of the state machine.

For example, in our call to `create_provision_request` we can set:

```
# arg6 = additionalValues (ws_values)
args << {'cloud_network' => '10000000000031'
         'cloud_tenant'  => '10000000000012'}
```

We can then copy *ManageIQ/Cloud/VM/Provisioning/StateMachines/Methods/open-stack_CustomizeRequest* into our own domain, and edit as follows:

```
#
# Description: Customize the OpenStack provisioning request
#
def find_object_for(rsc_class, id_or_name)
  obj = $evm.vmdb(rsc_class, id_or_name.to_s) ||
        $evm.vmdb(rsc_class).find_by_name(id_or_name.to_s)
  $evm.log(:warn, "Couldn\'t find an object of class #{rsc_class} \
                   with an ID or name matching \'#{id_or_name}\'") if obj.nil?
  obj
end

# Get provisioning object
prov = $evm.root["miq_provision"]
ws_values = prov.options.fetch(:ws_values, {})

if ws_values.has_key?(:cloud_network)
  cloud_network = find_object_for('CloudNetwork', ws_values[:cloud_network])
  prov.set_cloud_network(cloud_network)
end
if ws_values.has_key?(:cloud_tenant)
  cloud_tenant = find_object_for('CloudTenant', ws_values[:cloud_tenant])
  prov.set_cloud_tenant(cloud_tenant)
end

$evm.log("info", "Provisioning ID:<#{prov.id}> \
                  Provision Request ID:<#{prov.miq_provision_request.id}> \
                  Provision Type: <#{prov.provision_type}>")
```

Summary

Being able to create provisioning requests programmatically gives us complete control over the process and has many uses. For example, when managing a scalable cloud application, we can configure a CloudForms alert to detect high CPU utilization on any of the existing cloud instances making up the workload. We could use the alert to send a management event that runs an Automate method to scale out the workload by provisioning additional instances (see Chapter 11).

We can also use create_provision_request to create custom service catalog items, when the out-of-the-box service provisioning state machines do not provide the functionality that we need (see Chapter 39).

Further Reading

Provision Request Attribute Groups (*http://bit.ly/1sz7Jrp*)

## CHAPTER 28

Integrating with Satellite 6 During Provisioning

It is a relatively common requirement to register newly provisioned Red Hat Enterprise Linux virtual machines directly with Satellite 6 as part of the provisioning process. This ensures that the resultant VM is patched and up to date, and is configured by Puppet according to a server role.

This chapter describes the steps involved in adapting the provisioning workflow so that Red Hat virtual machines are automatically registered with Satellite 6 as part of the provisioning operation. We'll be preparing the Satellite environment slightly for the automation, and we'll call the Satellite RESTful API to perform some of the integration steps. This is a relatively simple use case that demonstrates the capability of CloudForms to *integrate* with our wider enterprise.

Hosts and Content Hosts

Registering a new system with Satellite 6.1 currently requires two operations. We need to create a Satellite *host* entry, which registers the server as a configuration management client, manageable by Puppet. We also need to use `subscription_manager` to activate the server as a *content host*, which associates one or more Red Hat subscriptions with the server and makes software package repository content available.

The Challenge of Triggering the Client Operations

For this example, we'll be provisioning into a VMware provider and cloning from fully installed *fat* templates (i.e., no kickstarting).

Cloning from a template (infrastructure providers) or image (cloud providers) presents us with the challenge of how to initiate several commands on the new VM, including `subscription-manager register`, using dynamic arguments such as `--activationkey` or `--org`.

There are several ways of remotely running commands in a newly created VM, including:

- Using the VMware VIX SDK library to connect to VMware tools running in a guest (VMware providers only)
- Using cloud-init (RHEV, OpenStack, and Amazon providers)
- Using ssh, including Ansible (all providers)

For flexibility (at the expense of some added complexity), we'll be triggering the subscription manager registration of the newly provisioned system using an Ansible playbook, dynamically created as part of the provisioning workflow.

The Satellite 6 Host Entry

A host entry in Satellite 6 requires certain parameters:

- Hostname
- Host's MAC address
- Location
- Organizaton
- Puppet environment
- Architecture
- Operating system
- Media
- Partition table
- Domain
- Root password

We can, however, define a *host group* in Satellite, containing defaults for several of these parameters. When we create the host entry, we can specify a host group as a configuration template.

Non-CloudForms Preparation

We need to do some preparation of our environment. To keep the example simple, we'll allow for provisioning Red Hat Enterprise Linux 6 and 7 servers (both x86_64), but we'll create a single generic host group and activation key for each operating system version.

Creating the Host Groups in Satellite 6

We'll create two host groups in Satellite 6: `Generic_RHEL6_Servers` and `Generic_RHEL7_Servers` (see Figure 28-1).

Figure 28-1. Preparation of two Satellite 6 host groups

These host groups will define defaults for:

- Puppet environment
- Architecture
- Operating system
- Media
- Partition table
- Domain
- Root password

The host group will also install the `motd` and `ntp` Puppet modules.

Creating the Activation Keys in Satellite 6

When a newly provisioned system registers with Satellite as a *content host*, it can include an activation key name as an argument to subscription_manager.

We'll create two activation keys in Satellite 6: RHEL6-Generic and RHEL7-Generic (see Figure 28-2).

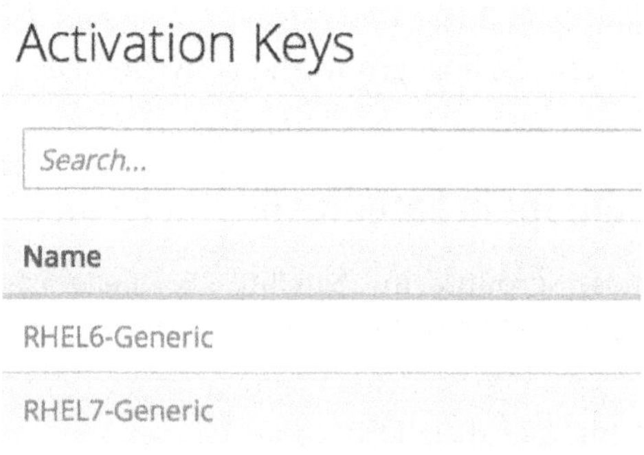

Figure 28-2. Preparation of two Satellite 6 activation keys

These activation keys will define defaults for:

- Content view and lifecycle environment (*Production*)
- Red Hat subscriptions
- Repository content sets

Adding an SSH Key to the VMware Template

We're going to be using Ansible from the CloudForms server to set the new VM's hostname, register the new VM with Satellite, and install and run Puppet. We need to copy root's public key from the CloudForms server to the VMware template and add it to */root/.ssh/authorized_keys*.

Installing and Configuring Ansible on the CloudForms Appliance

For convenience we'll install Ansible from the EPEL repository. We need to add the *rhel-7-server-optional-rpms* repository, and then the EPEL installation RPM on the CloudForms appliances with the Automation Engine role set:

```
subscription-manager repos --enable=rhel-7-server-optional-rpms
rpm -ivh https://dl.fedoraproject.org/pub/epel/epel-release-latest-7.noarch.rpm
```

Installing extra packages from the EPEL repository may leave your CloudForms installation unstable and unsupported by Red Hat.

Now we can install Ansible:

```
yum -y install ansible
Loaded plugins: product-id, search-disabled-repos, subscription-manager
Resolving Dependencies
--> Running transaction check
---> Package ansible.noarch 0:1.9.4-1.el7 will be installed
--> Processing Dependency: sshpass for package: ansible-1.9.4-1.el7.noarch
--> Processing Dependency: python-paramiko for package: ansible-1.9.4-1.el7.no...
--> Processing Dependency: python-keyczar for package: ansible-1.9.4-1.el7.noa...
--> Processing Dependency: python-jinja2 for package: ansible-1.9.4-1.el7.noarch
--> Processing Dependency: python-httplib2 for package: ansible-1.9.4-1.el7.no...
--> Running transaction check
---> Package python-httplib2.noarch 0:0.7.7-3.el7 will be installed
---> Package python-jinja2.noarch 0:2.7.2-2.el7 will be installed
--> Processing Dependency: python-babel >= 0.8 for package: python-jinja2-2.7....
--> Processing Dependency: python-markupsafe for package: python-jinja2-2.7.2-...
---> Package python-keyczar.noarch 0:0.71c-2.el7 will be installed
--> Processing Dependency: python-crypto for package: python-keyczar-0.71c-2.e...
---> Package python-paramiko.noarch 0:1.15.1-1.el7 will be installed
--> Processing Dependency: python-ecdsa for package: python-paramiko-1.15.1-1....
---> Package sshpass.x86_64 0:1.05-5.el7 will be installed
--> Running transaction check
---> Package python-babel.noarch 0:0.9.6-8.el7 will be installed
---> Package python-ecdsa.noarch 0:0.11-3.el7 will be installed
---> Package python-markupsafe.x86_64 0:0.11-10.el7 will be installed
---> Package python2-crypto.x86_64 0:2.6.1-9.el7 will be installed
--> Processing Dependency: libtomcrypt.so.0()(64bit) for package: python2-cry...
--> Running transaction check
---> Package libtomcrypt.x86_64 0:1.17-23.el7 will be installed
--> Processing Dependency: libtommath >= 0.42.0 for package: libtomcrypt-1.17-...
--> Processing Dependency: libtommath.so.0()(64bit) for package: libtomcrypt-1...
--> Running transaction check
---> Package libtommath.x86_64 0:0.42.0-4.el7 will be installed
--> Finished Dependency Resolution
...
```

We probably want to disable the EPEL repo after installing this to ensure that we don't accidentally pull anything else down from it:

```
sed -i -e 's/enabled=1/enabled=0/' /etc/yum.repos.d/epel.repo
```

Uncomment host_key_checking in */etc/ansible/ansible.cfg*:

```
# uncomment this to disable SSH key host checking
host_key_checking = False
```

Modifying the CloudForms Provisioning Workflow

We need to make two additions to the *VMProvision_VM* state machine. The first is to add a RegisterSatellite state to register the new VM with Satellite 6 as a host. The second is to add an ActivateSatellite state to create the Ansible playbook and initiate the subscription-manager activation of the new system as a content host.

Both of these states must be added at some point *after* the VM has been provisioned. The registration must include the MAC address of the new VM, and the activation uses Ansible to connect via ssh to the running VM.

Figure 28-3 shows the new states added.

Figure 28-3. RegisterSatellite and ActivateSatellite states added to the VM provision state machine

RegisterSatellite

Our new *RegisterSatellite* instance schema can store some more defaults. In this case we'll create per-organization/location instances, so that we can store the organization name and location in the schema (see Figure 28-4).

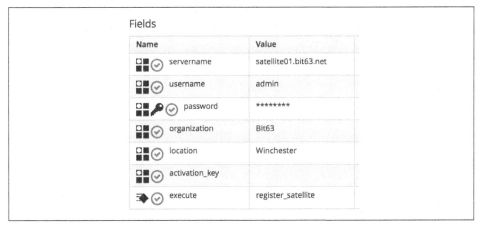

Figure 28-4. RegisterSatellite instance schema

The *register_satellite* method can access these in the usual way, from `$evm.object`:

```
servername    = $evm.object['servername']
username      = $evm.object['username']
password      = $evm.object.decrypt('password')
organization  = $evm.object['organization']
location      = $evm.object['location']
```

We need to ensure that we register only Linux VMs with Satellite, and we can select a host group by testing the VM `operating_system` object's `product_name` attribute (we're only provisioning RHEL 6 or 7, both x86_64):

```
...
prov = $evm.root['miq_provision']
template = prov.source
vm = prov.destination

if template.platform == "linux"
  #
  # Pick a host group based on the operating system being provisioned
  #
  if vm.operating_system.product_name == 'Red Hat Enterprise Linux 6 (64-bit)'
    hostgroup = 'Generic_RHEL6_Servers'
  elsif vm.operating_system.product_name == 'Red Hat Enterprise Linux 7 (64-bit)'
    hostgroup = 'Generic_RHEL7_Servers'
  else
    raise "Unrecognised Operating System Name"
  end
...
```

In a more advanced example we could present a selection of host groups to register with in a service dialog drop-down list (see Chapter 38).

We'll be creating the new host entry using the Satellite API, and this requires us to use the internal Satellite ID for each parameter, rather than a name. We define a generic query_id method and call it three times to retrieve the IDs for the location, organization, and host group:

```ruby
def query_id (uri, field, content)

  url = URI.escape("#{@uri_base}/#{uri}?search=#{field}=\"#{content}\"")
  request = RestClient::Request.new(
    method: :get,
    url: url,
    headers: @headers,
    verify_ssl: OpenSSL::SSL::VERIFY_NONE
  )

  id = nil
  rest_result = request.execute
  json_parse = JSON.parse(rest_result)

  subtotal = json_parse['subtotal'].to_i
  if subtotal == 1
    id = json_parse['results'][0]['id'].to_s
  elsif subtotal.zero?
    $evm.log(:error, "Query to #{url} failed, no result")
    id = -1
  elsif subtotal > 1
    $evm.log(:error, "Query to #{url} returned multiple results")
    id = -1
  else
    $evm.log(:error, "Query to #{url} failed, unknown condition")
    id = -1
  end
  id
end


...
$evm.log(:info, "Getting hostgroup id for '#{hostgroup}' from Satellite")
hostgroup_id = query_id("hostgroups", "name", hostgroup)
raise "Cannot determine hostgroup id for '#{hostgroup}'" if hostgroup_id == -1
$evm.log(:info, "hostgroup_id: #{hostgroup_id}")
```

Finally, we create the host record. We specify the :build parameter as false because we don't want Satellite to provision the VM:

```
#
# Create the host record
#
hostinfo = {
    :name              => vm.name,
    :mac               => vm.mac_addresses[0],
    :hostgroup_id      => hostgroup_id,
    :location_id       => location_id,
    :organization_id   => organization_id,
    :build             => 'false'
    }
$evm.log(:info, "Creating host record in Satellite")

uri = "#{@uri_base}/hosts"
request = RestClient::Request.new(
    method: :post,
    url: uri,
    headers: @headers,
    verify_ssl: OpenSSL::SSL::VERIFY_NONE,
    payload: { host: hostinfo }.to_json
  )
rest_result = request.execute
```

ActivateSatellite

Our new *ActivateSatellite* instance schema can also store some defaults. In this case we'll create per-organization instances, and we'll store the organization name in the schema (see Figure 28-5).

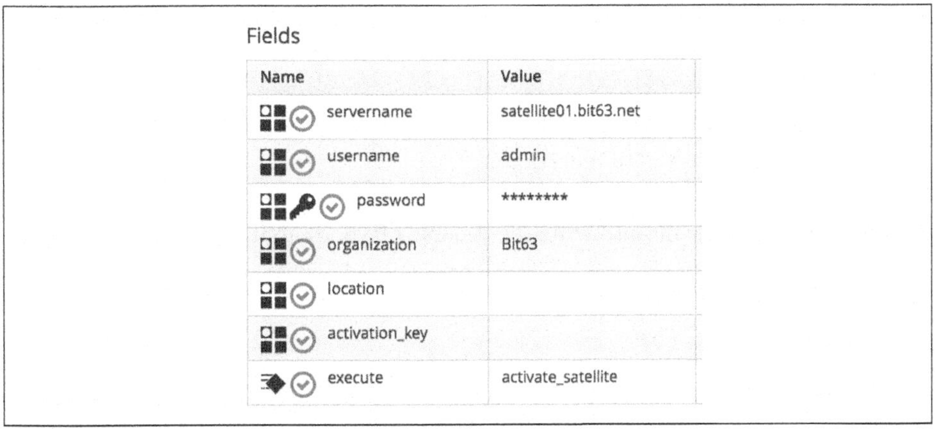

Fields	
Name	Value
servername	satellite01.bit63.net
username	admin
password	********
organization	Bit63
location	
activation_key	
execute	activate_satellite

Figure 28-5. ActivateSatellite instance schema

Once again we check that the system being provisioned is running Linux and select the activation key based on the operating system version:

```
if template.platform == "linux"
  #
  # Pick an activation key based on the operating system being provisioned
  #
  if vm.operating_system.product_name == 'Red Hat Enterprise Linux 6 (64-bit)'
    activationkey = 'RHEL6-Generic'
  elsif vm.operating_system.product_name == 'Red Hat Enterprise Linux 7 (64-bit)'
    activationkey = 'RHEL7-Generic'
  else
    raise "Unrecognised Operating System Name"
  end
```

We need to check that the VM is booted and has an IP address:

```
if vm.ipaddresses.length.zero?
  $evm.log(:info, "VM doesnt have an IP address yet - retrying in 1 minute")
  $evm.root['ae_result'] = 'retry'
  $evm.root['ae_retry_interval'] = '1.minute'
  exit MIQ_OK
end
ip_address = vm.ipaddresses[0]
```

For this example, we'll be connecting to the newly provisioned VM by IP address rather than hostname, so we have to add the new IP address to */etc/ansible/hosts* if it doesn't already exist:

```
unless File.foreach('/etc/ansible/hosts') \
.grep(/#{Regexp.escape(ip_address)}/).any?
  open('/etc/ansible/hosts', 'a') do |f|
    f.puts "#{ip_address}"
    f.close
  end
end
```

We need to remove the hosts key for that IP address if it already exists:

```
cmd = "ssh-keygen -R #{ip_address}"
`#{cmd}`
```

We create a temporary file and write the Ansible playbook to it:

```
tempfile = Tempfile.new('ansible-')

playbook = []
this_host = {}
this_host['hosts'] = []
this_host['hosts'] = "#{ip_address}"
this_host['tasks'] << { 'name'      => 'Set hostname',
                        'hostname'  => "name=#{vm.name}"
                      }
this_host['tasks'] = []
this_host['tasks'] << { 'name'      => 'Install Cert',
                        'command'   => "/usr/bin/yum -y localinstall \
                  http://#{servername}/pub/katello-ca-consumer-latest.noarch.rpm"
```

```
                      }
this_host['tasks'] << { 'name'       => 'Register with Satellite',
                        'command'    => "/usr/sbin/subscription-manager register \
                        --org #{organization} --activationkey #{activationkey}",
                        'register'   => 'registered'
                      }
this_host['tasks'] << { 'name'       => 'Enable Repositories',
                        'command'    => "subscription-manager repos \
                                    --enable=rhel-*-satellite-tools-*-rpms",
                        'when'       => 'registered|success'
                      }
this_host['tasks'] << { 'name'       => 'Install Katello Agent',
                        'yum'        => 'pkg=katello-agent state=latest',
                        'when'       => 'registered|success',
                        'notify'     => ['Enable Katello Agent', \
                                                    'Start Katello Agent']
                      }
this_host['tasks'] << { 'name'       => 'Install Puppet',
                        'yum'        => 'pkg=puppet state=latest',
                        'when'       => 'registered|success',
                        'register'   => 'puppet_installed',
                        'notify'     => ['Enable Puppet']
                      }
this_host['tasks'] << { 'name'       => 'Configure Puppet Agent',
                        'command'    => "/usr/bin/puppet config set server \
                                           #{servername} --section agent",
                        'when'       => 'puppet_installed|success'
                      }
this_host['tasks'] << { 'name'       => 'Run Puppet Test',
                        'command'    => '/usr/bin/puppet agent --test --noop \
                                            --onetime --waitforcert 60',
                        'when'       => 'puppet_installed|success'
                      }
this_host['tasks'] << { 'name'       => 'Start Puppet',
                        'service'    => 'name=puppet state=started'
                      }
this_host['tasks'] << { 'name'       => 'Update all packages',
                        'command'    => '/usr/bin/yum -y update'
                      }
this_host['handlers'] = []
this_host['handlers'] << { 'name'    => 'Enable Katello Agent',
                           'service' => 'name=goferd enabled=yes'
                         }
this_host['handlers'] << { 'name'    => 'Start Katello Agent',
                           'service' => 'name=goferd state=started'
                         }
this_host['handlers'] << { 'name'    => 'Enable Puppet',
                           'service' => 'name=puppet enabled=yes'
                         }
playbook << this_host
```

```
tempfile.write("#{playbook.to_yaml}\n")
tempfile.close
```

Finally, we run `ansible-playbook`:

```
cmd = "ansible-playbook -s #{tempfile.path}"
ansible_results = `#{cmd}`
$evm.log(:info, "Finished ansible-playbook, results: #{ansible_results}")
tempfile.unlink
```

The full scripts are available on GitHub (*http://bit.ly/1VOFeSa*).

Testing the Integration: Provisioning a New VM

First we check that we have no hosts with *test* in their name in our Satellite (see Figure 28-6).

Figure 28-6. The number of "test" hosts in Satellite before provisioning

We'll provision a RHEL 6 virtual machine and call it *rhel6test* (see Figure 28-7).

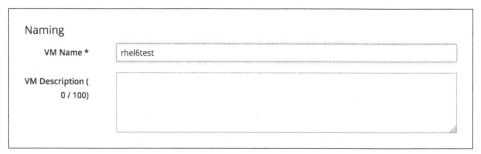

Figure 28-7. Provisioning a new virtual machine called rhel6test

Once the VM has finished cloning, we see the output from `register_satellite` in *automation.log*:

```
<AEMethod register_satellite> Getting hostgroup id for 'Generic_RHEL6_Servers' \
                                                          from Satellite
<AEMethod register_satellite> hostgroup_id: 3
<AEMethod register_satellite> Getting location id for 'Winchester' from Satellite
<AEMethod register_satellite> location_id: 4
<AEMethod register_satellite> Getting organization id for 'Bit63' from Satellite
<AEMethod register_satellite> organization_id: 3
<AEMethod register_satellite> Creating host record in Satellite with the \
          following details: {:name=>"rhel6test", :mac=>"00:50:56:b8:51:da", \
                             :hostgroup_id=>"3", :location_id=>"4", \
                             :organization_id=>"3", :build=>"false"}
<AEMethod register_satellite> return code => 200
```

In Satellite we see the new host entry, but the *N* icon indicates that no reports have been received from it yet (see Figure 28-8).

Figure 28-8. Newly added host record

Soon afterward we see the output from *activate_satellite* in *automation.log*:

```
activate_satellite> VM doesnt have an IP address yet - retrying in 1 minute
...
activate_satellite> IP Address is: 192.168.1.185
activate_satellite> Running ansible-playbook using /tmp/ansible-20151026-26705...
<AEMethod activate_satellite> Finished ansible-playbook, results:
PLAY [192.168.1.185] ********************************************************

GATHERING FACTS ************************************************************
ok: [192.168.1.185]

TASK: [Set hostname] *******************************************************
changed: [192.168.1.185]

TASK: [Install Cert] *******************************************************
changed: [192.168.1.185]

TASK: [Register with Satellite] ********************************************
changed: [192.168.1.185]
```

```
TASK: [Enable Repositories] *************************************************
changed: [192.168.1.185]

TASK: [Install Katello Agent] ***********************************************
changed: [192.168.1.185]

TASK: [Install Puppet] ******************************************************
changed: [192.168.1.185]

TASK: [Configure Puppet Agent] **********************************************
changed: [192.168.1.185]

TASK: [Run Puppet Test] *****************************************************
changed: [192.168.1.185]

TASK: [Start Puppet] ********************************************************
changed: [192.168.1.185]

TASK: [Update all packages] *************************************************
changed: [192.168.1.185]

NOTIFIED: [Enable Katello Agent] ********************************************
ok: [192.168.1.185]

NOTIFIED: [Start Katello Agent] *********************************************
ok: [192.168.1.185]

NOTIFIED: [Enable Puppet] ***************************************************
changed: [192.168.1.185]

PLAY RECAP ******************************************************************
192.168.1.185                : ok=14   changed=11   unreachable=0   failed=0
```

In Satellite we now see the new content host entry, showing that all packages have been updated (see Figure 28-9).

Figure 28-9. Newly added content host record

We also see that the new host record is shown as active, showing that the Puppet agent is connecting to the Puppet Master (see Figure 28-10).

Figure 28-10. Host record activated

Summary

This chapter has shown how we can integrate our virtual machine provisioning work-flow with our wider enterprise, in this case by registering new VMs with a Satellite 6 server. The example is deliberately simple in having only one host group and activa-tion key per operating system version, but hopefully this simplicity conveys the rela-tive ease of integration.

If we prefer to provision our new virtual machine by PXE boot/kickstart, we simply pass any additional parameters that are required for the kickstart in the hostinfo hash and set the key :build to be true, as follows:

```
hostinfo = {
    :name                => vm.name,
    :mac                 => vm.mac_addresses[0],
    :hostgroup_id        => hostgroup_id,
    :location_id         => location_id,
    :organization_id     => organization_id,
    :operatingsystem_id  => operatingsystem_id,
    :architecture_id     => architecture_id,
    :domain_id           => domain_id,
    :subnet_id           => subnet_id,
    :root_pass           => root_password,
    :ip                  => ip_address,
    :disk                => partition_layout,
    :build               => 'true'
}
```

In this example we've also installed Ansible directly onto our CloudForms appliance. At the time of writing it seems likely that a future version of CloudForms will have a dedicated Ansible provider, thereby rendering this step unnecessary.

Further Reading

How to Provision VMs with Foreman and ManageIQ (*http://bit.ly/1XeBSZL*)

Check Provisioning State in ManageIQ with Foreman (*http://bit.ly/25SoYlU*)

Foreman API—Create a Host (*http://bit.ly/1OhbVpE*)

PART III

Working with Services

We saw in Part II how we can provision virtual machines from the WebUI. This process involves entering values for the many provisioning dialog options, such as our name and email address, and the desired configuration of the virtual machine—the number of CPUs, amount of memory, disk format, and vLAN, for example.

CloudForms also enables us to create service catalogs with which we can provision preconfigured virtual machines from a single Order button (see Figure III-1).

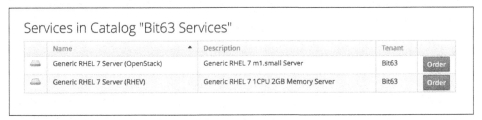

Figure III-1. Simple service catalog

In Part III we'll learn about creating and using services.

## CHAPTER 29

Service Dialogs

When we design our services in CloudForms, we try to simplify the ordering process for our users as much as possible. We preconfigure as many provisioning choices as we can and, ideally, offer a small selection of options in the form of a service dialog to allow our users to customize their service request. An example might be to offer a simple *T-shirt size* ordering style to specify the size of a virtual machine (see Figure 29-1).

Figure 29-1. Ordering VMs in T-shirt sizes

We have already seen how to create a simple service dialog in Chapter 5. This chapter will discuss service dialogs in more detail and show how we can create *dynamic elements* that are populated at runtime when the user orders the catalog item.

Dialog Elements

The service dialog that we created in Chapter 5 used two simple *text box* elements. In addition to text boxes, there are several other element types that we can use (see Figure 29-2).

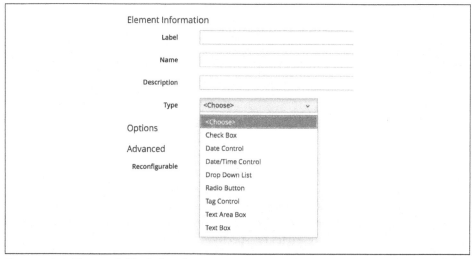

Figure 29-2. The available dialog element types

Service dialog elements gained several useful new features with recent versions of CloudForms, as we'll see in this chapter.

Dynamic Elements

Prior to CloudForms 3.2 only one element type was capable of dynamic (runtime) population, the Dynamic Drop Down List. CloudForms 3.2 extended the dynamic population capability to most other dialog element types, so the Dynamic Drop Down List has been removed as a separate element type.

Dynamic elements are populated from a method, called either when the service dialog is initially displayed or from an optional Refresh button (dynamic elements can also be autorefreshed, as we'll see shortly). The URI to the method is specified when we add the element and select the checkbox to make it dynamic.

Populating the Dynamic Fields

The dynamic element has its own $evm.object. We need to populate some predefined hash key/value pairs in this object to define the dialog field settings, and to load the data to be displayed. Here is an example of how we do this:

```
dialog_field = $evm.object

# sort_by: value / description / none
dialog_field["sort_by"] = "value"

# sort_order: ascending / descending
dialog_field["sort_order"] = "ascending"

# data_type: string / integer
dialog_field["data_type"] = "integer"

# required: true / false
dialog_field["required"] = "true"

dialog_field["values"] = {2 => "2GB", 4 => "4GB", 16 => "16GB"}
dialog_field["default_value"] = 2
```

If the dynamic element type is a drop-down list, the values key of this hash is also a hash of key/value pairs. Each key/value pair in this hash represents a value to be displayed in the element, and the corresponding data_type value to be returned to Automate as the dialog_* option if that choice is selected.

Here is another, more real-world example of the versatility of dynamic elements:

```
values_hash = {}
values_hash['!'] = '-- select from list --'
user_group = $evm.root['user'].ldap_group
#
# Everyone can provision to DEV and UAT
#
values_hash['dev'] = "Development"
values_hash['uat'] = "User Acceptance Test"
if user_group.downcase =~ /administrators/
  #
  # Administrators can also provision to PRE-PROD and PROD
  #
  values_hash['pre-prod'] = "Pre-Production"
  values_hash['prod'] = "Production"
end

list_values = {
  'sort_by'    => :value,
  'data_type'  => :string,
  'required'   => true,
  'values'     => values_hash
}
list_values.each { |key, value| $evm.object[key] = value }
```

This example populates a dynamic drop-down list with infrastructure lifecycle environments into which a user can provision a new virtual machine. If the user is a member of group containing the string administrators, then a further two environments, Pre-Production and Production, are added to the list.

Read-Only and Protected Elements

CloudForms 3.1 added the ability to mark a text box as protected, which results in any input being obfuscated. This is particularly useful for inputting passwords (see Figure 29-3).

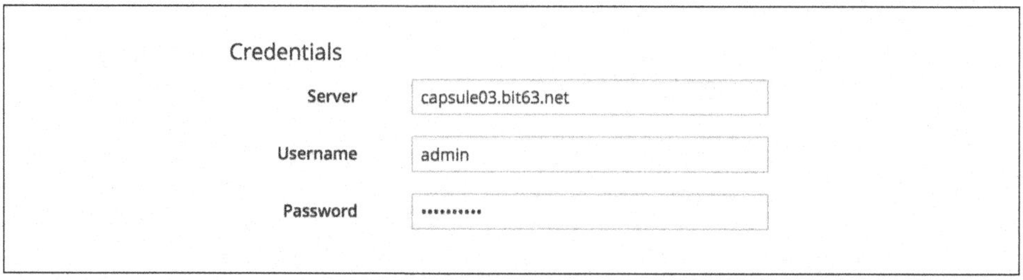

Figure 29-3. Dialog that prompts for a password in a protected element

CloudForms 3.2 introduced the concept of read-only elements for service dialogs that cannot be changed once displayed. Having a text box dynamically populated, but read-only, makes it ideal for displaying messages.

Programmatically Populating a Read-Only Text Box

We can use dynamically populated read-only text or text area boxes as status boxes to display messages. Here is an example of populating a text box with a message, depending on whether the user is provisioning into Amazon or not:

```
if $evm.root['vm'].vendor.downcase == 'amazon'
  status = "Valid for this VM type"
else
  status = 'Invalid for this VM type'
end
list_values = {
   'required'   => true,
   'protected'  => false,
   'read_only'  => true,
   'value'      => status,
 }
list_values.each do |key, value|
   $evm.object[key] = value
end
```

Element Validation

CloudForms 3.2 introduced the ability to add input field validation to dialog elements. Currently the only validator types are None or Regular Expression, but regular expressions are useful for validating input for values such as IP addresses (see Figure 29-4).

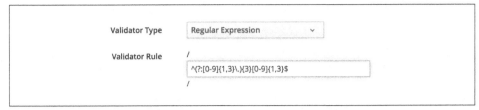

Figure 29-4. Validator rule for an IP address element

Using the Input from One Element in Another Element's Dynamic Method

We can link elements in such a way that a user's input in one element can be used by subsequent dynamic elements that are *refreshable*. The subsequent dynamic method, when refreshed, can use $evm.root['dialog_*elementname*'] or $evm.object['dia log_*elementname*'] to access the first element's input value. Elements can be refreshed with a Refresh button, but CloudForms 4.0 added the ability to mark dynamic elements with the "Auto refresh" characteristic. There is a corresponding characteristic, "Auto Refresh other fields when modified," that we can apply to the initial element at the start of this refresh chain.

We can use this in several useful ways, such as to populate a dynamic list based on a value input previously, or to create a validation method.

Example

Requirement

We have a service dialog containing a text box element called tenant_name. Into this element the user should type the name of a new OpenStack tenant to be created in each of several OpenStack providers. The tenant name should be unique and not currently exist in any provider.

We would like to add a validation capability to the service dialog to check that the tenant name doesn't already exist before the user clicks on the Submit button.

Solution

In the following example a read-only text area box element called validation is used to display a validation message. Users are instructed to click the Refresh button to validate their input to the tenant_name field.

Until the Refresh button is clicked, the validation text area box displays "Validation…". Once the Refresh button is clicked, the validation message changes according to whether the tenant exists or not:

```
display_string = "Validation...\n"
tenant_found = false

tenant_name = $evm.root['dialog_tenant_name']
unless tenant_name.length.zero?
  lowercase_tenant = tenant_name.gsub(/\W/,'_').downcase
  tenant_objects = $evm.vmdb('CloudTenant').find(:all)
  tenant_objects.each do | tenant |
    if tenant.name.downcase == lowercase_tenant
      tenant_found = true
      display_string += "   Tenant \'#{tenant.name}\' exists in OpenStack "
      display_string += "Provider: #{$evm.vmdb('ems', tenant.ems_id).name}\n"
    end
  end
  unless tenant_found
    display_string += "   Tenant \'#{lowercase_tenant}\' is available for use"
  end
end

list_values = {
  'required'   => true,
  'protected'  => false,
  'read_only'  => true,
  'value'      => display_string,
}
list_values.each do |key, value|
  $evm.log(:info, "Setting dialog variable #{key} to #{value}")
  $evm.object[key] = value
end
exit MIQ_OK
```

Summary

This chapter has shown the flexibility we have when we build our service dialogs. We can use dynamic methods to preload appropriate options into dialog elements, thereby customizing the dialog options on a per-user basis. We can also create confirmation text boxes that allow users to validate their inputs and thus allow them to make changes if necessary before clicking Submit.

It is worth noting that dynamic dialog methods always run on the WebUI appliance that we are logged into, whether or not this appliance has the Automation Engine server role set. This can have unexpected consequences. Our real-world CloudForms installations may comprise several appliances distributed among multiple zones, often with firewalls between (see Figure 29-5).

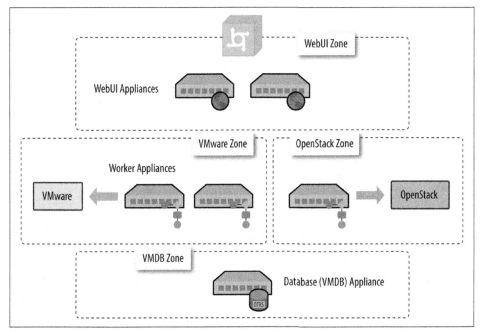

Figure 29-5. Typical real-world CloudForms installation with multiple appliances and zones

If we write a dynamic dialog method to retrieve any information from an external system, we might expect the method to run on any of our provider zone *worker* appliances, but it doesn't. We must ensure that the WebUI zone firewalls allow our WebUI appliances to directly connect to any external systems that our dialog methods need access to.

Further Reading

Service Dialogs (*http://red.ht/24Gw22p*)

Service Dialog Enhancements (*https://github.com/ManageIQ/manageiq/pull/2479*)

## CHAPTER 30

The Service Provisioning State Machine

As might be expected, CloudForms uses a state machine to intelligently handle the workflow for provisioning a service. Although we rarely modify the service provisioning state machine, it is useful to have an understanding of its steps and the functions that it performs. This more theoretical chapter examines the state machine and discusses its role in passing into the provisioning workflow the service dialog values that the user has input.

Class and Instances

The service provisioning state machine (the *ServiceProvision_Template* class) controls the sequence of steps involved in provisioning the service. The *ManageIQ* domain contains four instances of this state machine (see Figure 30-1).

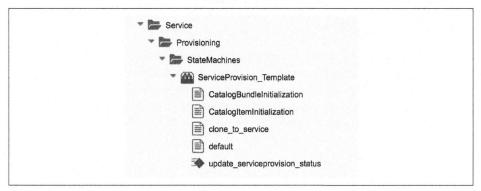

Figure 30-1. ServiceProvision_Template class, instances, and method

The *ServiceProvision_Template* class schema contains a number of states. Figure 30-2 shows the `default` instance of this state machine.

Name	Value
pre1	
pre2	
pre3	
pre4	
pre5	
configurechilddialog	#/Service/Provisioning/StateMachines/Methods/ConfigureChildDialog
provision	/Service/Provisioning/StateMachines/Methods/Provision
checkprovisioned	/Service/Provisioning/StateMachines/Methods/CheckProvisioned
post1	
post2	
post3	
post4	
post5	
EmailOwner	/Service/Provisioning/Email/ServiceProvision_complete?event=service_provisioned
Finished	/System/CommonMethods/StateMachineMethods/service_provision_finished

Figure 30-2. ServiceProvision_Template class schema

As we can see, most of the fields are *pre* and *post* placeholders around the main provi
sion and checkprovisioned states, to allow for optional processing if required. The
configurechilddialog state (by default commented out) can be used to populate the
options[:dialog] hash in the child task if required.

Passing Service Dialog Options to the Child and Grandchild Tasks

One of the more complex tasks that must be achieved by some state in the service
provisioning state machine is to pass the values received from the service dialog (if
there is one) to the actual tasks performing the provisioning of the virtual
machine(s). The complexity arises from the three *generations* of task object involved
in creating the service, the service resources, and the actual VMs (see Figure 30-3).

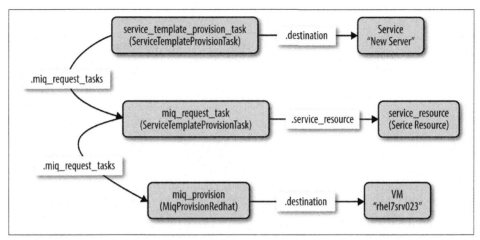

Figure 30-3. Task object hierarchy

This object hierarchy is represented at the highest level by the service template provision task. We access this from:

```
$evm.root['service_template_provision_task']
```

The `service_template_provision_task` has an assocation, `miq_request_tasks`, containing the `miq_request_task` objects representing the creation of the *service resource(s)*. These are the items or resources making up the service request (even a single service catalog item is treated as a bundle containing one service resource).

Each *child* (service resource) `miq_request_task` also has an `miq_request_tasks` association containing the VM provisioning tasks associated with creating the actual VMs for the service resource. This `miq_request_task` is provider-specific.

It is to the second level of `miq_request_task` (also known as the *grandchild task*) that we must pass the service dialog values that affect the provisioning of the VM (such as `:vm_memory` or `:vm_target_name`).

Chapter 35 discusses the service object structure in more detail.

Accessing the Service Dialog Options

If a service dialog has been used in the creation of an automation request (either from a button or from a service), then the key/value pairs from the service dialog are added to the request and subsequent task objects. These are available in two places: as individual keys accessible from `$evm.root`, and from the task object's options hash as the `:dialog` key:

```
$evm.root['service_template_provision_task'].options[:dialog] = \
        {
        "dialog_option_0_service_name"        => "New Server",
        "dialog_option_0_service_description" => "My New Server",
        "dialog_option_0_vm_name"             => "rhel7srv023",
        "dialog_tag_0_department"             => "engineering",
        "request"                             => "clone_to_service"
        }
```

or:

```
$evm.root['dialog_option_0_service_description'] = My New Server
$evm.root['dialog_option_0_service_name'] = New Server
$evm.root['dialog_option_0_vm_name'] = rhel7srv023
$evm.root['dialog_tag_0_department'] = engineering
```

Accessing the dialog options from options[:dialog] is easier when we don't necessarily know the option name.

ConfigureChildDialog

When we have several generations of child task object (as we do when provisioning VMs from a service), we also need to pass the dialog options from the parent object (the service template provision task) to the various child objects; otherwise, they won't be visible to the children.

This is generally done at the configurechilddialog state of the state machine. In the *Default* instance of the *ServiceProvision_Template* state machine, this state is not used (the value is commented out in the class schema), but we can uncomment it or add our own instance/method if we wish to use this functionality.

If we do decide to add our own method at this stage, we can insert the key/value pairs from the service dialog into the options[:dialog] hash of a child task object using the set_dialog_option method.

For example:

```
stp_task = $evm.root["service_template_provision_task"]
vm_size = $evm.root['dialog_vm_size']
stp_task.miq_request_tasks.each do |child_task|
  case vm_size
  when "Small"
    memory_size = 4096
  when "Large"
    memory_size = 8192
  end
  child_task.set_dialog_option('dialog_memory', memory_size)
end
```

This enables the child and grandchild virtual machine provision workflows (which run through the standard VM provision state machine that we have already studied) to access their own task object `options[:dialog]` hash and set the custom provisioning options accordingly.

Summary

This has been a brief overview of the service provisioning state machine, showing its relative simplicity.

One of the main tasks of the state machine is to pass values from the service dialog into the provisioning workflow, and we've seen how to navigate down the three generations of task object involved in a service provision operation in order to achieve this. Two out-of-the-box state machine instances have been created to simplify this task for us, and we will study those in the next chapter.

Although not immediately obvious, the service provision state machine is run in *task* context, so any access-control group profile processing, including naming and approval, has already taken place by the time any of our state machine methods run (we have `$evm.root['service_template_provision_task']` rather than `$evm.root['service_template_provision_request']`).

VM Naming for Services

As we're working in the *task* context of the provisioning process, the input variables to the naming process—`:vm_name`, `:vm_prefix`, and so on—are of no use to us (see Chapter 23). The naming process has already been run; they will not be referenced again.

We can, however, directly update the `:vm_target_name` and `:vm_target_hostname` values in the task object's options hash at any point before the `Provision` state of the *VMProvision_VM* state machine, like so:

```
task.set_option(:vm_target_name, "server001")
task.set_option(:vm_target_hostname, "server001")
```

Unfortunately, at this stage we don't have the ability to add the $n{2}–style syntax to our VM name either, hoping that the Automate Engine will assign us the next unique number. If we wanted to guarantee uniqueness, we'd have to use something like the following code:

```
for i in (1..999)
  new_vm_name = "#{vm_prefix}#{function}#{i.to_s.rjust(2, "0")}#{suffix}"
  break if $evm.vmdb('vm_or_template').find_by_name(new_vm_name).blank?
end
```

This loop iterates through all numbers from 1 to 999, appending each number as a zero-padded three-digit suffix to the virtual machine name prefix part. The script performs a service model lookup of a `vm_or_template` object containing that name/suffix combination, and if a virtual machine of that name doesn't exist, the loop exits with the variable `new_vm_name` set accordingly.

## CHAPTER 31

Catalog{Item,Bundle}Initialization

In Chapter 30 we saw that two of the service provisioning state machine instances are called *CatalogItemInitialization* and *CatalogBundleInitialization*. These two state machines greatly simplify the process of creating service catalog items and bundles, fronted by rich service dialogs, without the need for any Ruby scripting.

> A service catalog *item* generally provisions a single type of virtual machine (although it may result in multiple VMs of the same type being provisioned). A service catalog *bundle* can provision multiple service items in one go, allowing us to deploy multitier server workloads from a single click.

In this chapter we'll take a look at these two state machine instances in detail. We'll see how they allow us to name our service dialog elements in such a way that values are automatically passed into the provisioning workflow, with no need for further automation scripting.

CatalogItemInitialization

We can specify the *CatalogItemInitialization* state machine as the provisioning entry point when we create a service catalog item.

The state machine has been written to simplify the process of customizing the provisioned VMs, using values read from the service dialog. It does this by setting options hash values or tags in the child and grandchild `miq_request_task` objects, from specially constructed service dialog element names. It also allows us to specify a new unique name and description for the resulting service.

The schema for the *CatalogItemInitialization* instance is shown in Figure 31-1.

Fields		
Name	**Value**	
🦆✅ pre1	/Service/Provisioning/StateMachines/Methods/DialogParser	
🦆✅ pre2	/Service/Provisioning/StateMachines/Methods/CatalogItemInitialization	
🦆✅ pre3		
🦆✅ pre4		
🦆✅ pre5		
🦆✅ configurechilddialog	#/Service/Provisioning/StateMachines/Methods/ConfigureChildDialog	
🦆✅ provision	/Service/Provisioning/StateMachines/Methods/Provision	
🦆✅ checkprovisioned	/Service/Provisioning/StateMachines/Methods/CheckProvisioned	
🦆✅ post1		
🦆✅ post2		
🦆✅ post3		
🦆✅ post4		
🦆✅ post5		
🦆✅ EmailOwner	/Service/Provisioning/Email/ServiceProvision_complete?event=service_provisioned	
🦆✅ Finished	/System/CommonMethods/StateMachineMethods/service_provision_finished	

Figure 31-1. The schema of the CatalogItemInitialization state machine instance

We can see that the schema uses the `pre1` state to add a dialog parser (common between the *CatalogItemInitialization* and *CatalogBundleInitialization* state machines). It also uses the `pre2` state to specify the *CatalogItemInitialization* method, which sets the child object `options_hash` values and/or tags accordingly.

The *CatalogItemInitialization* method itself relies on the dialog inputs having been parsed correctly by *dialog_parser*, and this requires us to use a particular naming convention for our service dialog elements.

Service Dialog Element Naming Convention

To perform the service dialog → options hash or tag substitution correctly, we must name our service dialog elements in a particular way.

Single options hash key

The simplest service dialog element to process is one that prompts for the value of a single `options_hash` key. We name the service dialog element as:

`option_0_key_name` (for backward compatibility with CloudForms 3.1)

or just:

`key_name` (valid for CloudForms 3.2 and later)

For example, we can create a service dialog element as shown in Figure 31-2.

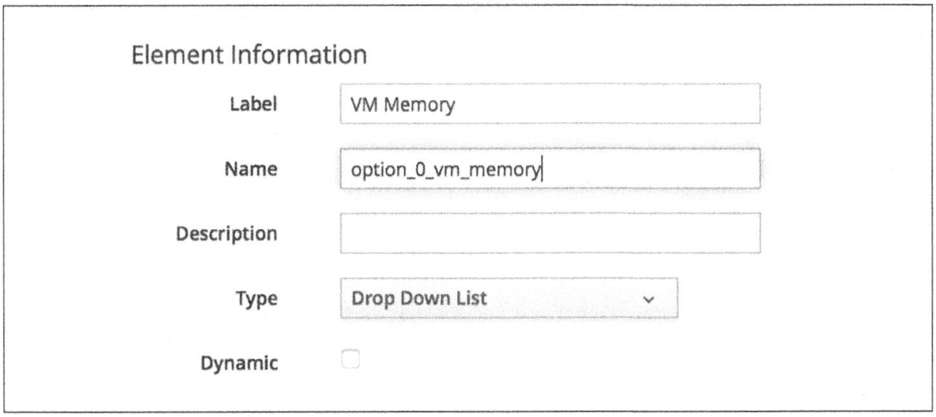

Figure 31-2. Service dialog element to prompt for an options hash key

The resulting value input from this dialog at runtime will be propagated to the child task's options hash as:

```
miq_request_task.options[:vm_memory]
```

The 0 in the dialog name refers to the item sequence number during provisioning. For a service dialog fronting a single catalog *item*, this will always be zero. For a service dialog fronting a catalog *bundle* comprising several items, the sequence number indicates which of the component items the dialog option should be passed to (an element with a name sequence of 0 will be propagated to all items).

Several key_name values are recognized and special-cased by the *CatalogItemInitialization* method. We can name a text box element as either vm_name or vm_target_name, and the resulting text string input value will be propagated to all of:

```
miq_request_task.options[:vm_target_name]
miq_request_task.options[:vm_target_hostname]
miq_request_task.options[:vm_name]
miq_request_task.options[:linux_host_name]
```

If we name a text box element as service_name, then the resulting service will be named from the text value of this element.

If we name a text box element as service_description, then the resulting service description will be updated from the text value of this element.

Single tag

We can also create a text box service dialog element to apply a single tag. The naming format is similar to that of naming an option but uses a prefix of tag_ and a suffix of the tag category name.

For example, we can prompt for a tag in the department category by naming the service dialog element as `tag_0_department` (see Figure 31-3).

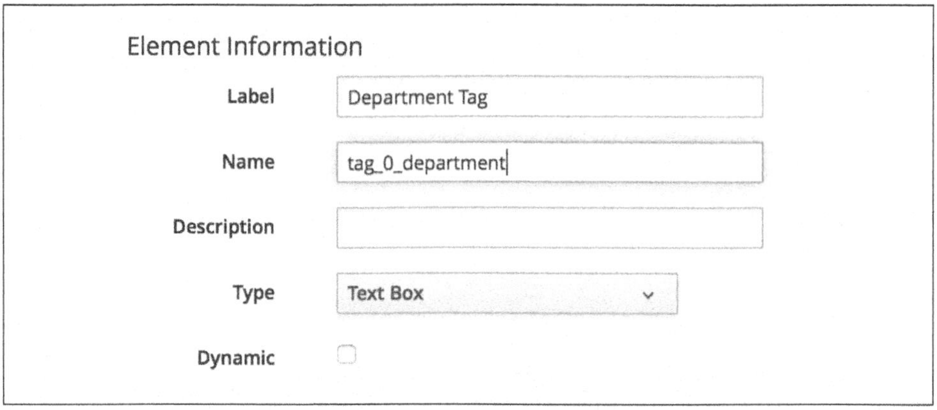

Element Information

Label	Department Tag
Name	tag_0_department
Description	
Type	Text Box ⌄
Dynamic	☐

Figure 31-3. Service dialog element to prompt for a tag value

The value input into the service dialog element at runtime should be a tag within this tag category. When an element of this type is processed by the *CatalogItemInitialization* method, if either the category or tag doesn't currently exist, it will be created.

CatalogBundleInitialization

The *CatalogBundleInitialization* state machine should be specified when we create a service catalog bundle.

The schema for the *CatalogBundleInitialization* instance is the same as for *CatalogItemInitialization*, except that the `pre2` stage calls the *CatalogBundleInitialization* method.

The *CatalogBundleInitialization* method passes the service dialog element values on to each catalog item's *CatalogItemInitialization* method, which is still required in order to set the `miq_request_task`'s options hash keys for the provision of that catalog item.

Summary

This chapter has introduced the two service provision state machines that we can use to create service catalog items and bundles, with no need for any Ruby scripting. We can create simple but impressive service catalogs in minutes using these entry points, and we'll see a practical example of this in Chapter 33.

Further Reading

It is worth familiarizing ourselves with the three methods that perform the parsing and transposing of the dialog values. These are *DialogParser*, *CatalogItemInitialization*, and *CatalogBundleInitialization*:

`DialogParser` method (*http://bit.ly/25kbN06*)

`CatalogItemInitialization` method (*http://bit.ly/1Wg9h66*)

`CatalogBundleInitialization` method (*http://bit.ly/1TUEyVQ*)

## CHAPTER 32

Approval and Quota

We discovered in Chapters 18 and 19 that the virtual machine provisioning process includes an approval stage—to allow administrators to optionally approve large VM requests—and a quota-checking stage that enforces quotas applied to access-control groups or tenants. We also learned that these workflows were triggered from *MiqProvisionRequest_created* and *MiqProvisionRequest_starting* policy instances. When we create a virtual machine from a service catalog item, however, our request object is different, so we cannot rely on the existing approval and quota workflow triggers.

This chapter examines the approval and quota workflows for when we provision a virtual machine from a service catalog.

Triggering Events

When we order a new virtual machine from a service catalog, our request still needs to be approved and matched against our current tenant or group quota. As with virtual machine provisioning, each of the corresponding service provision workflows is triggered by the `request_created` and `request_approved` events, but the request object type is different. It is now a `service_template_provision_request`.

Approval

The approval process for a service provision request starts with the */System/Policy/ ServiceTemplateProvisionRequest_created* instance being run as a result of a `request_created` event. This instance contains two relationships, `rel5` and `rel6`.

The `rel5` relationship performs a service provisioning profile lookup to read the value of the `auto_approval_state_machine` attribute, which by default is *ServiceProvisionRequestApproval* for a service provision request.

The `rel6` relationship runs the `Default` instance of this state machine (see Figure 32-1).

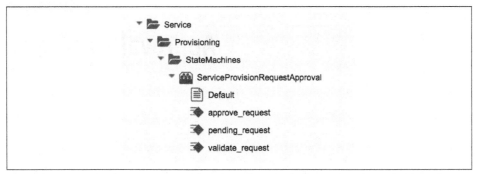

Figure 32-1. ServiceProvisionRequestApproval state machine instance and methods

The schema for the *ServiceProvisionRequestApproval/Default* state machine is shown in Figure 32-2.

Fields					
Name	Value	On Entry	On Exit	On Error
approval_type	auto			
ValidateRequest		validate_request		pending_request
ApproveRequest		approve_request		

Figure 32-2. ServiceProvisionRequestApproval/Default state machine schema

The methods *pending_request* and *approve_request* are the same as their counterparts for virtual machine provisioning approval. The default value of `validate_request` does nothing, so this state machine instance will auto-approve all service provisioning requests.

Customizing Approval

If universal auto-approval is not the required behavior, we can copy the *ServiceProvisionRequestApproval/Default* state machine methods to our own domain and edit them as necessary.

Quota

Quota checking for a service provision request in CloudForms 4.0 uses the same consolidated quota mechanism as described in Chapter 19.

The quota-checking process for a service provision request starts with the */System/Policy/ServiceTemplateProvisionRequest_starting* instance being run as a result of a `request_starting` event. This policy instance runs the */System/CommonMethods/QuotaStateMachine/quota* state machine from its `rel2` relationship.

Email

The email instances that handle the sending of "approval denied/pending" and "quota exceeded" emails are in the *RedHat* domain but by default are not *wired in* to any policy instances.

If we wish to use them we can add a policy instance called */System/Policy/ServiceTemplateProvisionRequest_denied* to our own domain. This should contain a relationship to the */Service/Provisioning/Email/ServiceTemplateProvisionRequest_Denied* email instance in the *RedHat* domain.

 We should ideally copy the *Email/ServiceTemplateProvisionRequest_Denied* instance into our own domain so that we can customize the `from_email_address`, `to_email_address`, and `signature` schema attributes.

Summary

We have seen how the approval and quota-checking mechanism for services mirrors that for virtual machines but uses different policy instances to trigger the workflows. The out-of-the-box approval workflow auto-approves all service requests, but we can copy the instance to our own domain to customize the behavior if we wish.

In practice we rarely need to customize these workflows. As virtualization administrators, when we provide a self-service catalog to our users, we generally accept the delegation of control and degree of responsibility that we pass to our users. This is, after all, one of the many benefits of implementing an Infrastructure as a Service cloud model. We almost certainly allocate quotas, but we rarely need to implement per-order approval as well. The default behavior of auto-approval of all service requests is valid in most situations.

## CHAPTER 33

Creating a Service Catalog Item

In this chapter we'll go through the steps involved in creating a service catalog item to provision a virtual machine into Red Hat Enterprise Virtualization (RHEV). We'll create a service dialog that allows the user to specify a name for both the new virtual machine and the service, and specify the number of CPUs and memory size of the provisioned virtual machine from a drop-down list.

Although for this example we'll be provisioning into RHEV, the same procedure can be used to create a service catalog item to provision into other providers.

The Service Dialog

We're going to create a service dialog to prompt for the number of CPUs and the amount of memory for the new virtual machine. These two characteristics will be added to the provisioning task object for the new VM, and we know that such items are stored in the task object's options hash for a provisioning operation. The *CatalogItemInitialization* state machine can handle the insertion of our dialog values into the options hash for us, as long as we name our dialog elements correctly.

Finding the Correct Element Names

We saw from Chapter 31 that *CatalogItemInitialization* recognizes and special-cases some element names, including vm_name and service_name, so we can create two of our elements with these names. If this is all we wish to prompt for, then we can move straight on to creating the service dialog.

For our use case, however, we are also prompting for number of CPUs and memory size. Any service dialog fields that we create with the intention of altering the final VM configuration (such as the number of CPUs or memory size) must also be named in a particular way. The element name must match the key in the provisioning task's options hash that we wish to overwrite.

We can find this key name in either of two ways: by examining the YAML code that makes up the provisioning dialog, or by performing an interactive provision of a virtual machine and examining the provisioning task's options hash during the provisioning process.

Searching the provisioning dialog

The simplest way to search the provisioning dialog is to copy the appropriate one, edit, and then select and paste the contents to a flat file that can be grepped, like so:

```
grep -i "memory\|cpu\|core\|socket" miq_provision_redhat_dialogs_template.yaml
  :number_of_sockets:
    :description: Number of Sockets
  :cores_per_socket:
    :description: Cores per Socket
  :vm_memory:
    :description: Memory (MB)
```

This shows that we probably need to name our elements `cores_per_socket` and `vm_memory`.

Examining the options hash during provisioning

As an alternative (or confirmation) to finding the key names from the provisioning dialog, we can use one of the techniques that we learned in Chapter 10 to dump the contents of the provisioning task's options hash during a normal interactive provision. Here is an example of calling `object_walker` after the `Placement` stage in the *VMProvision_VM/template* state machine (see Figure 33-1).

Figure 33-1. State added to the VM provisioning state machine to run ObjectWalker

Using the *object_walker_reader* after we've provisioned a virtual machine, we see that the same values are in the `miq_provision` task's options hash:

```
object_walker_reader.rb | grep 'miq_provision' | grep "memory\|cpu\|core\|socket"
    |    $evm.root['miq_provision'].options[:cores_per_socket] = [1, "1"]
    |    $evm.root['miq_provision'].options[:memory_reserve] = nil
    |    $evm.root['miq_provision'].options[:number_of_sockets] = [1, "1"]
    |    $evm.root['miq_provision'].options[:vm_memory] = ["1024", "1024"]
```

Some commonly used element names

Table 33-1 lists some commonly used element names for typical VM characteristics that can be modified from a service dialog.

Table 33-1. Element names of modifiable VM characteristics

VM characteristic to be modified	Element name
VM name	vm_name
Number of CPUs	cores_per_socket &/or number_of_sockets
VM memory	vm_memory
Root password	root_password
MAC address (first NIC)	mac_address
IP address (first NIC)	ip_addr
OpenStack flavor	instance_type

Any of the options hash values that set a parameter inside the virtual machine's operating system (such as root_password or ip_addr) needs a mechanism to inject these parameters into the VM once it's booted. We typically do this using a VMware customization specification in conjunction with VMware tools, or cloud-init.

We can define a template cloud-init script that contains substitution variables (from Infrastructure → PXE in the WebUI). Our value from options[:root_password] will be substituted into a cloned version of this script at runtime and used when cloud_init is executed in the guest:

```
...
<% root_password = evm[:root_password] %>
chpasswd:
    list: |
        root:<%=root_password%>
    expire: False
...
```

Creating the Service Dialog

We know from the preceding investigation that we must name our service dialog elements vm_name, service_name, option_0_cores_per_socket, and option_0_vm_memory.

We'll create a new service dialog called *RHEL7 VM*. Our new service dialog will be similar to the example that we created in Chapter 5, but this time we'll create two boxes—Service and VM Names, and VM Characteristics—each containing two elements (see Figure 33-2).

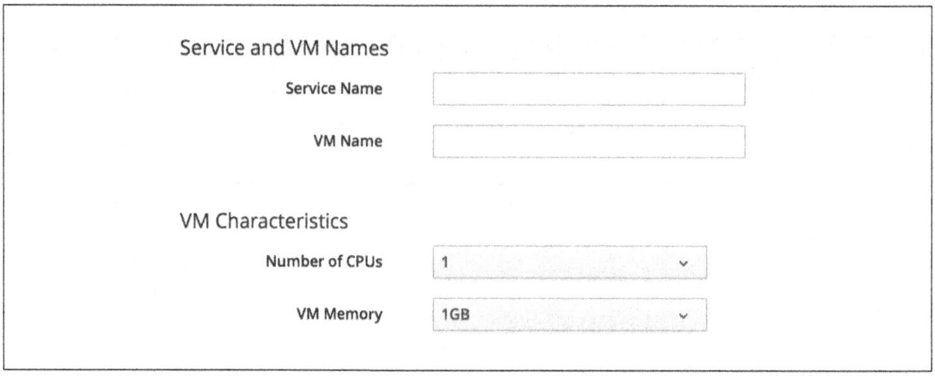

Figure 33-2. Service dialog with two boxes and four elements

The Service Name and VM Name elements in the first box are both of type Text Box and have the names service_name and vm_name, respectively.

The Number of CPUs element in the second box is of type Drop Down List (see Figure 33-3).

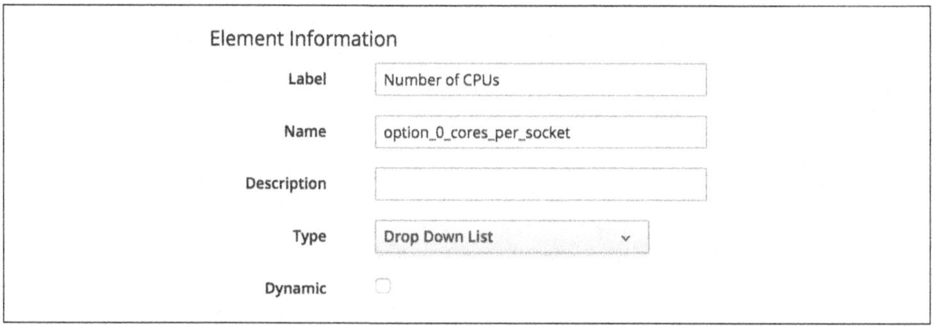

Figure 33-3. Number of CPUs element

We'll populate the list with options to provision one, two, or four CPUs (see Figure 33-4).

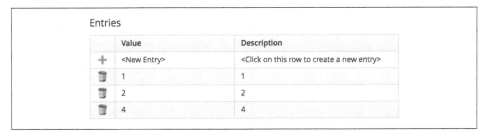

Figure 33-4. Defining the selection of available CPUs

The VM Memory element in the second box is of type Drop Down List (see Figure 33-5).

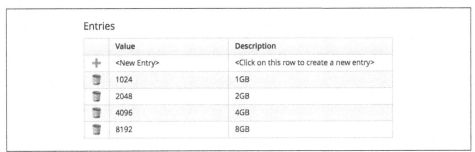

Figure 33-5. VM Memory element

We'll populate the list with options to provision 1, 2, 4, or 8 GB of memory (see Figure 33-6).

	Value	Description
+	<New Entry>	<Click on this row to create a new entry>
🗑	1024	1GB
🗑	2048	2GB
🗑	4096	4GB
🗑	8192	8GB

Entries

Figure 33-6. Defining the selection of available memory

Creating the Service Catalog Item

We need to create a service catalog item, but we'll also create a new service catalog to put the item into.

Create a Catalog

The first thing we should do is create a service catalog to store the service item. We can have many catalogs; they are used to organize or categorize our service items and bundles.

Navigate to the Catalogs section in the accordion, and select Configuration → Add a New Catalog (see Figure 33-7).

Figure 33-7. Adding a new catalog

Give the catalog a name (for this example we'll use **Generic Servers**), leave everything else as the default, and click Add.

Creating the Catalog Item

Navigate to the Catalog Items section in the accordion, highlight the newly created Generic Servers catalog, and then select Configuration → Add a New Catalog Item (see Figure 33-8).

Figure 33-8. Adding a new catalog item

Select RHEV from the Catalog Item Type drop-down list (see Figure 33-9).

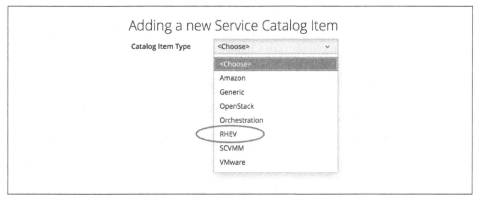

Figure 33-9. Selecting the catalog item type

Enter a name and description for the catalog item, and select the Display in Catalog checkbox to expose the remaining fields to be filled in. Select our newly created Generic Servers catalog and RHEL7 VM dialog in the appropriate drop-downs. For the Provisioning Entry Point field, navigate to *ManageIQ/Service/Provisioning/State-Machines/ServiceProvision_Template/CatalogItemInitialization* (see Figure 33-10).

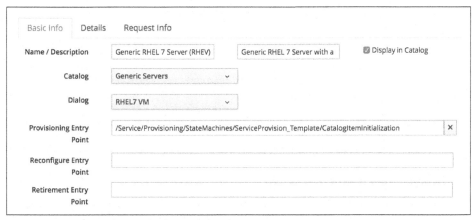

Figure 33-10. Completing the basic info tab

Click on the Details tab, and enter some HTML-formatted text to describe the catalog item to anyone viewing in the catalog:

```
<h1>Generic RHEL 7 Server</h1>
<hr>
<p>This catalog item will deploy a <strong>Red Hat Enterprise Linux 7</strong>
server, built from the @Base package set, and patched to 01-March-2016.

A selection of CPU count and memory size can be made when ordering</p>
```

Click on the Request Info tab and fill in the details. Select an appropriate template and Environment, Hardware, and Network tab settings that are known to work when a VM is provisioned interactively (see Chapter 39). The VM name will be overwritten during the provisioning process, so here we just set it as **changeme** (see Figure 33-11).

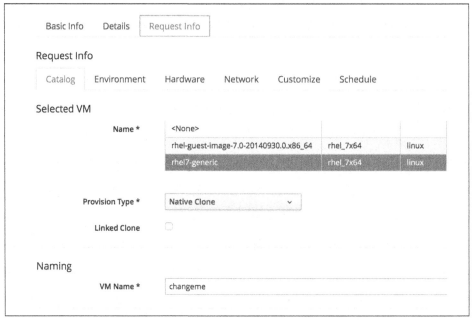

Figure 33-11. Completing the Request Info tab

Finally, click the Add button.

Select a suitably sized icon for a custom image, and save.

Ordering the Catalog Item

Navigate to the Service Catalogs section in the accordion, expand the Generic Servers catalog, and highlight the Generic RHEL 7 Server (RHEV) catalog item (see Figure 33-12).

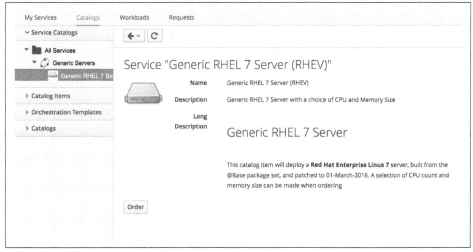

Figure 33-12. Navigating to the service catalog item

Click Order, and fill out the service dialog values (see Figure 33-13).

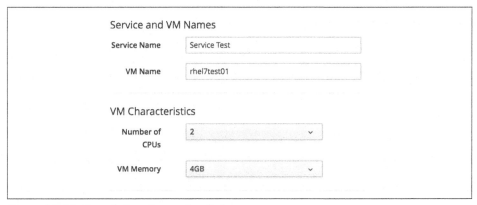

Figure 33-13. Completing the service dialog

Click Submit.

After a few minutes, the new service should be visible in My Services, containing the new VM (see Figure 33-14).

Figure 33-14. *The finished service*

If we examine the details of the VM, we see that it has been created with our requested CPU count and memory size (see Figure 33-15).

Properties	
Name	rhel7test01
Hostname	
IP Address	
Container	RedHat: 2 CPUs (1 socket x 2 cores), 4096 MB
Parent Host Platform	rhel
Platform Tools	N/A
Operating System	rhel_7x64

Figure 33-15. *Confirmation of VM configuration*

Summary

This example has described the procedure for creating a service catalog item to provision a single virtual machine. We can follow the same procedure to populate a service catalog with many types of virtual machine, both Windows and Linux. Although the service dialog used in this example was quite basic, it is typical of many generic services that we can create for our users. We can add further dialog elements, but we must be careful to balance the trade-off between simplicity of design and presenting additional choices to our users. Using dynamic elements can help in this regard. They enable us to create dialogs with "intelligent" elements that offer a reduced selection of choices, filtered by relevance for the requesting user. Rather than offering a drop-down list of all possible networks to provision the virtual machine onto, for example, we might filter based on the requesting user's group membership, or based on the input from another dialog element indicating that the VM should be tagged as *Development*.

Further Reading

Provisioning Virtual Machines and Hosts—Chapter 5, Catalogs and Services (*http://red.ht/1TUGDBa*)

## CHAPTER 34

Creating a Service Catalog Bundle

We learned in Chapter 33 how to create service catalog items that enable our users to provision fully configured virtual machines from a single Order button.

We can populate our service catalog with useful items (see Figure 34-1).

Services in Catalog "Intranet Servers"

	Name ▲	Description	Tenant	
	Database Server	RHEL6 PostgreSQL Database Server	Bit63	Order
	Middleware Server	RHEL6 JBoss EAP6 Middleware Server	Bit63	Order
	Web Server	RHEL6 Apache Web Server	Bit63	Order

Figure 34-1. A service catalog containing three services

In these examples the virtual machines are provisioned from fully installed VMware templates, preconfigured with the application packages. The service dialog purely prompts for the Service and VM Names (see Figure 34-2).

Service and VM Names

Service Name

VM Name

Figure 34-2. The service dialog for each catalog item

The next logical step is to be able to provision several items together as a single *service catalog bundle*.

Creating the Service Dialog for the Bundle

When we create a service catalog bundle, we handle the dialog input for each of the catalog items in a single service dialog that we create for the bundle. For our web, middleware, and database server items, we must prompt for the VM name of each, but we'll also prompt for a service name (see Figure 34-3).

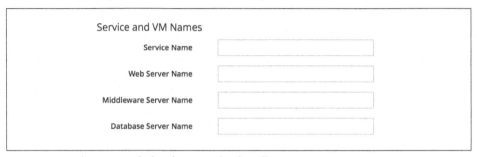

Figure 34-3. The service dialog for a catalog bundle

We name the dialog elements according to the sequence in which we want our individual items provisioned. Our sequence will be:

1. Database Server

2. Middleware Server

3. Web Server

Our four dialog elements are therefore constructed as follows. We'll create a text box element to prompt for Service Name (see Figure 34-4).

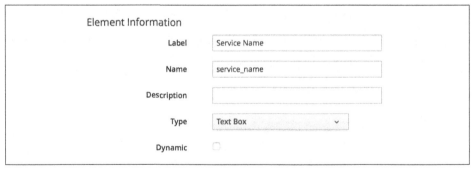

Figure 34-4. Dialog element to prompt for Service Name

We add a second text box element to prompt for Web Server Name (see Figure 34-5).

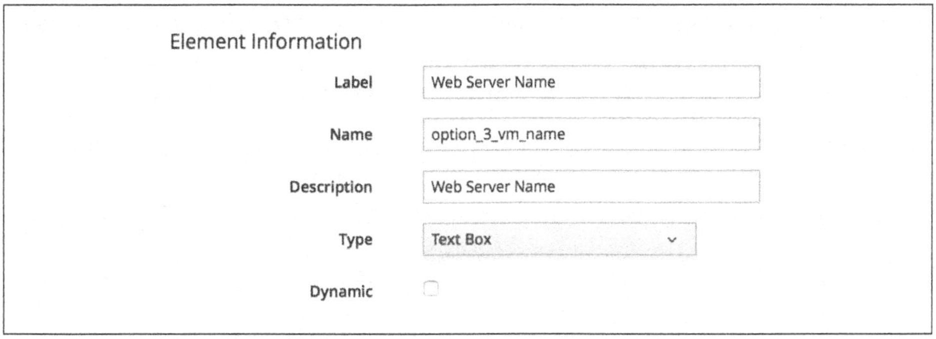

Figure 34-5. Dialog element to prompt for Web Server Name

We add a third text box element to prompt for Middleware Server Name (see Figure 34-6).

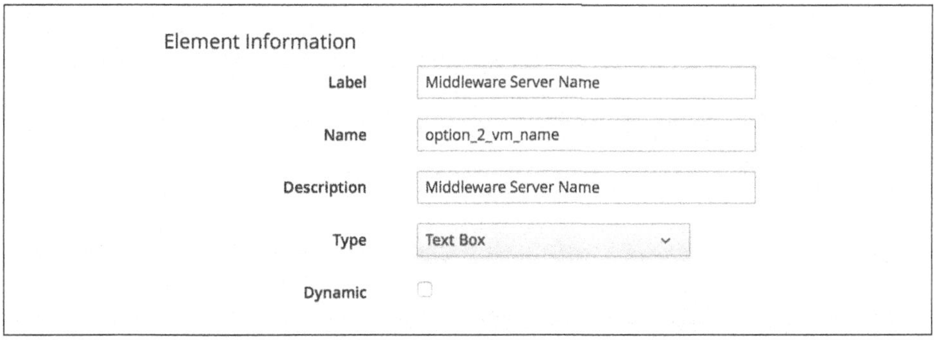

Figure 34-6. Dialog element to prompt for Middleware Server Name

Finally, we add a fourth text box element to prompt for Database Server Name (see Figure 34-7).

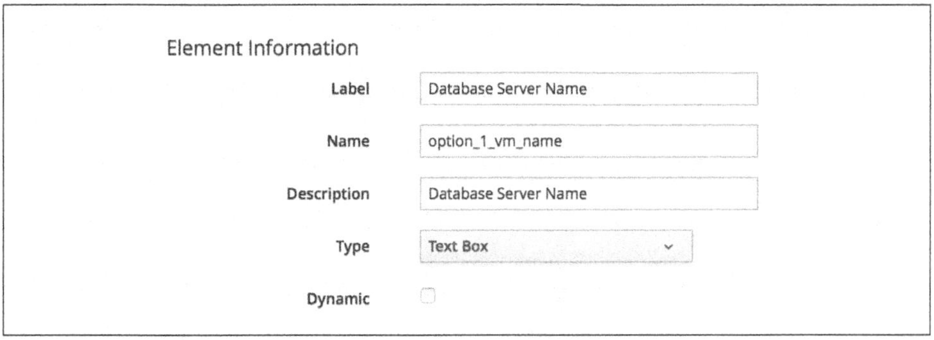

Figure 34-7. Dialog element to prompt for Database Server Name

The number in the element name reflects the sequence number, and the *CatalogItemInitialization* and *CatalogBundleInitialization* methods use this sequence number to pass the dialog value to the correct grandchild `miq_request_task` (see Chapter 30).

The value `option_n_vm_name` is recognized and special-cased by *CatalogItemInitialization*, which sets both the `:vm_target_name` and `:vm_target_hostname` keys in the `miq_request_task`'s options hash to the value input.

The `:vm_target_name` key sets the name of the resulting virtual machine.

The `:vm_target_hostname` key can be used to inject a Linux *hostname* (i.e., FQDN) into a VMware customization specification, which can then set this in the virtual machine using VMware tools on first boot.

Preparing the Service Catalog Items

As we will be handling dialog input when the bundle is ordered, we need to edit each catalog item to set the Catalog to <Unassigned> and the Dialog to <No Dialog>. We also *deselect* the Display in Catalog option, as we no longer want this item to be individually orderable (see Figure 34-8).

Figure 34-8. Preparing the existing service catalog items

Once we've done this, the items will appear as Unassigned (see Figure 34-9).

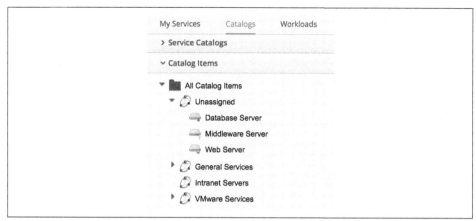

Figure 34-9. Unassigned catalog items

Creating the Service Catalog Bundle

Now we can go ahead and create our catalog bundle. Highlight a catalog name, and select Configuration → Add a New Catalog Bundle (see Figure 34-10).

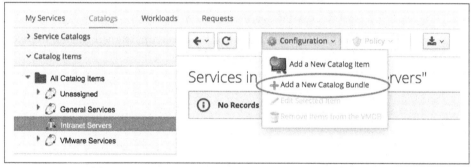

Figure 34-10. Adding a new catalog bundle

Enter a name and description for the bundle, then select the Display in Catalog checkbox. Select an appropriate catalog and the newly created bundle dialog from the appropriate drop-downs.

For the Provisioning Entry Point, navigate to *ManageIQ/Service/Provisioning/State-Machines/ServiceProvision_Template/CatalogBundleInitialization* (see Figure 34-11).

Figure 34-11. Service bundle basic info

Click on the Details tab, and enter some HTML-formatted text to describe the catalog item to anyone viewing in the catalog:

```
<h1>Three Tier Web Server Bundle</h1>
<hr>
<p>Deploy a <strong>Web, Middleware</strong> and <strong>Database</strong> \
            server together as a single service</p>
```

Click on the Resources tab, and select each of the three unassigned catalog items to add them to the bundle (see Figure 34-12).

Figure 34-12. Adding resources to the bundle

Change the Action Order and Provisioning Order according to our desired sequence (*3* won't be visible until *2* is set for an option); see Figure 34-13. The sequence should match the option_n_vm_name sequence that we gave our dialog elements.

Selected Resources							
Name	Action Order	Provision Order	Action		Delay (mins)	
			Start	Stop	Start	Stop
Database Server	1	1	Power On	Shutdown	None	None
Middleware Server	2	2	Power On	Shutdown	None	None
Web Server	3	3	Power On	Shutdown	None	None

Figure 34-13. Setting the action and provision orders

Finally, click the Add button.

Select a suitably sized icon for a custom image, and save.

Ordering the Catalog Bundle

Navigate to the Service Catalogs section in the accordion, expand the VMware Services catalog, and highlight the Three Tier Web Server Bundle catalog item (see Figure 34-14).

Figure 34-14. Ordering the catalog bundle

Click Order, and fill out the service dialog values (see Figure 34-15).

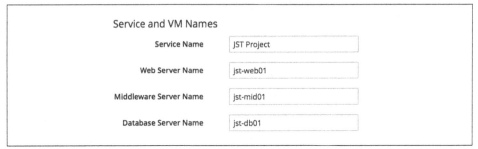

Figure 34-15. Entering the service and server names in the service dialog

Click Submit.

After a few minutes, the new service should be visible in My Services, containing the new VMs (see Figure 34-16).

Figure 34-16. The completed service

If we weren't watching the order that the VMs were created in, we could look in the database to check that our desired provisioning sequence was followed:

```
vmdb_production=# select id,name from vms order by id asc;
      id       |                    name
---------------+---------------------------------------------
...
 1000000000177 | jst-db01
 1000000000178 | jst-mid01
 1000000000179 | jst-web01
```

Here we see that the VMs were created (and named) in the correct order.

Summary

This has been a useful example that shows the flexibility of service catalogs to deploy entire application bundles. When we link this concept to a configuration management tool such as Puppet running from Red Hat Satellite 6, we start to really see the power of automation in our enterprise. We can deploy complex workloads from a single button click.

One of the cool features of service bundles is that we can mix and match catalog items that provision into different providers. For example, we may have a Bimodal IT (*http://www.gartner.com/it-glossary/bimodal/*) infrastructure comprising RHEV for our traditional Mode 1 workloads, and an in-house OpenStack private cloud for our more cloud-ready Mode 2 workloads. Using CloudForms service bundles, we could provision our relatively static servers into RHEV, and our dynamically scalable mid-tier and frontend servers into OpenStack.

Further Reading

Filtering out service catalog items during deployment (*http://bit.ly/1ZF4kSH*)

## CHAPTER 35

Service Objects

We saw in Chapter 26 that provisioning operations always include a *request* object, and a *task* object that links to *source* and *destination* objects.

When we provision a virtual machine from a service there are many more objects involved, because we are creating and referencing more items (creating both a service and potentially several new component VMs). When we provision from a service *bundle*, there will be several individual *items* to provision as part of the bundle. Even when we provision from a single service *item*, however, the objects are structured as if we were provisioning a bundle containing only one item.

In this chapter we will look at some of the objects involved in provisioning a single VM from a service catalog item. The objects are visible to us during the processing of the *CatalogItemInitialization* state machine.

For this example:

- We are using CloudForms 3.2.
- The provider is VMware.
- The service catalog item name that we've ordered from is called "Web Server."
- The service catalog item was created to clone from a VMware template called rhel65-template.
- The new service name is "My New Service."
- The resulting service contains a VM called test05.

We can use object_walker with the following @walk_association_whitelist to dump the objects:

```
{ 'MiqAeServiceServiceTemplateProvisionTask'    => ['source',
                                                    'destination',
                                                    'miq_request',
                                                    'miq_request_tasks',
                                                    'service_resource'],
  'MiqAeServiceServiceTemplateProvisionRequest' => ['miq_request',
                                                    'miq_request_tasks',
                                                    'requester',
                                                    'resource',
                                                    'source'],
  'MiqAeServiceServiceTemplate'                 => ['service_resources'],
  'MiqAeServiceServiceResource'                 => ['resource',
                                                    'service_template'],
  'MiqAeServiceMiqProvisionVmware'              => ['source',
                                                    'destination',
                                                    'miq_request'],
  'MiqAeServiceMiqProvisionRequestTemplate'     => ['source',
                                                    'destination'],
  'MiqAeServiceVmVmware'                        => ['service'] }
```

We'll call the *ObjectWalker* instance from the post5 state/stage of the *CatalogItemInitialization* state machine.

Object Structure

We can illustrate the main object structure in Figure 35-1 (some objects and links/relationships have been omitted for clarity).

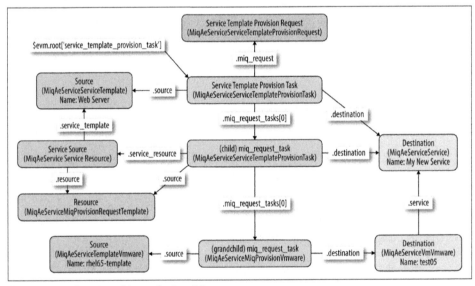

Figure 35-1. Service object relationship

Service Template Provision Task

Our entry point into the object structure from $evm is to the main ServiceTemplate
ProvisionTask object. We access this from:

```
$evm.root['service_template_provision_task']
```

From here we can access any of the other objects by following associations.

Source

The source is accessed from:

```
$evm.root['service_template_provision_task'].source
```

This is the ServiceTemplate object representing the service catalog item that has
been ordered from.

Destination

The destination is accessed from:

```
$evm.root['service_template_provision_task'].destination
```

This is the Service object representing the new service that will be created under My
Services.

Service Template Provisioning Request

The service template provisioning request is accessed from:

```
$evm.root['service_template_provision_task'].miq_request
```

This is the initial ServiceTemplateProvisionRequest object that was created when
we first ordered the new service. It is the request object for the entire service provision operation, including all VMs created as part of the service. This request object
has associations to each of the task objects involved in assembling the service, and
they in turn have backlinks to this request object.

Child miq_request_task

The child miq_request_task is accessed from:

```
$evm.root['service_template_provision_task'].miq_request_tasks.each do |child|
```

This is also a ServiceTemplateProvisionTask object and is the task object that represents the creation of an item for the new service. There will be a child
miq_request_task for each item (e.g., virtual machine) that makes up the final service, so for a service bundle containing three VMs, there will be three child
miq_request_tasks.

Service resource

The service resource is accessed from:

```
child_task.service_resource
```

This `ServiceResource` object stores details about this particular service item and its place in the overall service structure. A `ServiceResource` object has attributes such as:

```
service_resource.group_idx
service_resource.provision_index
...
service_resource.start_action
service_resource.start_delay
service_resource.stop_action
service_resource.stop_delay
```

These are generally zero or `nil` for a single-item service but represent the values selected in the WebUI for a multiitem service bundle (see Figure 35-2).

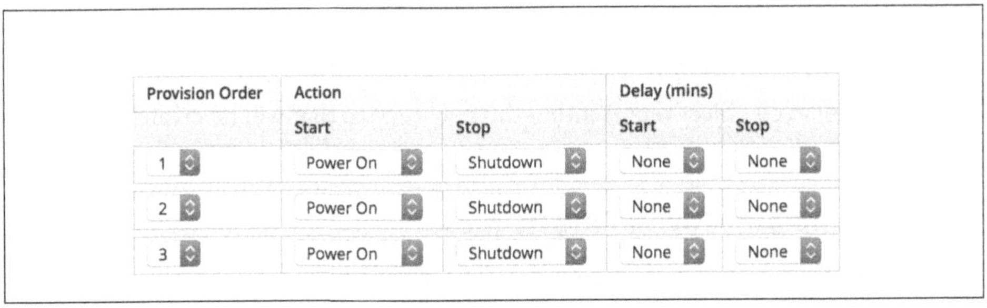

Provision Order	Action		Delay (mins)	
	Start	Stop	Start	Stop
1	Power On	Shutdown	None	None
2	Power On	Shutdown	None	None
3	Power On	Shutdown	None	None

Figure 35-2. Start and stop actions and delays in a multiitem bundle

The service resource has a relationship to the `ServiceTemplate` object via `child_task.service_resource.service_template`.

Source

The source is accessed from:

```
child_task.source
```

or:

```
child_task.service_resource.resource
```

This is the `MiqProvisionRequestTemplate` object that describes how the resulting VM will be created. The object looks very similar to a traditional VM provisioning request object and contains an options hash populated from the dialog options that were selected when the service item was created (e.g., placement options, memory size, CPUs, etc.).

Destination

The destination is accessed from:

```
child_task.destination
```

This is the same `Service` object that is accessible from `$evm.root['service_tem` `plate_provision_task'].destination`.

Grandchild miq_request_task

The grandchild `miq_request_task` is accessed from:

```
child_task.miq_request_tasks.each do |grandchild_task|
```

This is an `MiqProvisionVmware` `miq_request_task` object (renamed to `ManageIQ_Pro` `viders_Vmware_InfraManager_Provision` in CloudForms 4.0) and is the task object that represents the creation of the VM. This is exactly the same as the task object described in Chapter 26.

It is the grandchild `miq_request_task` that contains the options hash for the VM to be provisioned; this is being cloned from the options hash in the `MiqProvisionRe` `questTemplate` object. If we have a service dialog that prompts for properties affecting the provisioned VM (such as VM name, number of CPUs, memory, etc.), we must pass these dialog values to the grandchild task options hash.

Source

The source is accessed from:

```
grandchild_task.source
```

This is the `TemplateVmware` object (renamed to `ManageIQ_Providers_Vmware_Infra` `Manager_Template` in CloudForms 4.0) that represents the VMware template that the new VM will be cloned from.

Destination

The destination is accessed from:

```
grandchild_task.destination
```

or:

```
grandchild_task.vm
```

This is the `VmVmware` object (renamed to `ManageIQ_Providers_Vmware_InfraMan` `ager_Vm` in CloudForms 4.0) that represents the newly created VM. This VM object has an association `service` that links to the newly created service object.

Summary

In this chapter we've taken a detailed look at the various objects that are involved in provisioning a virtual machine from a service. This is the object view from any method running as part of the service provision state machine.

The lowest layer of objects in Figure 35-1—the grandchild `miq_request_task` with its source and destination objects—corresponds to the virtual machine provisioning objects that we discussed in Chapter 26. When the service provision state machine hands over to the VM provision state machine, these are indeed the objects that are referenced at this latter stage, just like any other VM provision workflow. Any VM provision state machine methods that we may have written that access the attributes of these objects will see no difference. The only change is in the type of request object; `$evm.root['miq_provision'].miq_provision_request` will in this case be a `ser vice_template_provision_request` object.

## CHAPTER 36

Log Analysis During Service Provisioning

The workflow of provisioning a virtual machine from a service catalog involves a request, an approval stage, several tasks, and multiple concurrently running state machines.

If we are curious to discover more about their interaction, we can follow this workflow by examining the log lines written to *automation.log* during the service provisioning operation. This can reveal some interesting details about the interleaving of the various operations and state machines.

For this example we've grepped for the Following.. Followed message pairs in *automation.log* on CloudForms 3.2 (the workflow is similar in CloudForms 4.0). The service provisioning request was from a nonadmin user in the Bit63Group_vm_user group, so we see some group-specific profile processing. For the brevity, service_tem plate_provision is abbreviated to stp in the following outputs.

Initial Request

We see the initial automation request being created though the */System/Request/ UI_PROVISION_INFO* entry point:

```
Following /System/Request/UI_PROVISION_INFO
Following /unknown/VM/Provisioning/Profile/Bit63Group_vm_user#get_domains
Followed  /unknown/VM/Provisioning/Profile/Bit63Group_vm_user#get_domains
Followed  /System/Request/UI_PROVISION_INFO
Following /System/Event/request_created
Following /System/Policy/request_created
Following /System/Process/parse_provider_category
Followed  /System/Process/parse_provider_category
Following /System/Policy/ \
                        ServiceTemplateProvisionRequest_created
```

Profile Lookup

We see a service provisioning profile lookup to get the auto-approval state machine, and some events raised and processed:

```
Following /service/Provisioning/Profile/ \
          Bit63Group_vm_user#get_auto_approval_state_machine
Followed /service/Provisioning/Profile/ \
          Bit63Group_vm_user#get_auto_approval_state_machine
Following /service/Provisioning/StateMachines/ServiceProvisionRequestApproval/ \
                    Default
Followed /service/Provisioning/StateMachines/ServiceProvisionRequestApproval/ \
                    Default
Followed /System/Policy/ServiceTemplateProvisionRequest_created
Followed /System/Policy/request_created
Followed /System/Event/request_created
Following /System/Event/request_approved
Following /System/Policy/request_approved
Following /System/Process/parse_provider_category
Followed /System/Process/parse_provider_category
```

Request Processing and Approval

We see the request approval and the creation of the service template provisioning request (service_template_provision_request_11). We see some processing in request context:

```
Following /System/Policy/ServiceTemplateProvisionRequest_Approved
Following /Service/Provisioning/Email/ServiceTemplateProvisionRequest_Approved
([stp_request_11]) Following /System/Event/request_starting
([stp_request_11]) Following /System/Policy/request_starting
([stp_request_11]) Following /System/Process/parse_provider_category
Followed /Service/Provisioning/Email/ServiceTemplateProvisionRequest_Approved
Followed /System/Policy/ServiceTemplateProvisionRequest_Approved
Followed /System/Policy/request_approved
Followed /System/Event/request_approved
([stp_request_11]) Followed /System/Process/parse_provider_category
([stp_request_11]) Following /System/Policy/ \
                    ServiceTemplateProvisionRequest_starting
([stp_request_11]) Following /service/ \
                    Provisioning/Profile/Bit63Group_vm_user#get_quota_state_machine
([stp_request_11]) Followed /service/ \
                    Provisioning/Profile/Bit63Group_vm_user#get_quota_state_machine
([stp_request_11]) Following /service/Provisioning/StateMachines/ \
                    ServiceProvisionRequestQuotaVerification/Default
([stp_request_11]) Followed /service/Provisioning/StateMachines/ \
                    ServiceProvisionRequestQuotaVerification/Default
([stp_request_11]) Followed /System/Policy/ \
                    ServiceTemplateProvisionRequest_starting
([stp_request_11]) Followed /System/Policy/request_starting
([stp_request_11]) Followed /System/Event/request_starting
```

```
([stp_request_11]) Following /System/Request/UI_PROVISION_INFO
([stp_request_11]) Following /infrastructure/ \
                        VM/Provisioning/Profile/Bit63Group_vm_user#get_vmname
([stp_request_11]) Following /Infrastructure/VM/Provisioning/Naming/Default
([stp_request_11]) Followed /Infrastructure/VM/Provisioning/Naming/Default
([stp_request_11]) Followed /infrastructure/ \
                        VM/Provisioning/Profile/Bit63Group_vm_user#get_vmname
([stp_request_11]) Followed /System/Request/UI_PROVISION_INFO
```

Notice that this request processing runs the naming method, which is therefore processed *before CatalogItemInitialization* (which is processed in task context).

Service Template Provisioning Tasks

Next we see two service template provisioning tasks created: our top-level and child task objects (`service_template_provision_task_31` and `service_template_provi sion_task_32`):

> The two tasks are actually running through two separate state machines.
>
> Task `service_template_provision_task_31` is running through /
> *Service/Provisioning/StateMachines/ServiceProvision_Template/*
> *CatalogItemInitialization.*
>
> Task `service_template_provision_task_32` is running through /
> *Service/Provisioning/StateMachines/ServiceProvision_Template/*
> *clone_to_service.*

```
([stp_task_31]) Following /Service/Provisioning/StateMachines/Methods/ \
                                        DialogParser
([stp_task_31]) Followed /Service/Provisioning/StateMachines/Methods/DialogParser
([stp_task_31]) Following /Service/Provisioning/StateMachines/Methods/ \
                    CatalogItemInitialization
([stp_task_31]) Followed /Service/Provisioning/StateMachines/Methods/ \
                    CatalogItemInitialization
([stp_task_31]) Following /Service/Provisioning/StateMachines/Methods/Provision
([stp_task_31]) Followed /Service/Provisioning/StateMachines/Methods/Provision
([stp_task_31]) Following /Service/Provisioning/StateMachines/Methods/ \
                    CheckProvisioned
([stp_task_31]) Followed /Service/Provisioning/StateMachines/Methods/ \
                    CheckProvisioned
([stp_task_32]) Following /Service/Provisioning/StateMachines/Methods/ \
                    GroupSequenceCheck
([stp_task_32]) Followed /Service/Provisioning/StateMachines/Methods/ \
                    GroupSequenceCheck
([stp_task_32]) Following /Service/Provisioning/StateMachines/Methods/Provision
([stp_task_32]) Followed /Service/Provisioning/StateMachines/Methods/Provision
([stp_task_32]) Following /Service/Provisioning/StateMachines/Methods/ \
                    CheckProvisioned
```

```
([stp_task_32]) Followed /Service/Provisioning/StateMachines/Methods/ \
                         CheckProvisioned
```

VM Provisioning Task

We see our grandchild miq_provision task object created (miq_provision_33), and it processes the *Infrastructure/VM/Provisioning/StateMachines* methods in the state machine defined in our user profile:

```
([miq_provision_33]) Following /infrastructure/VM/Lifecycle/Provisioning
([miq_provision_33]) Following /Infrastructure/ \
                 VM/Provisioning/Profile/Bit63Group_vm_user#get_state_machine
([miq_provision_33]) Followed /Infrastructure/ \
                 VM/Provisioning/Profile/Bit63Group_vm_user#get_state_machine
([miq_provision_33]) Following /Infrastructure/ \
                 VM/Provisioning/StateMachines/VMProvision_vm/template
([miq_provision_33]) Following /Infrastructure/ \
                 VM/Provisioning/StateMachines/Methods/CustomizeRequest#VMware
([miq_provision_33]) Followed /Infrastructure/ \
                 VM/Provisioning/StateMachines/Methods/CustomizeRequest#VMware
([miq_provision_33]) Following /Infrastructure/ \
                             VM/Provisioning/Placement/default#VMware
([miq_provision_33]) Followed /Infrastructure/ \
                             VM/Provisioning/Placement/default#VMware
([miq_provision_33]) Following /Infrastructure/ \
                  VM/Provisioning/StateMachines/Methods/PreProvision#VMware
([miq_provision_33]) Followed /Infrastructure/ \
                  VM/Provisioning/StateMachines/Methods/PreProvision#VMware
([miq_provision_33]) Following /Infrastructure/ \
                    VM/Provisioning/StateMachines/Methods/Provision
([miq_provision_33]) Followed /Infrastructure/ \
                    VM/Provisioning/StateMachines/Methods/Provision
([miq_provision_33]) Following /Infrastructure/ \
                 VM/Provisioning/StateMachines/Methods/CheckProvisioned
([miq_provision_33]) Followed /Infrastructure/ \
                 VM/Provisioning/StateMachines/Methods/CheckProvisioned
([miq_provision_33]) Followed /Infrastructure/ \
                 VM/Provisioning/StateMachines/VMProvision_vm/template
([miq_provision_33]) Followed /infrastructure/VM/Lifecycle/Provisioning
([miq_provision_33]) Following /System/Request/UI_PROVISION_INFO
([miq_provision_33]) Following /infrastructure/ \
                 VM/Provisioning/Profile/Bit63Group_vm_user#get_host_and_storage
([miq_provision_33]) Followed /infrastructure/ \
                 VM/Provisioning/Profile/Bit63Group_vm_user#get_host_and_storage
([miq_provision_33]) Followed /System/Request/UI_PROVISION_INFO
```

Service State Machine CheckProvisioned

We see both top-level and child service template provisioning tasks running their *CheckProvisioned* methods:

```
([stp_task_31]) Following /Service/Provisioning/StateMachines/Methods/ \
                    CheckProvisioned
([stp_task_31]) Followed /Service/Provisioning/StateMachines/Methods/ \
                    CheckProvisioned
([stp_task_32]) Following /Service/Provisioning/StateMachines/Methods/ \
                    CheckProvisioned
([stp_task_32]) Followed /Service/Provisioning/StateMachines/Methods/ \
                    CheckProvisioned
```

VM State Machine CheckProvisioned

We see the VM provision state machine running its *CheckProvisioned* method. We can see the entire */Infrastructure/VM/Provisioning/StateMachines* state machine being reinstantiated for each call of its *CheckProvisioned* method, including the profile lookup:

```
Following /infrastructure/VM/Lifecycle/Provisioning
Following /Infrastructure/VM/Provisioning/Profile/ \
         Bit63Group_vm_user#get_state_machine
Following /Infrastructure/VM/Provisioning/StateMachines/VMProvision_vm/template
Following /Infrastructure/VM/Provisioning/StateMachines/Methods/CheckProvisioned
```

 Recall that if a state exits with $evm.root['ae_result'] = 'retry', the entire state machine is relaunched after the retry interval, starting at the state to be retried.

We see the service and VM provisioning state machines both running their *CheckProvisioned* methods:

```
([miq_provision_33]) Following /infrastructure/VM/Lifecycle/Provisioning
([miq_provision_33]) Following /Infrastructure/ \
                    VM/Provisioning/Profile/Bit63Group_vm_user#get_state_machine
([miq_provision_33]) Followed /Infrastructure/ \
                    VM/Provisioning/Profile/Bit63Group_vm_user#get_state_machine
([miq_provision_33]) Following /Infrastructure/ \
                    VM/Provisioning/StateMachines/VMProvision_vm/template
([miq_provision_33]) Following /Infrastructure/ \
                    VM/Provisioning/StateMachines/Methods/CheckProvisioned
([miq_provision_33]) Followed /Infrastructure/ \
                    VM/Provisioning/StateMachines/Methods/CheckProvisioned
([miq_provision_33]) Followed /Infrastructure/ \
                    VM/Provisioning/StateMachines/VMProvision_vm/template
([miq_provision_33]) Followed /infrastructure/VM/Lifecycle/Provisioning
([stp_task_31]) Following /Service/Provisioning/StateMachines/Methods/ \
                    CheckProvisioned
([stp_task_31]) Followed /Service/Provisioning/StateMachines/Methods/ \
                    CheckProvisioned
([stp_task_32]) Following /Service/Provisioning/StateMachines/Methods/ \
```

```
                               CheckProvisioned
([stp_task_32]) Followed /Service/Provisioning/StateMachines/Methods/ \
                               CheckProvisioned
([miq_provision_33]) Following /infrastructure/VM/Lifecycle/Provisioning
([miq_provision_33]) Following /Infrastructure/ \
                 VM/Provisioning/Profile/Bit63Group_vm_user#get_state_machine
([miq_provision_33]) Followed /Infrastructure/ \
                 VM/Provisioning/Profile/Bit63Group_vm_user#get_state_machine
([miq_provision_33]) Following /Infrastructure/ \
                 VM/Provisioning/StateMachines/VMProvision_vm/template
([miq_provision_33]) Following /Infrastructure/ \
                 VM/Provisioning/StateMachines/Methods/CheckProvisioned
([miq_provision_33]) Followed /Infrastructure/ \
                 VM/Provisioning/StateMachines/Methods/CheckProvisioned
([miq_provision_33]) Followed /Infrastructure/ \
                 VM/Provisioning/StateMachines/VMProvision_vm/template
([miq_provision_33]) Followed /infrastructure/VM/Lifecycle/Provisioning
([stp_task_31]) Following /Service/Provisioning/StateMachines/Methods/ \
                               CheckProvisioned
([stp_task_31]) Followed /Service/Provisioning/StateMachines/Methods/ \
                               CheckProvisioned
([stp_task_32]) Following /Service/Provisioning/StateMachines/Methods/ \
                               CheckProvisioned
([stp_task_32]) Followed /Service/Provisioning/StateMachines/Methods/ \
                               CheckProvisioned
...
```

Virtual Machine Provision Complete

We see the *Infrastructure/VM* provisioning state machine *CheckProvisioned* method
return success and continue with the remainder of the state machine:

```
([miq_provision_33]) Following /infrastructure/VM/Lifecycle/Provisioning
([miq_provision_33]) Following /Infrastructure/VM/ \
                   Provisioning/Profile/Bit63Group_vm_user#get_state_machine
([miq_provision_33]) Followed /Infrastructure/VM/ \
                   Provisioning/Profile/Bit63Group_vm_user#get_state_machine
([miq_provision_33]) Following /Infrastructure/VM/ \
                   Provisioning/StateMachines/VMProvision_vm/template
([miq_provision_33]) Following /Infrastructure/VM/ \
                   Provisioning/StateMachines/Methods/CheckProvisioned
([miq_provision_33]) Followed /Infrastructure/VM/ \
                   Provisioning/StateMachines/Methods/CheckProvisioned
([miq_provision_33]) Following /Infrastructure/VM/ \
                   Provisioning/StateMachines/Methods/PostProvision#VMware
([miq_provision_33]) Followed /Infrastructure/VM/ \
                   Provisioning/StateMachines/Methods/PostProvision#VMware
([miq_provision_33]) Following /Infrastructure/VM/ \
           Provisioning/Email/MiqProvision_Complete?event=vm_provisioned
([stp_task_31]) Following /Service/Provisioning/ \
                               StateMachines/Methods/CheckProvisioned
([miq_provision_33]) Followed /Infrastructure/VM/ \
```

```
                    Provisioning/Email/MiqProvision_Complete?event=vm_provisioned
([stp_task_31]) Followed /Service/Provisioning/ \
                                    StateMachines/Methods/CheckProvisioned
([miq_provision_33]) Following /System/CommonMethods/ \
                                    StateMachineMethods/vm_provision_finished
([miq_provision_33]) Following /System/Event/service_provisioned
([miq_provision_33]) Followed /System/Event/service_provisioned
([miq_provision_33]) Followed /System/CommonMethods/ \
                                    StateMachineMethods/vm_provision_finished
([miq_provision_33]) Followed /Infrastructure/VM/ \
                    Provisioning/StateMachines/VMProvision_vm/template
([miq_provision_33]) Followed /infrastructure/VM/Lifecycle/Provisioning
```

Service Provision Complete

Finally, we see both of the service provisioning state machine *CheckProvisioned* methods return success and continue with the remainder of their state machines:

```
([stp_task_32]) Following /Service/Provisioning/ \
                                    StateMachines/Methods/CheckProvisioned
([stp_task_32]) Followed /Service/Provisioning/ \
                                    StateMachines/Methods/CheckProvisioned
([stp_task_32]) Following /Service/Provisioning/Email/ \
                    ServiceProvision_complete?event=service_provisioned
([stp_task_32]) Followed /Service/Provisioning/Email/ \
                    ServiceProvision_complete?event=service_provisioned
([stp_task_32]) Following /System/CommonMethods/ \
                            StateMachineMethods/service_provision_finished
([stp_task_32]) Followed /System/CommonMethods/ \
                            StateMachineMethods/service_provision_finished
([stp_task_31]) Following /Service/Provisioning/ \
                                    StateMachines/Methods/CheckProvisioned
([stp_task_31]) Followed /Service/Provisioning/ \
                                    StateMachines/Methods/CheckProvisioned
([stp_task_31]) Following /Service/Provisioning/Email/ \
                    ServiceProvision_complete?event=service_provisioned
([stp_task_31]) Followed /Service/Provisioning/Email/ \
                    ServiceProvision_complete?event=service_provisioned
([stp_task_31]) Following /System/CommonMethods/ \
                            StateMachineMethods/service_provision_finished
([stp_task_31]) Followed /System/CommonMethods/ \
                            StateMachineMethods/service_provision_finished
```

Summary

Tracing the steps of various workflows though *automation.log* can reveal a lot about the inner workings of the Automation Engine. All students of automation are encouraged to investigate the Following.. Followed message pairs in the logs to get a feel for how state machines sequence tasks and handle retry operations.

## CHAPTER 37

Service Hierarchies

We have seen how service catalogs made up of catalog items and bundles can simplify the process of ordering infrastructure or cloud instance and virtual machines. Simplicity of ordering is not the only benefit of services, however.

When we order one or more virtual machines from a service catalog, a new service is created for us that appears in All Services in the WebUI. This service gives us a useful summary of its resources in the Totals for Service VMs section. We can use this feature to extend the utility of services into tracking and organizing resources. We could, for example, use a service to represent a project comprising many dozens of virtual machines. We would be able to see the total virtual machine resource consumption for the entire project in a single place in the WebUI.

In line with this organizational use, we can arrange services in hierarchies for further convenience (see Figure 37-1).

Figure 37-1. A service hierarchy

In this example we have three child services, representing the three tiers of our simple intranet platform. Figure 37-2 shows the single server making up the database tier of our architecture.

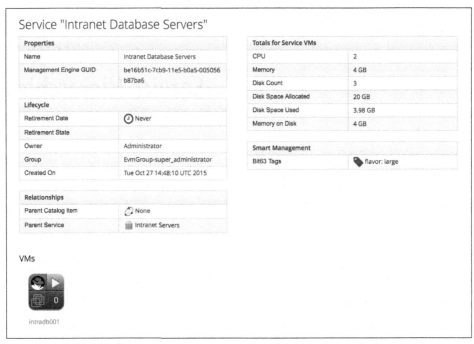

Figure 37-2. The database tier

Figure 37-3 shows the two servers making up the middleware tier of our architecture.

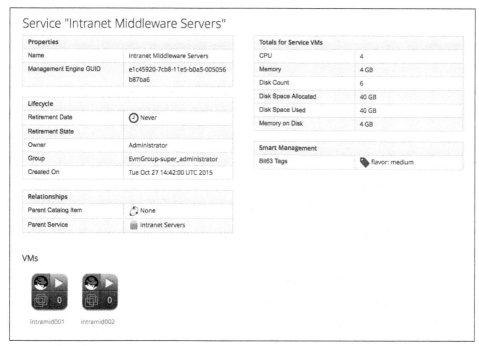

Service "Intranet Middleware Servers"

Properties	
Name	Intranet Middleware Servers
Management Engine GUID	e1c45920-7cb8-11e5-b0a5-005056b87ba6

Lifecycle	
Retirement Date	Never
Retirement State	
Owner	Administrator
Group	EvmGroup-super_administrator
Created On	Tue Oct 27 14:42:00 UTC 2015

Relationships	
Parent Catalog Item	None
Parent Service	Intranet Servers

Totals for Service VMs	
CPU	4
Memory	4 GB
Disk Count	6
Disk Space Allocated	40 GB
Disk Space Used	40 GB
Memory on Disk	4 GB

Smart Management	
Bit63 Tags	flavor: medium

VMs

intramid001   intramid002

Figure 37-3. The middleware tier

Figure 37-4 shows the four servers making up the web tier of our architecture.

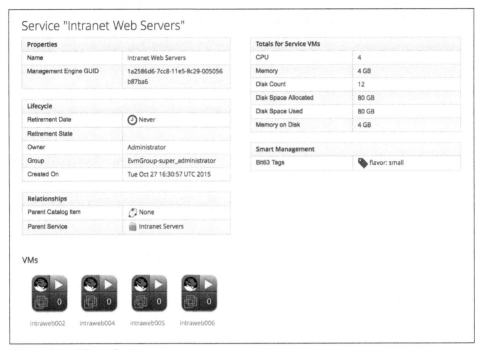

Service "Intranet Web Servers"

Properties	
Name	Intranet Web Servers
Management Engine GUID	1a2586d6-7cc8-11e5-8c29-005056 b87ba6

Lifecycle	
Retirement Date	⏰ Never
Retirement State	
Owner	Administrator
Group	EvmGroup-super_administrator
Created On	Tue Oct 27 16:30:57 UTC 2015

Relationships	
Parent Catalog Item	None
Parent Service	Intranet Servers

Totals for Service VMs	
CPU	4
Memory	4 GB
Disk Count	12
Disk Space Allocated	80 GB
Disk Space Used	80 GB
Memory on Disk	4 GB

Smart Management	
Bit63 Tags	🏷 flavor: small

VMs

intraweb002	intraweb004	intraweb005	intraweb006

Figure 37-4. The web tier

When we view the parent service, we see that it contains details of all child services, including the cumulative CPU, memory, and disk counts (see Figure 37-5).

Figure 37-5. *Parent service view*

Organizing Our Services

To make maximum use of service hierarchies, it is useful to be able to create empty services, and to be able to move both services and VMs into existing services.

Creating an Empty Service

We could create a new service directly from automation, using the lines:

```
new_service = $evm.vmdb('service').create(:name => "My New Service")
new_service.display = true
```

For this example, though, we'll create our new empty service from a service catalog.

State machine

First we'll copy *ManageIQ/Service/Provisioning/StateMachines/ServiceProvision_Template/default* into our own domain and rename it *EmptyService*. We'll add a pre5 relationship to a new instance that we'll create, called */Service/Provisioning/ StateMachines/Methods/RenameService* (see Figure 37-6).

Name	Value
Automate Instance "EmptyService" was saved	
pre1	
pre2	
pre3	
pre4	
pre5	/Service/Provisioning/StateMachines/Methods/RenameService
configurechilddialog	#/Service/Provisioning/StateMachines/Methods/ConfigureChildDialog
provision	/Service/Provisioning/StateMachines/Methods/Provision
checkprovisioned	/Service/Provisioning/StateMachines/Methods/CheckProvisioned
post1	
post2	
post3	
post4	
post5	
EmailOwner	/Service/Provisioning/Email/ServiceProvision_complete?event=service_provisioned
Finished	/System/CommonMethods/StateMachineMethods/service_provision_finished

Figure 37-6. Schema of the EmptyService state machine

Method

The pre5 stage of this state machine is a relationship to a *RenameService* instance. This instance calls a *rename_service* method containing the following code:

```
begin
  service_template_provision_task = $evm.root['service_template_provision_task']
  service = service_template_provision_task.destination
  dialog_options = service_template_provision_task.dialog_options
  if dialog_options.has_key? 'dialog_service_name'
    service.name = "#{dialog_options['dialog_service_name']}"
  end
  if dialog_options.has_key? 'dialog_service_description'
    service.description = "#{dialog_options['dialog_service_description']}"
  end
```

```
  $evm.root['ae_result'] = 'ok'
  exit MIQ_OK
rescue => err
  $evm.log(:error, "[#{err}]\n#{err.backtrace.join("\n")}")
  $evm.root['ae_result'] = 'error'
  $evm.root['ae_reason'] = "Error: #{err.message}"
  exit MIQ_ERROR
end
```

Service dialog

We create a simple service dialog called New Service with element names `ser vice_name` and `service_description` (see Figure 37-7).

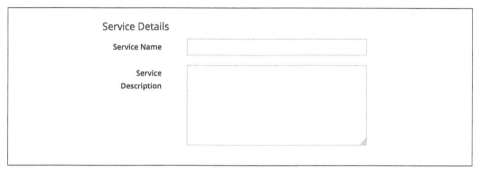

Figure 37-7. Service dialog

Putting it all together

Finally, we assemble all of these parts by creating a new service catalog called General Services and a new catalog item of type Generic called Empty Service (see Figure 37-8).

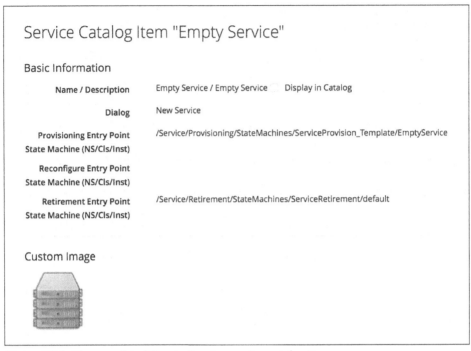

Figure 37-8. *The completed Empty Service service catalog item*

We can order from this service catalog item to create our new empty services.

Adding VMs and Services to Existing Services

We'll provide the ability to move both services and virtual machines into existing services from a button. The button will present a drop-down list of existing services that we can add as a new parent service (see Figure 37-9).

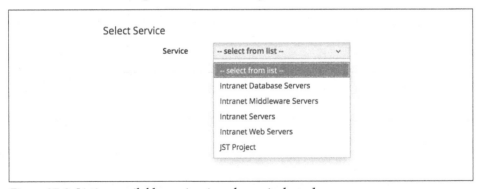

Figure 37-9. *Listing available services in a dynamic drop-down*

Adding the Button

As before, the process of adding a button involves the creation of the button dialog and a button script. For this example, however, our dialog will contain a dynamic drop-down list, so we must create a dynamic element method as well to populate this list.

Button dialog

We create a simple button dialog with a dynamic drop-down element named *service* (see Figure 37-10).

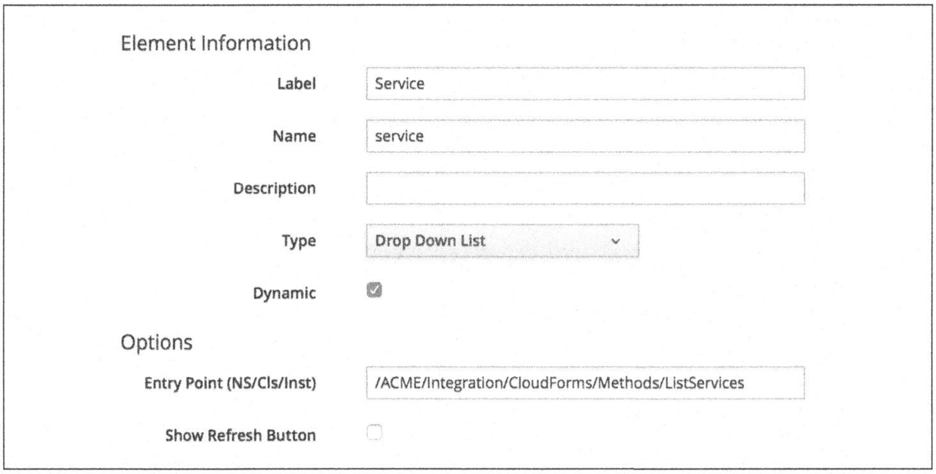

Element Information	
Label	Service
Name	service
Description	
Type	Drop Down List ⌄
Dynamic	☑
Options	
Entry Point (NS/Cls/Inst)	/ACME/Integration/CloudForms/Methods/ListServices
Show Refresh Button	☐

Figure 37-10. Button dialog

Dialog element method

The dynamic drop-down element in the service dialog calls a method called *list_services*. We only wish to display a service in the drop-down list if the user has permissions to see it via their role-based access control (RBAC) filter. We define two methods: `get_current_group_rbac_array` to retrieve a user's RBAC filter array, and `service_visible?` to check that a service has a tag that matches the filter:

```ruby
def get_current_group_rbac_array(user, rbac_array=[])
  unless user.current_group.filters.blank?
    user.current_group.filters['managed'].flatten.each do |filter|
      next unless /(?<category>\w*)\/(?<tag>\w*)$/i =~ filter
      rbac_array << {category=>tag}
    end
  end
  rbac_array
end

def service_visible?(rbac_array, service)
```

```
      $evm.log(:info, "Evaluating Service #{service.name}")
      if rbac_array.length.zero?
        $evm.log(:info, "No Filter, service: #{service.name} is visible to this user")
        return true
      else
        rbac_array.each do |rbac_hash|
          rbac_hash.each do |category, tag|
            if service.tagged_with?(category, tag)
              $evm.log(:info, "Service: #{service.name} is visible to this user")
              return true
            end
          end
        end
        false
      end
    end
```

When we enumerate the services, we check on visibility to the user before adding to the drop-down list:

```
$evm.vmdb(:service).find(:all).each do |service|
  if service['display']
    $evm.log(:info, "Found service: #{service.name}")
    if service_visible?(rbac_array, service)
      visible_services << service
    end
  end
end
if visible_services.length > 0
  if visible_services.length > 1
    values_hash['!'] = '-- select from list --'
  end
  visible_services.each do |service|
    values_hash[service.id] = service.name
  end
else
  values_hash['!'] = 'No services are available'
end
```

Here we use a simple technique of keeping the string `'-- select from list --'` at the top of the list, by using a key string of `'!'`, which is the first ASCII printable non-whitespace character.

Button method

The main instance and method called from the button are called *AddToService* and *add_to_service*, respectively. This method adds the current virtual machine or service into the service selected from the drop-down list. As we wish to be able to call this from a button on either a Service object type or a "VM and Instance" object type, we identify our context using `$evm.root['vmdb_object_type']`.

If we are adding a virtual machine to an existing service, we should allow for the fact that the virtual machine might itself have been provisioned from a service. We detect any existing service membership, and if the old service is empty after we move the virtual machine, we delete the service from the VMDB:

```
begin
  parent_service_id = $evm.root['dialog_service']
  parent_service = $evm.vmdb('service').find_by_id(parent_service_id)
  if parent_service.nil?
    $evm.log(:error, "Can't find service with ID: #{parent_service_id}")
    exit MIQ_ERROR
  else
    case $evm.root['vmdb_object_type']
    when 'service'
      $evm.log(:info, "Adding Service #{$evm.root['service'].name} to \
                                          #{parent_service.name}")
      $evm.root['service'].parent_service = parent_service
    when 'vm'
      vm = $evm.root['vm']
      #
      # See if the VM is already part of a service
      #
      unless vm.service.nil?
        old_service = vm.service
        vm.remove_from_service
        if old_service.v_total_vms.zero?
          old_service.remove_from_vmdb
        end
      end
      $evm.log(:info, "Adding VM #{vm.name} to #{parent_service.name}")
      vm.add_to_service(parent_service)
    end
  end
  exit MIQ_OK
rescue => err
  $evm.log(:error, "[#{err}]\n#{err.backtrace.join("\n")}")
  exit MIQ_ERROR
end
```

The scripts in this chapter are available on GitHub (*http://bit.ly/1VOFeSa*).

Putting it all together

Finally, we create two Add to Service buttons: one on a Service object type, and one on a "VM and Instance" object type. We can go ahead and organize our service hierarchies.

Exercise

Filter the list of services presented in the drop-down to remove the *current* service—we would never wish to add a service as its own parent.

Summary

Organizing our services in this way changes the way that we think about our cloud or virtual infrastructure. We start to think in terms of service workloads, rather than individual virtual machines or instances. We can start to work in a more "cloudy" way, whereby we treat our virtual machines as anonymous entities, and scale out or scale back according to point-in-time application demand.

We can also use service bundles and hierachies of bundles to keep track of the resources in projects and subprojects. This can help from an organizational point of view; for example, we can tag services, and our method to add a virtual machine to a service can propagate any service tags to the virtual machine. In this way we can assign project-related chargeback costs to the tagged VMs or apply WebUI display filters that display project resources.

## CHAPTER 38

Service Reconfiguration

Our virtual machine or instance provisioning workflows have so far created new ready-configured virtual machines, or virtual machines integrated with Satellite 6 so that a Puppet configuration can be applied (see Chapter 28).

In these cases we must log in to two separate systems to get our provisioned and configured servers into operation. We log in to the CloudForms WebUI to start the provisioning operation and a second WebUI for the configuration management platform (such as Satellite) to set or reset the configuration parameters.

When we provision new virtual machines as services, however, we can consolidate the provisioning and configuration functions in a single user interface. We can set initial configuration parameters in a service dialog and then mark a service as *Reconfigurable* to allow these parameters to be updated from the same CloudForms service dialog.

This duel use of a service dialog for both initial configuration and reconfiguration works well if we are using a configuration management tool such as Satellite 6, and Puppet. We can specify Puppet *smart class parameters* in our service dialog that can be passed to Foreman and used to override the statically defined Puppet class parameters.

Reconfigure Entry Point

So far when we have created our service catalog items, we have specified a provisioning entry point state machine to handle the provisioning workflow for the new service. There are two other entry points that we can optionally hook into: a *retirement* entry point (see Chapter 41) and a *reconfigure* entry point (see Figure 38-1).

Figure 38-1. Setting the reconfigure entry point when creating a service item

If we create a service catalog item to have a reconfigure entry point state machine, then any service created from that catalog item will have a Reconfigure this Service option available under its Configuration menu (see Figure 38-2).

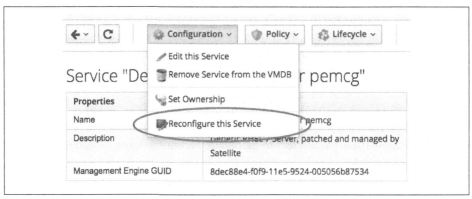

Figure 38-2. Reconfiguring a service

If we select this option, we are presented with the original service dialog once more. Entering new values and clicking the Submit button will create a `ServiceReconfigur eRequest` to perform the reconfiguration action, based on the revised values that we have have entered into the dialog.

Service Design

When we create a service that can be reconfigured in this way, we need to put extra thought into our service design and provisioning workflow. We need to make some of our service dialog elements *reconfigurable* so that we can enter new values when re-presented with the dialog on a service reconfiguration request (elements not marked as Reconfigurable will be greyed out). We need to create a *set_configuration* method that can be called from either the virtual machine provision or service reconfiguration state machines, and retrieve dialog values from the correct location in each case. This method must detect whether the VM provision was initiated from a service that passed the correct dialog values or an interactive VM provision request that did not.

Adding a Configuration Management Provider

We can add our Satellite 6 server as a CloudForms configuration management provider. This imports the Foreman host groups as CloudForms *configuration profiles*, saving us from having to make a REST call to the Satellite server to list them (see Figure 38-3).

Description	▲	Total Configured Systems	Environment
Generic_RHEL6_Servers		13	KT_Bit63_Production_RHEL6_Q4_2015_6
Generic_RHEL7_Servers		1	KT_Bit63_Production_RHEL7_Q4_2015_5
Generic_RHEL7_Servers/Database Servers		0	KT_Bit63_Production_RHEL7_Q4_2015_5
Generic_RHEL7_Servers/Middleware Servers		0	KT_Bit63_Production_RHEL7_Q4_2015_5
Generic_RHEL7_Servers/Web Servers		0	KT_Bit63_Production_RHEL7_Q4_2015_5

Figure 38-3. Configuration profiles imported from Satellite 6

Automate Datastore Components

Even though a service reconfiguration capability is provided for us by CloudForms, we still need to add several Automate Datastore components if we wish to use it.

Creating the Namespaces and State Machines

In our own domain, we'll create a */Service/Reconfiguration/StateMachines* namespace (see Figure 38-4).

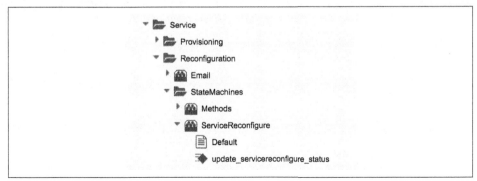

Figure 38-4. /Service/Reconfiguration/StateMachines namespace

We'll create a simple state machine class called *ServiceReconfigure*, with seven states (see Figure 38-5).

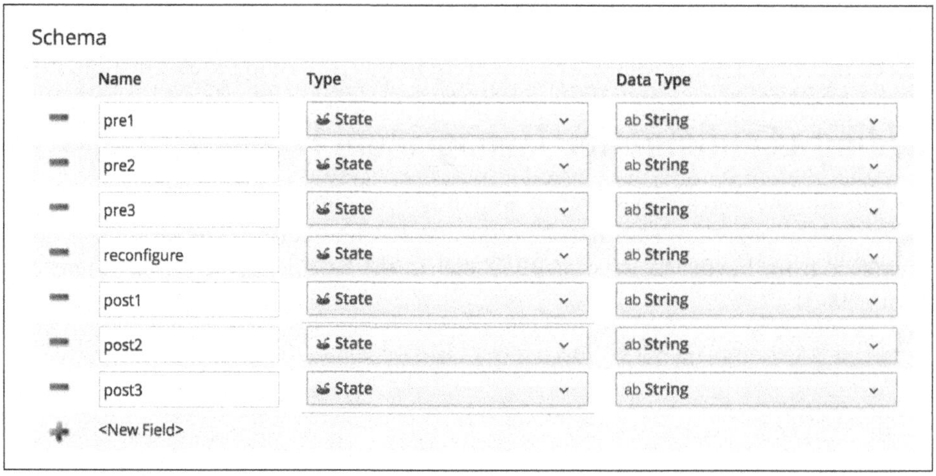

	Name	Type		Data Type	
	pre1	State	v	ab String	v
	pre2	State	v	ab String	v
	pre3	State	v	ab String	v
	reconfigure	State	v	ab String	v
	post1	State	v	ab String	v
	post2	State	v	ab String	v
	post3	State	v	ab String	v
	<New Field>				

Figure 38-5. ServiceReconfigure state machine class schema

pre{1-3} and post{1-3} are future-proofing placeholders in case we wish to enhance the functionality in future. For now we'll just be using the reconfigure state.

We'll copy the *ManageIQ/Service/Provisioning/StateMachines/ServiceProvision_Template/update_serviceprovision_status* method into our domain and rename it *update_servicereconfigure_status*. We change line 6 from:

```
prov = $evm.root['service_template_provision_task']
```

to:

```
reconfigure_task = $evm.root['service_reconfigure_task']
```

We also change the variable name in line 13 from *prov* to *reconfigure_task*.

We'll edit the On Entry, On Exit, and On Error columns in the state machine class schema to refer to the new *update_servicereconfigure_status* method (see Figure 38-6).

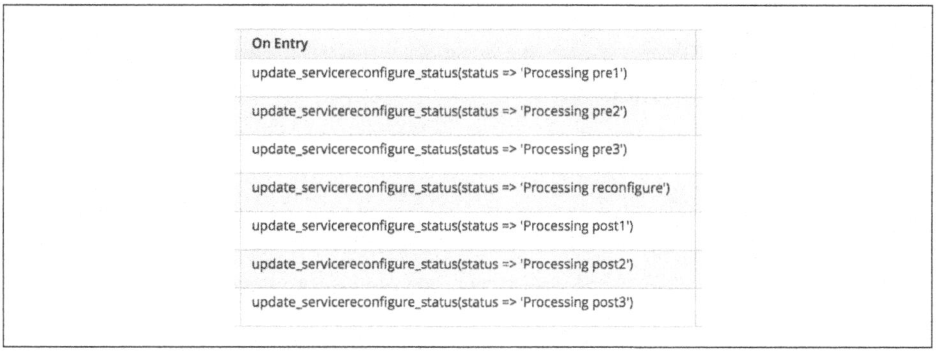

On Entry
update_servicereconfigure_status(status => 'Processing pre1')
update_servicereconfigure_status(status => 'Processing pre2')
update_servicereconfigure_status(status => 'Processing pre3')
update_servicereconfigure_status(status => 'Processing reconfigure')
update_servicereconfigure_status(status => 'Processing post1')
update_servicereconfigure_status(status => 'Processing post2')
update_servicereconfigure_status(status => 'Processing post3')

Figure 38-6. Setting the On Entry methods

We create a *Default* instance of the *ServiceReconfiguration* state machine class, and we'll point the `reconfigure` stage to the */Integration/Satellite/Methods/SetConfiguration* instance that we'll create (see Figure 38-7).

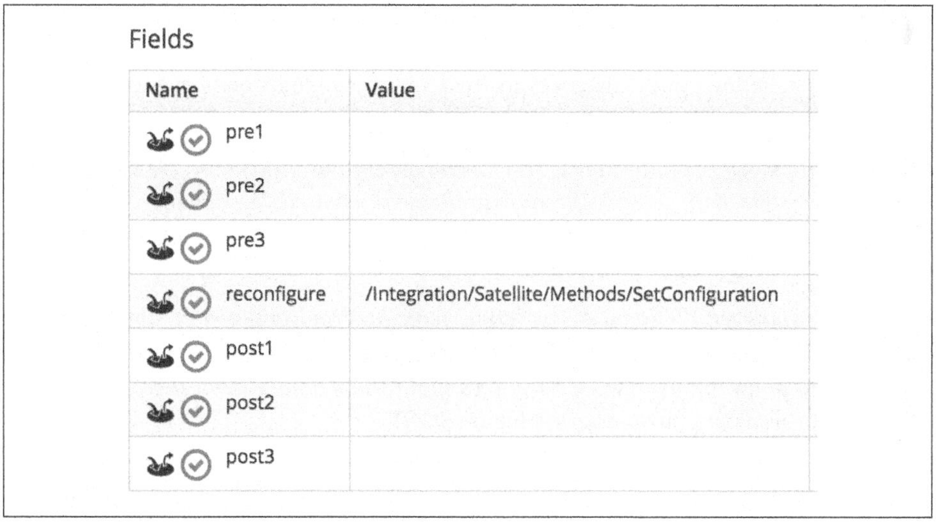

Fields

Name	Value
pre1	
pre2	
pre3	
reconfigure	/Integration/Satellite/Methods/SetConfiguration
post1	
post2	
post3	

Figure 38-7. Schema of the default instance

Email Classes

We need to create two new email instances with associated methods, to send emails when a service reconfigure is approved and completed. For convenience we'll just copy, rename, and edit the *ManageIQ/Service/Provisioning/Email* instances and methods (see Figure 38-8).

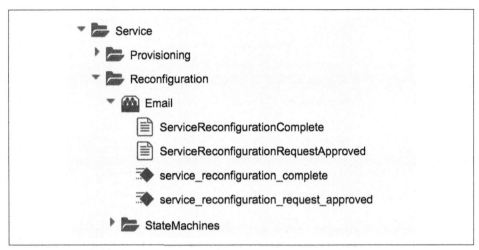

Figure 38-8. Copied and renamed email instances and methods

Policies

We need to generate policy instances for two ServiceReconfigure events: *ServiceReconfigureRequest_created* and *ServiceReconfigureRequest_approved*.

We copy *ManageIQ/System/Policy/ServiceTemplateProvisionRequest_created* into our domain as *System/Policy/ServiceReconfigureRequest_created*. We can leave the schema contents as they are because we'll use the same auto-approval state machine as when the service was originally provisioned.

We copy *ManageIQ/System/Policy/ServiceTemplateProvisionRequest_approved* into our domain as */System/Policy/ServiceReconfigureRequest_approved*, and we edit the rel5 state to point to our new */Service/Reconfiguration/Email/ServiceReconfigurationRequestApproved* email instance (see Figure 38-9).

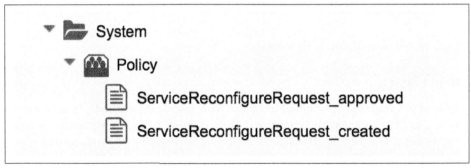

Figure 38-9. Copied and renamed policy instances

Modifying the VM Provision Workflow

We need to change our VM provision workflow to add a state to perform the initial configuration, using the values input from the service dialog. We'll take the state machine that we used in Chapter 28 and add a `SetConfiguration` stage after `Regis terSatellite`. `SetConfiguration` points to the same instance as our new *ServiceRe-configuration* state machine's `reconfigure` stage (see Figure 38-10).

🦆✅	PostProvision	/Infrastructure/VM/Provisioning/StateMachines/Methods/PostProvision#${/#miq_pro
🦆✅	RegisterSatellite	/Integration/Satellite/Methods/RegisterSatellite
🦆✅	SetConfiguration	/Integration/Satellite/Methods/SetConfiguration
🦆✅	RegisterDHCP	
🦆✅	ActivateCMDB	
🦆✅	ActivateSatellite	/Integration/Satellite/Methods/ActivateSatellite

Figure 38-10. Adding the SetConfiguration stage to the VM provision state machine

Service Dialog

We're going to create a completely dynamic service dialog, interacting with Satellite to retrieve information. The dialog will search the VMDB for configuration profiles (host groups) and present them in a drop-down list. For the host group selected, Satellite will be queried for the configured activation keys and Puppet classes, and these will be presented in drop-down lists. For the Puppet class selected, Satellite will be queried for the available smart class parameters, and these will be presented in a drop-down list. Finally, a text area box will be presented to optionally input an override parameter.

Elements

The service dialog will contain seven elements, of which the Puppet Class, Smart Class Parameter, and New Parameter Value elements will be marked as Reconfigurable. The dialog elements are summarized in Table 38-1.

Table 38-1. Dialog elements

Name	Type	Dynamic	Instance	Auto-refresh	Auto-refresh other fields	Reconfigurable
Service Name	Text Box	No	N/A	N/A	N/A	No
VM Name	Text Box	No	N/A	N/A	N/A	No
Host Group	Drop Down List	Yes	`ListHostGroups`	No	Yes	No
Activation Key	Drop Down List	Yes	`ListActivationKeys`	Yes	No	No
Puppet Class	Drop Down List	Yes	`ListPuppetClasses`	Yes	Yes	Yes
Smart Class Parameter	Drop Down List	Yes	`ListSmartClassPara` `meters`	Yes	No	Yes
New Parameter Value	Text Area Box	No	N/A	N/A	N/A	Yes

When ordered, the dialog will look like Figure 38-11.

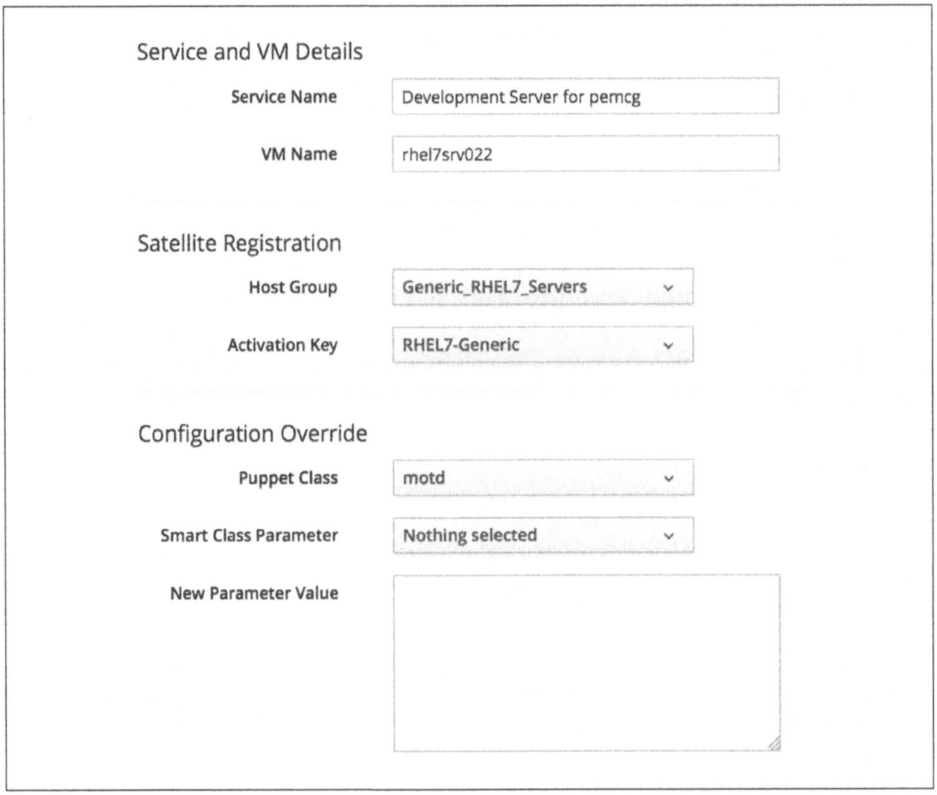

Figure 38-11. The final service dialog

Instances and Methods

We need to create a number of instances and methods to populate the dynamic dialog elements of the service dialog.

Dynamic Dialogs

The dynamic dialog instances and methods are defined under an */Integration/Satellite/DynamicDialogs* namespace in our domain (see Figure 38-12).

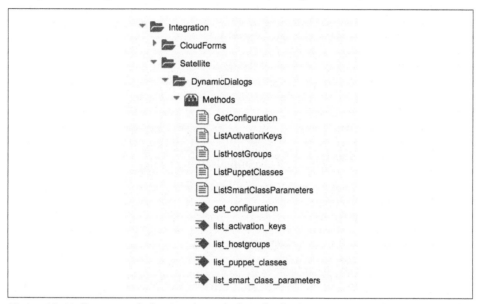

Figure 38-12. Dynamic dialog instances and methods

The schema for the *Methods* class holds variables containing the credentials to connect to our Satellite server (we first used this technique in Chapter 4).

Common functionality

Each of the dynamic methods has a simple `rest_action` method to perform the RESTful call to Satellite:

```
def rest_action(uri, verb, payload=nil)
  headers = {
    :content_type  => 'application/json',
    :accept        => 'application/json;version=2',
    :authorization => \
                   "Basic #{Base64.strict_encode64("#{@username}:#{@password}")}"
  }
  response = RestClient::Request.new(
    :method       => verb,
```

```
      :url        => uri,
      :headers    => headers,
      :payload    => payload,
      verify_ssl: false
    ).execute
    return JSON.parse(response.to_str)
  end
```

They each pull the credentials from the instance schema and define the base URI and an empty values_hash:

```
servername = $evm.object['servername']
@username  = $evm.object['username']
@password  = $evm.object.decrypt('password')

uri_base = "https://#{servername}/api/v2"
values_hash = {}
```

ListHostGroups

The *list_hostgroups* method does not need to connect to the Satellite RESTful API, as the Satellite server is registered as a configuration management provider. The method performs a simple VMDB lookup of all configuration profiles:

```
hostgroups = $evm.vmdb(:configuration_profile).all

if hostgroups.length > 0
  if hostgroups.length > 1
    values_hash['!'] = '-- select from list --'
  end
  hostgroups.each do |hostgroup|
    $evm.log(:info, "Found Host Group '#{hostgroup.name}' \
                                    with ID: #{hostgroup.manager_ref}")
    values_hash[hostgroup.manager_ref] = hostgroup.name
  end
else
  values_hash['!'] = 'No hostgroups are available'
end
```

ListActivationKeys

The *list_activationkeys* method retrieves the hostgroup_id from the Host Group element and makes a Satellite API call to get the hostgroup parameters:

```
hg_id = $evm.object['dialog_hostgroup_id']

if hg_id.nil?
  values_hash['!'] = "Select a Host Group and click 'Refresh'"
else
  rest_return = rest_action("#{uri_base}/hostgroups/#{hg_id}/parameters", :get)
  rest_return['results'].each do |hostgroup_parameter|
    if hostgroup_parameter['name'].to_s == "kt_activation_keys"
```

```
        hostgroup_parameter['value'].split(',').each do |activationkey|
          values_hash[activationkey] = activationkey
        end
      end
    end
    if values_hash.length > 0
      if values_hash.length > 1
        values_hash['!'] = '-- select from list --'
      end
    else
      values_hash['!'] = 'This Host Group has no Activation Keys'
    end
  end
```

ListPuppetClasses

The *list_puppetclasses* method retrieves the hostgroup_id from the Host Group element and makes a Satellite API call to get the Puppet classes associated with the host group:

```
hg_id = $evm.object['dialog_hostgroup_id']

if hg_id.nil?
  values_hash['!'] = "Select a Host Group and click 'Refresh'"
else
  rest_return = rest_action("#{uri_base}/hostgroups/#{hg_id}/puppetclasses",:get)
  if rest_return['total'] > 0
    if rest_return['total'] > 1
      values_hash['!'] = '-- select from list --'
    end
    rest_return['results'].each do |classname, classinfo|
      values_hash[classinfo[0]['id'].to_s] = classname
    end
  else
    values_hash['!'] = 'No Puppet Classes are defined for this Hostgroup'
  end
end
```

ListSmartClassParameters

The *list_smart_class_parameters* method retrieves the hostgroup_id and puppet class_id from previous elements and makes a Satellite API call to get the Puppet smart class parameters associated with the host group. For each parameter returned it then makes a further Satellite API call to cross-reference against the requested Puppet class:

```
hg_id           = $evm.object['dialog_hostgroup_id']
puppet_class_id = $evm.object['dialog_puppet_class_id']

if puppet_class_id.nil?
  values_hash['!'] = "Select a Puppet Class and click 'Refresh'"
```

```
else
  call_string = "#{uri_base}/hostgroups/#{hg_id}/smart_class_parameters"
  rest_return = rest_action(call_string, :get)
  rest_return['results'].each do |parameter|
    #
    # Retrieve the details of this smart class parameter
    # to find out which puppet class it's associated with
    #
    call_string = "#{uri_base}/hostgroups/#{hg_id}/"
    call_string += "smart_class_parameters/#{parameter['id']}"
    parameter_details = rest_action(call_string, :get)
    if parameter_details['puppetclass']['id'].to_s == puppet_class_id
      values_hash[parameter['id'].to_s] = parameter_details['parameter']
    end
  end
  if values_hash.length > 0
    if values_hash.length > 1
      values_hash['!'] = '-- select from list --'
    end
  else
    values_hash['!'] = 'This Puppet class has no Smart Class Parameters'
  end
end
```

Making several cross-referencing API calls to Satellite in this way can be slow if many Puppet classes with smart class variables are defined in our host group, but this technique is suitable for our example.

Configuration-Related Methods

We have three methods that handle the registration with Satellite and the setting of configuration.

RegisterSatellite

We edit the *register_satellite* method from Chapter 28 to take out the hardcoded selection of host group. We also bypass Satellite registration entirely if we don't find the hostgroup_id:

```
#
# Only register if the provisioning template is linux
#
if template.platform == "linux"
  #
  # Only register with Satellite if we've been passed a
  # hostgroup ID from a service dialog
  #
  hg_id = $evm.root['miq_provision'].get_option(:dialog_hostgroup_id)
  unless hg_id.nil?
    ...
```

ActivateSatellite

We edit the *activate_satellite* method from Chapter 28 to take out the hardcoded selection of activation key. We also bypass Satellite activation entirely if we don't find the activation key name:

```
#
# Only register if the provisioning template is linux
#
prov = $evm.root['miq_provision']
if template.platform == "linux"
  #
  # Only register and activate with Satellite if we've been passed an
  # activation key from a service dialog
  #
  activationkey = prov.get_option(:dialog_activationkey_name)
  unless activationkey.nil?
    ...
```

SetConfiguration

The *set_configuration* method will be called from two completely different state machines, once to perform an initial configuration during provisioning and possibly again during a service reconfigure request. The method must retrieve the service dialog values from either of two different places:

```
if $evm.root['vmdb_object_type'] == 'miq_provision'
  prov = $evm.root['miq_provision']
  parameter_id    = prov.get_option(:dialog_parameter_id)
  parameter_value = prov.get_option(:dialog_parameter_value)
  hg_id           = prov.get_option(:dialog_hostgroup_id)
  hostname        = prov.get_option(:dialog_vm_name)
elsif $evm.root['vmdb_object_type'] == 'service_reconfigure_task'
  parameter_id    = $evm.root['dialog_parameter_id']
  parameter_value = $evm.root['dialog_parameter_value']
  hg_id           = $evm.root['dialog_hostgroup_id']
  hostname        = $evm.root['dialog_vm_name']
end
```

If a smart class parameter override value has not been input, the method simply exits:

```
#
# Only set the smart class parameter if we've been passed a
# parameter value from a service dialog
#
unless parameter_value.nil?
  ...
```

The method must fetch the default domain name from the host group to assemble the correct FQDN for the match:

```
rest_return = rest_action("#{uri_base}/hostgroups/#{hg_id}", :get)
domain_name = rest_return['domain_name']
match = "fqdn=#{hostname}.#{domain_name}"
```

The method must also determine whether the override match already exists. If it doesn't exist, it must be created with a POST action; if it does exist, it must be updated with a PUT action:

```
call_string = "#{uri_base}/smart_class_parameters/"
call_string += "#{parameter_id}/override_values"
rest_return = rest_action(call_string, :get)
override_value_id = 0
if rest_return['total'] > 0
  rest_return['results'].each do |override_value|
    if override_value['match'] == match
      override_value_id = override_value['id']
    end
  end
end
if override_value_id.zero?
  payload = {
    :match => match,
    :value => parameter_value
  }
  call_string = "#{uri_base}/smart_class_parameters/"
  call_string += "#{parameter_id}/override_values"
  rest_return = rest_action(call_string, :post, JSON.generate(payload))
else
  payload = {
    :value => parameter_value
  }
  call_string = "#{uri_base}/smart_class_parameters/"
  call_string =+ "#{parameter_id}/override_values/#{override_value_id}"
  rest_return = rest_action(call_string, :put, JSON.generate(payload))
end
```

Here we see that match is the FQDN of the server. If an override match doesn't exist for this smart class parameter, we create one using the server FQDN and the value to override. If an override match based on the FQDN does exist, we simply update the override value.

The full code for the methods is available on GitHub (*http://bit.ly/1TxEtrE*).

Testing

We'll order a new service and select appropriate host group and activation keys from the drop-downs. We'll select the motd Puppet class and override the content smart class parameter (see Figure 38-13).

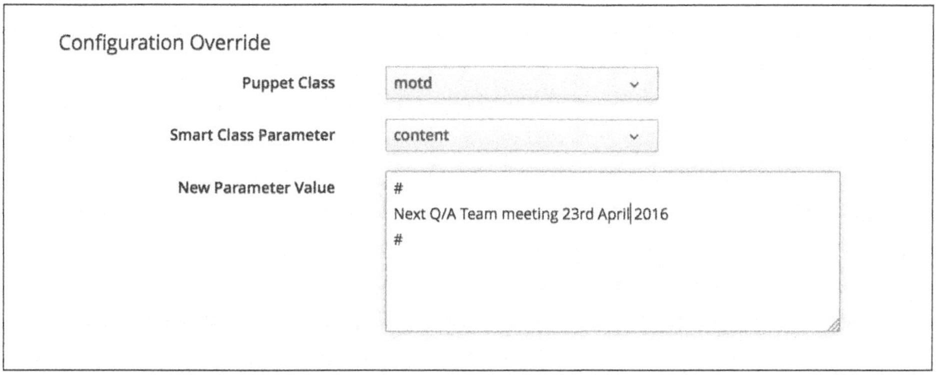

Figure 38-13. Setting an initial value for motd when provisoning a service

We click Submit and wait for our newly provisioned service.

Logging in to the newly provisioned server confirms that the motd has been set:

```
Last login: Wed Mar 23 17:14:34 2016 from cloudforms05.bit63.net
#
Next Q/A Team meeting 23rd April 2016
#
[root@rhel7srv034 ~]#
```

If we look at the details of our new service in My Services and select Configuration →
Reconfigure this Service, we are again presented with the service dialog, but the elements not marked as Reconfigurable are read-only (see Figure 38-14).

Figure 38-14. Setting a new value for motd when reconfiguring the service

We can select the motd Puppet class again, enter a new value for the content smart class parameter, and click Submit.

We receive an email informing us that the reconfiguration request has been approved:

```
Hello,
Your Service reconfiguration request was approved. If Service reconfiguration
is successful you will be notified via email when the Service is available.

Approvers notes: Auto-Approved

To view this Request go to: https://cloudforms05/miq_request/show/1000000000109

Thank you,
Virtualization Infrastructure Team
```

We can log in to the Satellite 6 user interface to confirm that the "Override value for specific hosts" contains our updated value against the match filter (see Figure 38-15).

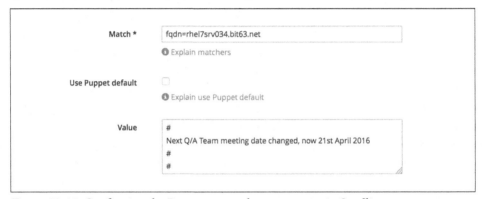

Figure 38-15. Confirming the Puppet smart class parameter in Satellite

Once the Puppet agent has run on the client again, we can log in and see the new message:

```
Last login: Wed Mar 23 17:35:50 2016 from cloudforms05.bit63.net
#
Next Q/A Team meeting date changed, now 21st April 2016
#
#[root@rhel7srv034 ~]#
```

Summary

This chapter has built on several topics and examples that we've worked through so far in the book. It extends the integration with Satellite 6 that we covered in Chapter 28, and shows how we can dynamically present lists of activation keys or Puppet classes with values retrieved from the Satellite server at runtime. We configured some of the service dialog elements to autorefresh, so that a selection made from one element automatically runs the refresh methods to populate other dependent elements. Some of the dialog elements were reconfigurable as well, so that their values can be updated. This is a pretty advanced example that shows what can be done from a service catalog.

Finally, this example builds on the concept of using services as workload orchestrators and shows how we can set and update our service configuration from a single tool. This is a powerful concept and means that we can use our service catalog as the single control point for deploying and configuring our workloads.

## CHAPTER 39

Service Tips and Tricks

There are three useful tips and tricks to be aware of when developing services, and we'll discuss them here.

Test Virtual Machine Provisioning First

Before developing a service catalog item to provision a virtual machine, test that an interactive provision (Infrastructure → Virtual Machines → Lifecycle → Provision VMs) from the same virtual machine template, using the same virtual machine settings, works successfully.

This should include the same placement type (auto or manually selected), and the same CPU count and memory size ranges that will be offered from the service dialog.

Troubleshooting a failing interactive VM provision is simpler than troubleshooting a failing service order.

Re-create the Service Item if the Template Changes

If any changes are made to the template that would result in a new internal template ID, then the service catalog item must be re-created (even if the new template has the same name as the old). The new template will be represented by a new object in the VMDB, so the service provision request template will need to be re-created with the new template ID.

Custom State Machines

There are times when an out-of-the-box service provision state machine does not provide the flexibility that we need to create the service that we require. An example of this would be wishing to present a service dialog offering a drop-down list prompting for the number of virtual machines to provision as part of the order from the catalog item (by default this number is fixed when the catalog item is created). Fortunately, we are not constrained to use the as-supplied state machines.

When we create a new service catalog item, we are presented with a drop-down list of catalog item types to choose from (see Figure 39-1).

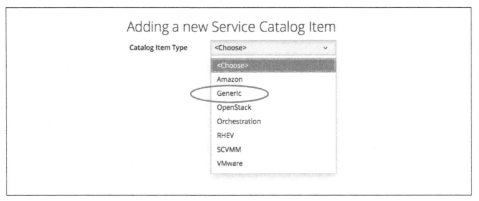

Figure 39-1. Selection of catalog item type

As Figure 39-1 shows, there's a Generic selection that we can use. If we select this catalog item type, we can create our own custom instance of the *ServiceProvision_Template* state machine class. This can handle the parsing of any service catalog elements and assemble arguments for a call to `$evm.execute('create_provision_request')` to complete the VM provision (see Chapter 27).

By hand-rolling the arguments to `create_provision_request` in this way, we have complete control over the VM provision request. We could easily prompt the user for the template name to provision from or the number of VMs to provision with the request, for example.[1]

Summary

This chapter has shown us three simple tips to consider when working with services. Generic services, in particular, are useful if we wish to create a single service catalog item to provision a new virtual machine into a choice of providers (such as VMware or OpenStack). With a traditional service catalog item, we must select a template first, and this decides the destination provider. With a Generic service type, we can present our users with a list of VMware templates or OpenStack Glance images to choose

---

[1] The CloudForms Essentials (*https://github.com/ramrexx/CloudForms_Essentials*) repository has several examples of such custom state machines that we can use or adapt.

from at runtime. Depending on the template or image selected, we can then supply the appropriate provider-specific arguments to `$evm.execute('create_provi sion_request')` in order to complete the request.

## PART IV

Retirement

The retirement process for virtual machines, instances, and services was substantially rewritten for CloudForms 3.2. Part IV describes the current retirement workflows for virtual machines and services.

## CHAPTER 40

Virtual Machine and Instance Retirement

CloudForms is a virtual machine and instance lifecycle management tool, and so far we have concentrated on the provisioning phase of that lifecycle. CloudForms also has a virtual machine retirement workflow that lets us manage the retirement and deletion of our virtual machines or instances, both from the provider and from the CloudForms VMDB if required.

The retirement process allows us to treat virtual machines that were provisioned with CloudForms differently from those that might have existed on the provider infrastructure before CloudForms was installed.

 We may wish to keep the VMDB record of a virtual machine long after its deletion from the provider, for recording and auditing purposes.

In this chapter we'll examine the retirement process for virtual machines and instances.

Initiating Retirement

Virual machine or instance retirement is initiated from the Lifecycle menu on the VM details page (see Figure 40-1).

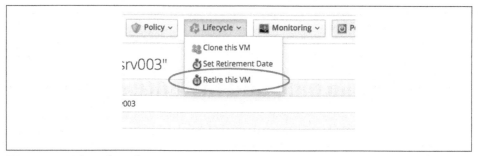

Figure 40-1. Virtual machine or instance retirement menu

Clicking on Retire this VM raises a `request_vm_retire` event that begins a chain of relationships through the datastore:

- `request_vm_retire` →
  - */System/Event/MiqEvent/POLICY/request_vm_retire* →
  - */{Cloud,Infrastructure}/VM/Lifecycle/Retirement* →
  - */{Cloud,Infrastructure}/VM/Retirement/StateMachines/VMRetirement/ {Default,Unregister}*

The relationship from *Lifecycle/Retirement* forwards the event processing into the preferred virtual machine retirement state machine: *Default* for cloud instances, and *Default* or *Unregister* for infrastructure virtual machines. We can select our preferred infrastructure state machine (*Default* is the default) by copying the */ Infrastructure/VM/Lifecycle/Retirement* instance to our own domain and editing accordingly.

Retirement-Related Attributes and Methods

A virtual machine object has a number of retirement-related methods:

```
$evm.root['vm'].start_retirement
$evm.root['vm'].finish_retirement
$evm.root['vm'].retire_now
$evm.root['vm'].retired?
$evm.root['vm'].retirement_state=
$evm.root['vm'].retirement_warn=
$evm.root['vm'].retires_on=
$evm.root['vm'].retiring?
```

It also has several attributes:

```
$evm.root['vm'].retired = nil
$evm.root['vm'].retirement_last_warn = nil
$evm.root['vm'].retirement_requester = nil
$evm.root['vm'].retirement_state = nil
```

```
$evm.root['vm'].retirement_warn = nil
$evm.root['vm'].retires_on = nil
```

During the retirement process some of these are set to indicate progress:

```
$evm.root['vm'].retirement_requester = admin    (type: String)
$evm.root['vm'].retirement_state = retiring    (type: String)
```

and completion:

```
$evm.root['vm'].retired = true    (type: TrueClass)
$evm.root['vm'].retirement_requester = nil
$evm.root['vm'].retirement_state = retired    (type: String)
$evm.root['vm'].retires_on = 2015-12-10    (type: Date)
```

VM Retirement State Machine

The VM retirement state machines(s) undo many of the operations performed by the VM provision state machine. They allow us to optionally deactivate a CI record from a CMDB; unregister from DHCP, Active Directory, and DNS; and release both MAC and IP addresses (see Figure 40-2).

Name	Value
StartRetirement	/Infrastructure/VM/Retirement/StateMachines/Methods/StartRetirement
PreRetirement	/Infrastructure/VM/Retirement/StateMachines/Methods/PreRetirement#${/#vm.vendor}
CheckPreRetirement	/Infrastructure/VM/Retirement/StateMachines/Methods/CheckPreRetirement#${/#vm.vendor}
DeactivateCMDB	
UnregisterDHCP	
UnregisterAD	
UnregisterDNS	
ReleaseMACAddress	
ReleaseIPAddress	
PreDeleteFromProvider	#/Infrastructure/VM/Retirement/StateMachines/Methods/PreDeleteFromProvider
RemoveFromProvider	/Infrastructure/VM/Retirement/StateMachines/Methods/RemoveFromProvider
PreDeleteEmailOwner	#/Infrastructure/VM/Retirement/Email/vm_retirement_emails?event=vm_entered_retirement
EmailOwner	/Infrastructure/VM/Retirement/Email/vm_retirement_emails?event=vm_retired
CheckRemovedFromProvider	/Infrastructure/VM/Retirement/StateMachines/Methods/CheckRemovedFromProvider
FinishRetirement	/Infrastructure/VM/Retirement/StateMachines/Methods/FinishRetirement
DeleteFromVMDB	/Infrastructure/VM/Retirement/StateMachines/Methods/DeleteFromVMDB

Figure 40-2. VM retirement state machine

StartRetirement

The *StartRetirement* instance calls the *start_retirement* state machine method, which checks whether the VM is already in the `retired` or `retiring` state, and if so it aborts. If the VM is in neither of these states, it calls the VM's `start_retirement` method, which sets the `retirement_state` attribute to `retiring`.

PreRetirement/CheckPreRetirement

The state machine allows us to have provider-specific instances and methods for these stages. The out-of-the-box infrastructure *PreRetirement* instance runs a vendor-independent *pre_retirement* method that just powers off the VM. The out-of-the-box cloud *PreRetirement* instance runs the appropriate vendor-specific *pre_retirement* method—that is, *amazon_pre_retirement*, *azure_pre_retirement*, or *open-stack_pre_retirement*.

CheckPreRetirement checks that the power off has completed. The cloud versions have corresponding vendor-specific *check_pre_retirement* methods.

RemoveFromProvider/CheckRemovedFromProvider

The `RemoveFromProvider` stage allows us some flexibility in handling the actual removal of the VM, and this is where the *Default* and *Unregister* state machines differ.

Default

The `RemoveFromProvider` stage of the *Default* state machine links to the *RemoveFromProvider* instance, which calls the *remove_from_provider* state machine method, passing the `removal_type` argument of `remove_from_disk`. This checks whether the VM was provisioned from CloudForms (`vm.miq_provision` is not `nil`) *or* if the VM is tagged with `lifecycle/retire_full`. If either of these is `true`, it fully deletes the VM from the underlying provider, including the disk image. Having done so, it sets the Boolean `vm_removed_from_provider` state variable to `true`.

If neither of these checks returns `true`, no action is performed.

Unregister

The `RemoveFromProvider` stage of the *Unregister* state machine links to the *UnregisterFromProvider* instance, which calls the *remove_from_provider* state machine method, passing the `removal_type` argument of `unregister`. This checks whether the VM was provisioned from CloudForms (`vm.miq_provision` is not `nil`) *or* if the VM is tagged with `lifecycle/retire_full`. If either of these is `true`, it deletes the VM from the underlying provider but retains the VM's disk image, allowing the VM to be re-created if required in the future. Having done so, it sets the Boolean `vm_removed_from_provider` state variable to `true`.

If neither of these checks is `true`, no action is performed.

FinishRetirement

The *FinishRetirement* instance calls the *finish_retirement* state machine method that sets the following VM object attributes:

```
:retires_on        => Date.today
:retired           => true
:retirement_state  => "retired"
```

It also raises a `vm_retired` event that can be caught by an Automate action or control policy.

DeleteFromVMDB

The *DeleteFromVMDB* instance calls the *delete_from_vmdb* state machine method that checks for the state variable `vm_removed_from_provider`, and if the variable is found (and `true`), it removes the virtual machine record from the VMDB.

Summary

This chapter has shown that retirement is a more complex process than simply deleting the virtual machine. We must potentially free up resources that were allocated when the VM was created, such as an IP address. We might need to delete a CI record from a CMDB, unregister from Active Directory, or even keep the VMDB object inside CloudForms for auditing purposes.

Fortunately, the retirement workflow allows us to fine-tune all of these options and handle retirement in a manner that suits us.

Further Reading

Provisioning Virtual Machines and Hosts, Chapter 6: Retirement (*http://red.ht/25hjYXC*)

Deleting VMs from Foreman During Retirement (*http://bit.ly/1UdAUZP*)

## CHAPTER 41

Service Retirement

We saw in Chapter 40 how individual virtual machines or instances can be retired from their Lifecycle menu button, and we can also retire services in the same way. The service retirement process follows a similar workflow to the VM retirement process, but we have the flexibility to specify per-service retirement state machines if we wish.

Defining a Service Retirement Entry Point

When we create a service catalog item, we can optionally specify a retirement entry point (see Figure 41-1).

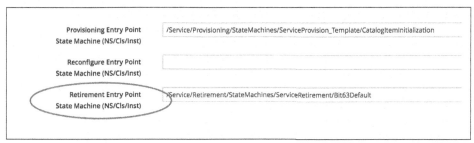

Provisioning Entry Point **State Machine (NS/Cls/Inst)**	/Service/Provisioning/StateMachines/ServiceProvision_Template/CatalogItemInitialization
Reconfigure Entry Point **State Machine (NS/Cls/Inst)**	
Retirement Entry Point **State Machine (NS/Cls/Inst)**	/Service/Retirement/StateMachines/ServiceRetirement/Bit63Default

Figure 41-1. Setting a service retirement entry point state machine

If we specify our own retirement entry point, then this state machine will be used to retire any services created from this catalog item. If we do not specify our own entry point here, then then the *Default* retirement state machine will be used.

Initiating Retirement

Service retirement is initiated from the Lifecycle menu on the service details frame (see Figure 41-2).

Figure 41-2. Service retirement menu

Clicking on Retire this Service raises a `request_service_retire` event that begins a chain of relationships through the datastore:

- `request_service_retire` →
  - */System/Event/MiqEvent/POLICY/request_service_retire* →
  - */Service/Retirement/StateMachines/Methods/GetRetirementEntrypoint*

GetRetirementEntrypoint runs a method called *get_retirement_entry_point* that returns the retirement entry point state machine defined when the service catalog item was created (see Figure 41-3). If this is empty, then */Service/Retirement/StateMachines/ServiceRetirement/Default* is returned.

Retirement-Related Attributes and Methods

A service object has a number of retirement-related methods:

```
$evm.root['service'].automate_retirement_entrypoint
$evm.root['service'].finish_retirement
$evm.root['service'].retire_now
$evm.root['service'].retire_service_resources
$evm.root['service'].retired?
$evm.root['service'].retirement_state=
$evm.root['service'].retirement_warn=
$evm.root['service'].retires_on=
$evm.root['service'].start_retirement
```

and attributes:

```
$evm.root['service'].retired = nil
$evm.root['service'].retirement_last_warn = nil
$evm.root['service'].retirement_requester = nil
$evm.root['service'].retirement_state = nil
$evm.root['service'].retirement_warn = nil
$evm.root['service'].retires_on = nil
```

Service Retirement State Machine

The *Default* service retirement state machine is simpler than its VM counterpart (see Figure 41-3).

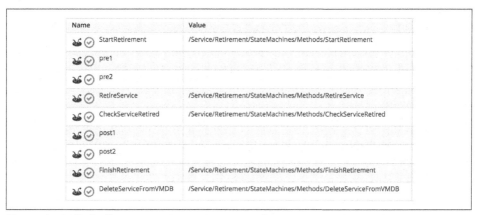

Figure 41-3. Default service retirement state machine

StartRetirement

The *StartRetirement* instance calls the *start_retirement* state machine method, which checks whether the service is already in the `retired` or `retiring` state, and if so it aborts. If the service is in neither of these states, it calls the service's `start_retire ment` method, which sets the `retirement_state` attribute to `retiring`.

RetireService/CheckServiceRetired

The *RetireService* instance calls the *retire_service* state machine method, which in turn calls the service object's `retire_service_resources` method. This method calls the `retire_now` method of every VM comprising the service, to initiate their retirement. *CheckServiceRetired* retries the stage until all VMs are retired or deleted.

FinishRetirement

The `FinishRetirement` stage sets the following service object attributes:

```
:retires_on        => Date.today
:retired           => true
:retirement_state  => "retired"
```

It also raises a `service_retired` event that can be caught by an Automate action or control policy.

DeleteServiceFromVMDB

The *DeleteServiceFromVMDB* instance calls the *delete_service_from_vmdb* state machine method, which removes the service record from the VMDB.

Summary

We have seen in this chapter how the process of retiring a service will also trigger the retirement of its virtual machines. If we are using service hierarchies, however, or services to manage cloud-style workloads as single entities, this might not be our desired behavior.

Fortunately, the service retirement mechanism is flexible enough that we can create per-service retirement state machines that we can customize to suit our individual use cases and workloads.

PART V
Integration

One of the powerful features of CloudForms is *integration*—its ability to orchestrate and coordinate with external services as part of a workflow. These services might include a corporate IP address management (IPAM) solution, ticketing system, or a configuration management database (CMDB), for example.

Part V looks at the integration capabilities of CloudForms Automate.

## CHAPTER 42

Calling Automation Using the RESTful API

Our first look at the integration capabilities of CloudForms examines how external systems can make *inbound* calls to CloudForms to run Automate instances using the RESTful API.[1]

Being able to call automation in this way enables our workflows to be utilized by other enterprise tools in a number of ways. For example, organizations may wish to use a help-desk ticketing system as their starting point for new virtual machine provisioning requests. The ticketing system can make a RESTful call to CloudForms Automate to initiate the workflow.

API Entry Point

We can call any Automate instance from the RESTful API, by issuing a POST call to */api/automation_requests* and enclosing a JSON-encoded parameter hash such as the following:

```
post_params = {
  :version => '1.1',
  :uri_parts => {
    :namespace => 'ACME/General',
    :class => 'Methods',
    :instance => 'HelloWorld'
  },
  :requester => {
    :auto_approve => true
  }
}.to_json
```

---

1 We need to enable the *Web Services* server role on any of our CloudForms appliances to which we wish to make RESTful calls.

We can call the RESTful API from an external Ruby script by using the `rest-client` gem:

```ruby
url = 'https://cloudforms_server'
query = '/api/automation_requests'
rest_return = RestClient::Request.execute(
                            method: :post,
                            url: url + query,
                            :user => username,
                            :password => password,
                            :headers => {:accept => :json},
                            :payload => post_params,
                            verify_ssl: false)
result = JSON.parse(rest_return)
```

The request ID is returned to us in the result from the initial call:

```ruby
request_id = result['results'][0]['id']
```

We call poll this to check on status:

```ruby
query = "/api/automation_requests/#{request_id}"
rest_return = RestClient::Request.execute(
                            method: :get,
                            url: url + query,
                            :user => username,
                            :password => password,
                            :headers => {:accept => :json},
                            verify_ssl: false)
result = JSON.parse(rest_return)
request_state = result['request_state']
until request_state == "finished"
  puts "Checking completion state..."
  rest_return = RestClient::Request.execute(
                            method: :get,
                            url: url + query,
                            :user => username,
                            :password => password,
                            :headers => {:accept => :json},
                            verify_ssl: false)
  result = JSON.parse(rest_return)
  request_state = result['request_state']
  sleep 3
end
```

Returning Results to the Caller

The automation request's options hash is included in the return from the Rest Client::Request call, and we can use this to our advantage, by using set_option to add return data in the form of key/value pairs to the options hash from our called automation method.

For example, from the *called* (Automate) method, we can include the following:

```
automation_request = $evm.root['automation_task'].automation_request
automation_request.set_option(:return, JSON.generate({:status => 'success',
                                                        :return => some_data}))
```

From the *calling* (external) method, we can then parse the `return` key from the returned options hash and print the contents, as follows:

```
result = JSON.parse(rest_return)
puts "Results: #{result['options']['return'].inspect}"
```

Using this technique, we can write our own pseudo-API calls for CloudForms to handle anything that the standard RESTful API doesn't support. We implement the "API" using a standard Automate method and call it using the RESTful automate call; and we can pass parameters to, and retrieve result back from, the called method.

Authentication and auto_approve

When we make a RESTful call, we must authenticate using a valid username and password. This user must be an admin or equivalent, however, if we wish to specify an `:auto_approve` value of `true` in our calling arguments (only admins can auto-approve automation requests).

If we try making a RESTful call as a nonadmin user, the automation request will be blocked, pending approval (as expected). If we want to submit an auto-approved automation request as a nonadmin user, we would need to write our own approval workflow (see Chapter 43).

Zone Implications

When we submit an automation request via the API, by default the Automate task is queued on the same appliance that the web service is running on. This will be dequeued to run by any appliance with the Automation Engine role set *in the same zone*. If we have separated out our UI/web service appliances into a different zone, this may not necessarily be our desired behavior.

We can add the parameter `:miq_zone` to the automation request to override this:

```
:requester => {
  :auto_approve => true
},
:parameters => {
    :miq_zone => 'Zone Name'
}
```

The behavior of this parameter is as follows:

- If the parameter is not passed, the request should use the zone of the server that receives the request.

- If passed but empty (e.g., *parameters* => "miq_zone="), the zone should be set to nil and any appliance can process the request.

- Passing a valid zone name parameter (e.g., *parameters* => "miq_zone=Test") should process the work in the Test zone.

- Passing an invalid zone name should raise an error of unknown zone *Zone_name* back to the caller.

run_via_api

The accompanying code on GitHub (*http://bit.ly/1VOFeSa*) contains an example script called *run_via_api.rb* that can be used to call any Automate instance, using arguments to pass server name, credentials, and URI parameters to the instance to be called. Its usage is as follows:

```
Usage: run_via_api.rb [options]
    -s, --server server              CloudForms server to connect to
    -u, --username username          Username to connect as
    -p, --password password          Password
    -d, --domain                     Domain
    -n, --namespace                  Namespace
    -c, --class                      Class
    -i, --instance                   Instance
    -P, --parameter <key,value>      Parameter (key => value pair) for the instance
    -h, --help
```

Edit the default values for server, username, and password if required. Run the script as:

```
./run_via_api.rb -s 192.168.1.1 -u cfadmin -p password -d ACME -n General \
-c Methods -i AddNIC2VM -P vm_id,1000000000195
-P nic_name,nic1 -P nic_network,vlan_712
```

Summary

This chapter has examined how we can make RESTful API calls into Automate and, if necessary, return results back to the caller. This is a very powerful feature that lets us harness the power of CloudForms Automate from external systems.

We can implement bidirectional workflows, for example, whereby CloudForms makes outgoing calls to integrate with some other enterprise tool, perhaps to initiate an asynchronous action that may take some time to complete. We can implement callback routines as REST-callable Automate instances that can be called to signal that the external processing has finished.

Further Reading

https:http://bit.ly/1szXHpL[API Reference—Automation Requests]

Trigger a Single Automation Request (*http://bit.ly/1YZHQLD*)

Trigger Multiple Automation Requests (*http://bit.ly/20BTyN6*)

## CHAPTER 43

Automation Request Approval

In Chapter 42 we looked at how external systems can make use of CloudForms Automate workflows by calling the RESTful API. In the examples we specified `:auto_approve => true` in the REST call so that our requests were immediately processed; however, we can only auto-approve our own requests if we authenticate as an admin user.

Embedding admin credentials in our external (calling) scripts is generally considered unwise, but if we still want our automation requests to be auto-approved, what can we do?

Fortunately, by this stage in the book we have learned enough to be able to implement our own approval workflow for automation requests. The example in this chapter uses an access-control group profile to control which groups can submit auto-approved automation requests.

Implementing a Custom Approval Workflow

Our automation request approval workflows will follow a very similar pattern to those for provision request approval, and we'll reuse and adapt several of the components. We'll implement two workflows: one triggered from a `request_created` event and one from a `request_pending` event (see Figure 43-1).

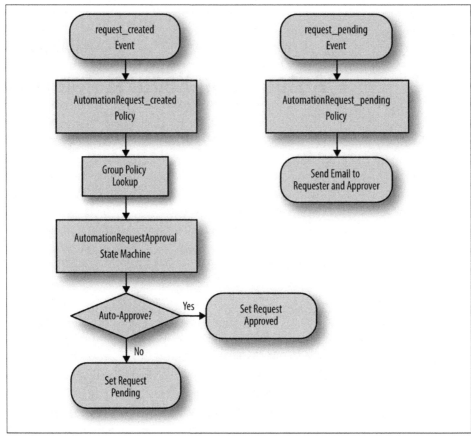

Figure 43-1. Event-triggered automation request approval workflows

Before we implement anything, we need to create some new Automate Datastore components to hold our workflow objects.

Namespace

We'll create a new namespace called *Automation* in our own domain.

Group Profile

We'll create a simple variant of the virtual machine provisioning group profile (we can copy this from the *ManageIQ* domain and edit it). Our profile class will contain two instances (profiles): *Bit63Group_vm_user* and *.missing* (see Figure 43-2).

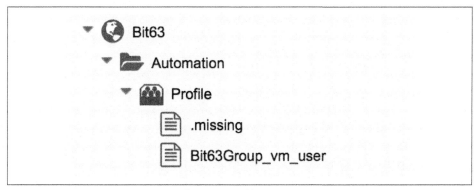

Figure 43-2. Automation approval group profiles

The profile merely contains the name of the auto-approval state machine instance that will be used to determine whether or not the request is auto-approved. The profile is queried using the message `get_auto_approval_state_machine_instance` and returns the Value field via a *collect* as `/state_machine_instance`.

We'll allow members of the `Bit63Group_vm_user` group to have their requests auto-approved, and everyone else (including admins who haven't specified `:auto_approve => true`) will require explicit approval.

The profile for the `Bit63Group_vm_user` group is shown in Figure 43-3.

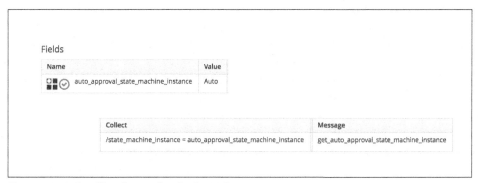

Figure 43-3. Profile schema for the Bit63Group_vm_user group

The *.missing* profile for all other groups is shown in Figure 43-4.

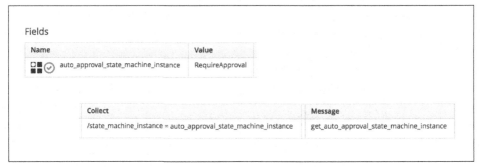

Figure 43-4. Profile schema for .missing

State Machine

Now we'll create a *StateMachines* namespace and a simple variant of the VM *ProvisionRequestApproval* class. We'll copy the *ProvisionRequestApproval* class from the *ManageIQ* domain into ours under the new *StateMachines* namespace and call it *AutomationRequestApproval*. We'll copy the associated instances and methods as well (see Figure 43-5).

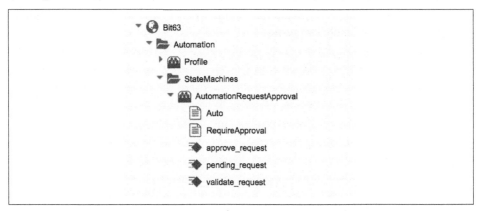

Figure 43-5. AutomationRequestApproval instances and methods

Instances

The *RequireApproval* instance has an `approval_type` value of `require_approval` (see Figure 43-6).

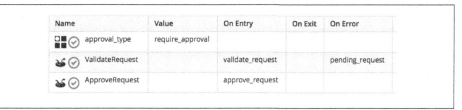

Name	Value	On Entry	On Exit	On Error
approval_type	require_approval			
ValidateRequest		valldate_request		pending_request
ApproveRequest		approve_request		

Figure 43-6. Schema of the RequireApproval instance

The *Auto* instance is similar but has an `approval_type` value of `auto`.

Methods

The *validate_request* method is as follows:

```
request = $evm.root['miq_request']
resource = request.resource
raise "Automation Request not found" if request.nil? || resource.nil?

$evm.log("info", "Checking for auto_approval")
approval_type = $evm.object['approval_type'].downcase
if approval_type == 'auto'
  $evm.root["miq_request"].approve("admin", "Auto-Approved")
  $evm.root['ae_result'] = 'ok'
else
  msg =  "Request was not auto-approved"
  resource.set_message(msg)
  $evm.root['ae_result'] = 'error'
  $evm.object['reason'] = msg
end
```

The *pending_request* method is as follows:

```
#
# This method is executed when the automation request is NOT auto-approved
#
# Get objects
msg = $evm.object['reason']
$evm.log('info', "#{msg}")

# Raise automation event: request_pending
$evm.root["miq_request"].pending
```

The method definition is also given an input parameter with input name `reason` and the data type `string`.

The *approve_request* method is as follows:

```
#
# This method is executed when the automation request is auto-approved
#
# Auto-Approve request
$evm.log("info", "AUTO-APPROVING automation request")
$evm.root["miq_request"].approve("admin", "Auto-Approved")
```

Email Classes

Next we create an *Email* class with an *AutomationRequest_Pending* instance and method (see Figure 43-7).

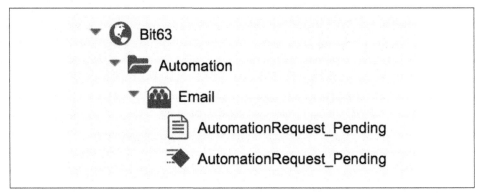

Figure 43-7. Email classes and methods

The method code is copied and adapted as appropriate from the VM *ProvisionRequest_Pending* method. We specify as the `to_email_address` a user that will act as approver for the automation requests.

The full code for the methods is on GitHub (*http://bit.ly/1XUDAPf*).

Policies

We need to generate policy instances for two `AutomationRequest` events: `Automation` `Request_created` and `AutomationRequest_approved`. We copy the standard */System/ Policy* class to our domain and add two instances (see Figure 43-8).

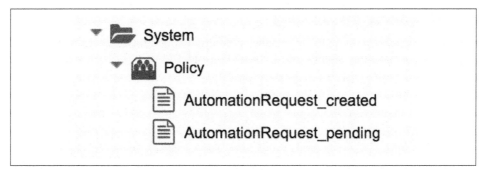

Figure 43-8. New policy instances

AutomationRequest_created

Our policy instance *AutomationRequest_created* has three entries: an assertion and two relationships. We need to recognize whether an automation request was made with the :auto_approve => true parameter. If it was, we need to skip our own approval workflow.

We know (from some investigative debugging using *ObjectWalker*) that when a request is made that specifies :auto_approve => true, we have an $evm.root['auto mation_request'].approval_state attribute with a value of approved. When a request is made that specifies :auto_approve => false, this value is pending_appro val. We can therefore create our assertion to look for $evm.root['automa tion_request'].approval_state == 'pending_approval' and continue with the instance only if the Boolean test returns true.

The rel1 relationship of this instance performs a profile lookup based on our user group, to find the auto-approval state machine instance that should be run. The rel2 relationship calls this state machine instance (see Figure 43-9).

Name	Value
guard	"${/#automation_request.approval_state}" == "pending_approval"
logical_event	
on_entry	
rel1	/Automation/Profile/${/#user.normalized_ldap_group}#get_auto_approval_state_machine_instance
meth1	
rel2	/Automation/StateMachines/AutomationRequestApproval/${/#state_machine_instance}

Figure 43-9. Schema of the AutomationRequest_created instance

AutomationRequest_pending

The *AutomationRequest_pending* instance contains a single relationship to our *AutomationRequest_pending* email instance (see Figure 43-10).

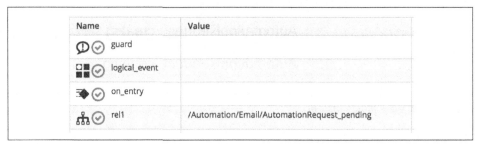

Name	Value
guard	
logical_event	
on_entry	
rel1	/Automation/Email/AutomationRequest_pending

Figure 43-10. Schema of the AutomationRequest_pending instance

Testing

We'll submit three automation requests via the RESTful API, calling a simple *Test* Instance. The calls will be made as follows:

- As user `admin`, specifying `:auto_approve => true`
- As user `admin`, specifying `:auto_approve => false`
- As a user who is a member of the `Bit63Group_vm_user` group

For the first call, our assertion correctly prevents our custom approval workflow from running (the request has already been auto-approved). From *automation.log* we see:

```
Evaluating substituted assertion ["approved" == "pending_approval"]
Assertion Failed: <"approved" == "pending_approval">
Followed  Relationship [miqaedb:/System/Policy/AutomationRequest_created#create]
Followed  Relationship [miqaedb:/System/Policy/request_created#create]
Followed  Relationship [miqaedb:/System/Event/request_created#create]
```

For the second call we see that the assertion evaulates to `true`, but the user `admin`'s group (`EVMGroup-super_administrator`) doesn't have a group profile. The `.missing` profile is used, and the automation request is not auto-approved.

The `admin` user receives an email:

```
Request was not auto-approved.

Please review your Request and update or wait for approval from an Administrator.

To view this Request go to: https://192.168.1.45/miq_request/show/125

Thank you,
Virtualization Infrastructure Team
```

The approving user also receives an email:

```
Approver,
An automation request received from admin@bit63.com is pending.

Request was not auto-approved.

For more information you can go to: https://192.168.1.45/miq_request/show/125

Thank you,
Virtualization Infrastructure Team
```

Clicking the link takes us to an approval page, and we can approve the request, which then continues.

For the third call we see that the assertion evaluates to true, but this time we see the valid group profile being used:

```
Evaluating substituted assertion ["pending_approval" == "pending_approval"]
Following Relationship [miqaedb:/Automation/Profile/Bit63Group_vm_user#get_auto..
```

This group's profile auto-approves the automation request, and the Test instance is successfully run:

```
Q-task_id([automation_task_186]) \
                        <AEMethod test> Calling the test method was successful!
```

Success!

Summary

In this chapter we've assembled many of the Automate components that we've studied throughout the book to create our own custom approval workflow. We've done it by copying and adapting slightly several existing components in the *ManageIQ* domain, and adding our own pieces where necessary.

We started off by creating our own namespace to work in, and we added an access-control group profile so that we can apply the auto-approval to specific groups. We cloned the *ProvisionRequestApproval* class and its methods to become our *AutomationRequestApproval* state machine, and we created two instances, one called *Auto* and one called *RequireApproval*. We added an email class and cloned and adapted the *ProvisionRequest_Pending* instance and method to become our *AutomationRequest_Pending* versions. Finally, we added two policy instances to handle the two automation request_created and request_pending events.

Creating an approval workflow such as this is really just a case of putting the pieces in place and wiring it together. We know that approval workflows start with an event, and that the event is translated to a policy. As long as our policy instances route the workflow into the appropriate handlers (generally a state machine or email class), all that is left is to adapt the method code to our specific purposes, and test.

## CHAPTER 44

Calling External Services

We saw in Chapter 42 how external systems can make *incoming* calls to CloudForms using the RESTful API and run automation instances, perhaps to initiate workflows that we've defined.

From Automate we can also make *outgoing* calls to external systems. We typically use SOAP or RESTful APIs to access theses external services, and there are several Ruby gems that make this easy for us, including `Savon` (SOAP client), `RestClient`, `XmlSim ple` and `Nokogiri` (XML parsers), and `fog` (a Ruby cloud services library).

We have already seen an example of making a RESTful API connection to the RHEV Manager in Chapter 22. Now we will look at some more ways that we can integrate with external services.[1]

Calling a SOAP API Using the Savon Gem

The following snippet makes a SOAP call to an f5 BIG-IP load balancer to add an IP address to a pool (some lines have been omitted for brevity/clarity):

```
def call_F5_Pool(soap_action, body_hash=nil)
  servername = nil || $evm.object['servername']
  username   = nil || $evm.object['username']
  password   = nil || $evm.object.decrypt('password')

  require "rubygems"
  gem 'savon', '=2.3.3'
  require "savon"
  require 'httpi'
```

---

[1] There are more and complete examples of integration code on GitHub (*https://github.com/ramrexx*).

```ruby
# configure httpi gem to reduce verbose logging
HTTPI.log_level = :info # changing the log level
HTTPI.log       = false # diable HTTPI logging
HTTPI.adapter   = :net_http # [:httpclient, :curb, :net_http]

soap = Savon.client do |s|
  s.wsdl "https://#{servername}/iControl/iControlPortal.cgi? \
                                    WSDL=LocalLB.Pool"
  s.basic_auth [username, password]
  s.ssl_verify_mode :none
  s.endpoint "https://#{servername}/iControl/iControlPortal.cgi"
  s.namespace 'urn:iControl:LocalLB/Pool'
  s.env_namespace :soapenv
  s.namespace_identifier :pool
  s.raise_errors false
  s.convert_request_keys_to :none
  s.log_level :error
  s.log false
end

response = soap.call soap_action do |s|
  s.message body_hash unless body_hash.nil?
end

# Convert xml response to a hash
return response.to_hash["#{soap_action}_response".to_sym][:return]
end
...
vm.ipaddresses.each do |vm_ipaddress|
  body_hash = {}
  body_hash[:pool_names] = {:item => [f5_pool]}
  body_hash[:members] = [{:items =>
                          { :member =>
                            {:address => vm_ipaddress,
                             :port => f5_port}
                          }
                        }]
  # call f5 and return a hash of pool names
  f5_return = call_F5_Pool(:add_member, body_hash)
end
```

This script defines a method, call_F5_Pool, that handles the connection to the load balancer. The method first retrieves the connecting credentials from the instance schema, then specifies a particular version of the *Savon* gem to use, and sets the required HTTP logging levels. It initializes the Savon client with the required parameters (including a WSDL path) and then makes the SOAP call. The method finally returns with the SOAP XML return string formatted as a Ruby hash.

The method is called in a loop, passing an IP address into the body_hash argument on each iteration.

Calling an OpenStack API Using the fog Gem

The `fog` gem is a multipurpose cloud services library that supports connectivity to a number of cloud providers.

The following code uses the `fog` gem to retrieve OpenStack networks from Neutron and present them as a dynamic drop-down dialog list. The code filters networks that match a tenant's name and assumes that the CloudForms user has a `tenant` tag containing the same name:

```
require 'fog'
begin
  tenant_name = $evm.root['user'].current_group.tags(:tenant).first
  $evm.log(:info, "Tenant name: #{tenant_name}")

  dialog_field = $evm.object
  dialog_field["sort_by"] = "value"
  dialog_field["data_type"] = "string"
  openstack_networks = {}
  openstack_networks[nil] = '< Select >'
  ems = $evm.vmdb('ems').find_by_name("OpenStack DC01")
  raise "ems not found" if ems.nil?

  neutron_service = Fog::Network.new({
    :provider => 'OpenStack',
    :openstack_api_key => ems.authentication_password,
    :openstack_username => ems.authentication_userid,
    :openstack_auth_url => "http://#{ems.hostname}:35357/v2.0/tokens",
    :openstack_tenant => tenant_name
  })

  keystone_service = Fog::Identity.new({
    :provider => 'OpenStack',
    :openstack_api_key => ems.authentication_password,
    :openstack_username => ems.authentication_userid,
    :openstack_auth_url => "http://#{ems.hostname}:35357/v2.0/tokens",
    :openstack_tenant => tenant_name
  })

  tenant_id = keystone_service.current_tenant["id"]
  $evm.log(:info, "Tenant ID: #{tenant_id}")
  networks = neutron_service.networks.all
  networks.each do |network|
    $evm.log(:info, "Found network #{network.inspect}")
    if network.tenant_id == tenant_id
      network_id = $evm.vmdb('CloudNetwork').find_by_ems_ref(network.id)
      openstack_networks[network_id] = network.name
    end
  end

  dialog_field["values"] = openstack_networks
```

```
    exit MIQ_OK

rescue => err
  $evm.log(:error, "[#{err}]\n#{err.backtrace.join("\n")}")
  exit MIQ_STOP
end
```

This example first retrieves the value of a `tenant` tag applied to the current user's access-control group. It then makes a `fog` connection to both Neutron and Keystone, using the `Fog::Network.new` and `Fog::Identity.new` calls, specifying a `:provider` type of `OpenStack`, the credentials defined for the CloudForms OpenStack provider, and the tenant name retrieved from the tag.

The script iterates though all of the Neutron networks, matching those with a `tenant_id` that matches our `tenant` tag. If a matching network is found, it retrieves the `CloudNetwork` service model object ID for the network and uses that as the key for the hash that populates the dynamic drop-down list. The corresponding hash value is the network name retrieved from Neutron.

Reading from a MySQL Database Using the MySQL Gem

We can add gems to our CloudForms appliance if we wish. The following code snippet uses the `mysql` gem to connect to a MySQL-based CMDB to extract project codes and create tags from them:

```
require 'rubygems'
require 'mysql'

begin
  server   = $evm.object['server']
  username = $evm.object['username']
  password = $evm.object.decrypt('password')
  database = $evm.object['database']

  con = Mysql.new(server, username, password, database)

  unless $evm.execute('category_exists?', "project_code")
    $evm.execute('category_create', :name => "project_code",
                                     :single_value => true,
                                     :description => "Project Code")
  end
  con.query('SET NAMES utf8')
  query_results = con.query('SELECT description,code FROM projectcodes')
  query_results.each do |record|
    tag_name = record[1]
    tag_display_name = record[0].force_encoding(Encoding::UTF_8)

    unless $evm.execute('tag_exists?', 'project_code', tag_name)
      $evm.execute('tag_create', "project_code", :name => tag_name,
```

```
                                      :description => tag_display_name)
      end
    end
  end
rescue Mysql::Error => e
  puts e.errno
  puts e.error
ensure
  con.close if con
end
```

This example first makes a connection to the MySQL database, using credentials stored in the instance schema. It then checks that the tag category exists, before specifying SET NAMES utf8[2] and making a SQL query to the database to retrieve a list of project codes and descriptions. Finally, the script iterates through the list of project codes returned, creating a tag for each corresponding code.

Summary

These examples show the flexibility that we have to integrate with other enterprise components. We have called a load balancer API as part of a provisioning operation to add new IP addresses to its pool. This enables us to completely automate the autoscaling of our application workload. We have called two OpenStack components to populate a dynamic drop-down list in a service dialog, and we have made a SQL call to a MySQL database to extract a list of project codes and create tags from them.

Further Reading

Heavy metal SOAP client (*https://github.com/savonrb/savon*)

The Ruby cloud services library (*https://github.com/fog/fog*)

MySQL API module for Ruby (*https://rubygems.org/gems/mysql/*)

---

2 This is required if the database contains "non-English" strings with character marks such as umlauts.

Miscellaneous

Part VI wraps up the book with some miscellaneous topics.

## CHAPTER 45

Distributed Automation Processing

As we start using CloudForms Automate to expand our workflows into the wider enterprise, we may find that we need to add further CloudForms appliances to spread the workload in our region.

CloudForms Automate has been designed to be scalable by supporting distributed worker appliances, each running the Automation Engine role and polling the VMDB database appliance for work. In this chapter we'll take an in-depth look at how the automation operations are distributed among appliances via a central queue. This is another background information chapter, so feel free to skip it on first read or bookmark it for later reference.

Nondistributed Automation Operations

Not all automation operations need to have a distributed capability. Some automation operations interact with a user through the WebUI, and these require an instance/method to be run directly on the WebUI node to which the user is logged in. Such operations include:

- Running an Automate instance from simulation
- Automate instances that are run to populate dynamic dialog elements

Some other automation operations need to be executed synchronously and in a specific order, and these are also run on a single appliance to guarantee execution order. An example of this is running a control policy *synchronous* action type of Invoke a Custom Automation.

The Automation Engine role does not need to be enabled for these nondistributed automation operations to run.

Distributed Automation Operations

Most automation operations benefit from being scalable and distributed, and capable of running on any appliance in our zone with the Automation Engine role set. These include:

- Running an Automate instance from a custom button
- A control policy *asynchronous* action type of Invoke a Custom Automation
- Any automation operations that involve separated requests and tasks

Distributed automation tasks are passed to the Automation Engine using the standard message-passing mechanism by which all workers communicate. This is via a queue, modeled in the database as the miq_queue table. Generic workers, running on appliances with the Automation Engine role set, monitor this queue for messages with a queue_name field of *generic* and a role field of *automate*. If such a message is found, it is dequeued and processed.

Tracing Queueing/Dequeueing Operations

We can examine *evm.log* to see the interworker message queueing/dequeueing activity when a custom button is clicked that launches an automation task (here the lines have been wrapped for clarity). The first activity that we see is the ResourceAction message (button activities are run as *resource actions*):

```
MIQ(ResourceAction#deliver_to_automate_from_dialog) \
        Queuing <ResourceAction:1000000000066> for <CustomButton:1000000000001>
```

This is immediately followed by the insertion of a new message (#1000000158789) into the queue, containing the task details. The Role: [automate] parameter signifies that the message is intended for the Automation Engine:

```
MIQ(MiqQueue.put) Message id: [1000000158789], \
        id: [], \
        Zone: [default], \
        Role: [automate], \
        Server: [], \
        Ident: [generic], \
        Target id: [], \
        Instance id: [], \
        Task id: [resource_action_1000000000066], \
        Command: [MiqAeEngine.deliver], \
        Timeout: [3600], \
        Priority: [20], \
        State: [ready], \
        Deliver On: [], \
        Data: [], \
        Args: [{:namespace=>"SYSTEM", \
```

```
    :class_name=>"PROCESS", \
    :instance_name=>"Request", \
    :automate_message=>nil, \
    :attrs=>{"class"=>"methods", \
            "instance"=>"objectwalker", \
            "namespace"=>"stuff", \
            "request"=>"call_instance", \
            "dialog_walk_association_whitelist"=>""}, \
    :object_type=>"VmOrTemplate", \
    :object_id=>1000000000024, \
    :user_id=>1000000000001, \
    :miq_group_id=>1000000000002, \
    :tenant_id=>1000000000001}] \
```

The next log line that mentions Message id: [1000000158789] shows it being dequeued by an MiqPriorityWorker thread:

```
MIQ(MiqPriorityWorker::Runner#get_message_via_drb) Message id: [1000000158789], \
    MiqWorker id: [1000000000504], \
    Zone: [default], \
    Role: [automate], \
    Server: [], \
    Ident: [generic], \
    Target id: [], \
    Instance id: [], \
    Task id: [resource_action_1000000000066], \
    Command: [MiqAeEngine.deliver], \
    Timeout: [3600], Priority: [20], \
    State: [dequeue], \
    Deliver On: [], \
    Data: [], \
    Args: [{:namespace=>"SYSTEM", \
        :class_name=>"PROCESS", \
        :instance_name=>"Request", \
        :automate_message=>nil, \
        :attrs=>{"class"=>"methods", \
                "instance"=>"objectwalker", \
                "namespace"=>"stuff", \
                "request"=>"call_instance", \
                "dialog_walk_association_whitelist"=>""}, \
        :object_type=>"VmOrTemplate", \
        :object_id=>1000000000024, \
        :user_id=>1000000000001, \
        :miq_group_id=>1000000000002, \
        :tenant_id=>1000000000001}], \
    Dequeued in: [3.494673879] seconds
```

From here we see the message payload being delivered to the Automation Engine. Notice that in the logfile the task action is now prefixed by Q-task_id, followed by the task ID in the message:

```
Q-task_id([resource_action_1000000000066]) MIQ(MiqQueue#deliver) \
                                    Message id: [1000000158789], Delivering...
Q-task_id([resource_action_1000000000066]) MIQ(MiqAeEngine.deliver) Delivering \
        {"class"=>"methods", \
        "instance"=>"objectwalker", \
        "namespace"=>"stuff", \
        "request"=>"call_instance", \
        "dialog_walk_association_whitelist"=>""} \
        for object [VmOrTemplate.1000000000024] with state [] to Automate
```

We see the Q-task_id string many times in *evm.log*. This is an indication that the log line was generated by a task that was created as a result of a dequeued message, and that the message contained a valid task ID.

Finally, the target instance itself is run by the Automation Engine:

```
Q-task_id([resource_action_1000000000066]) \
    <AutomationEngine> Instantiating [/SYSTEM/PROCESS/Request? \
        MiqServer%3A%3Amiq_server=1000000000001& \
        User%3A%3Auser=1000000000001& \
        VmOrTemplate%3A%3Avm=1000000000024& \
        class=methods& \
        dialog_walk_association_whitelist=& \
        instance=objectwalker& \
        namespace=stuff& \
        object_name=Request& \
        request=call_instance& \
        vmdb_object_type=vm]
```

Detailed Queue Analysis

At any time, the miq_queue table in the PostgreSQL database contains several messages:

```
vmdb_production=# select id,priority,method_name,state,queue_name,class_name,
vmdb_production=# zone,role,msg_timeout from miq_queue;
    id         | priority | method_name     | state  |    queue_name          |
---------------+----------+-----------------+--------+------------------------+...
 1000000160668 |      100 | perf_rollup     | ready  | ems_metrics_processor  | ...
 1000000160710 |       20 | deliver         | ready  | generic                | ...
 1000000160673 |      100 | perf_rollup     | ready  | ems_metrics_processor  | ...
 1000000126295 |      100 | refresh         | ready  | ems_1000000000004      | ...
 1000000160711 |       20 | deliver         | ready  | generic                | ...
 1000000153572 |      100 | perf_rollup     | ready  | ems_metrics_processor  | ...
 1000000154220 |      100 | perf_rollup     | ready  | ems_metrics_processor  | ...
 ...
```

Each worker type queries the miq_queue table to see if there is any work to be done for its respective role. The workers search for messages with a specific queue_name field; for automation-related messages this is generic.

When work is claimed by a worker, the message status is changed from `ready` to dequeue and the worker starts processing the message.

Monitoring the Queue During an Automation Operation

We can monitor the `miq_queue` table during an automation operation initiated from a RESTful call. The following SQL query enables us to see the relevant messages:

```
vmdb_production=# select id,priority,method_name,state,queue_name,
vmdb_production-# class_name,zone,role,msg_timeout from miq_queue where
vmdb_production-# class_name like '%Automation%' or class_name like '%MiqAe%';
```

Searching for specific `class_name` fields in this way enables us to also see auto mate_event messages, which aren't handled by the Automation Engine but are still relevant to an automation operation.

We see several messages created and dispatched over a short time period:

```
   id   | pri |       method_name       | state | queue   |     class_name     | ...
--------+-----+-------------------------+-------+---------+--------------------+----
...1068 | 100 | call_automate_event     | ready | generic | AutomationRequest  | ...
...1069 | 100 | call_automate_event     | ready | generic | AutomationRequest  | ...
...1070 | 100 | create_request_tasks    | ready | generic | AutomationRequest  | ...
(3 rows)

   id   | pri |       method_name       |  state  | queue   |     class_name     ...
--------+-----+-------------------------+---------+---------+-------------------+...
...1071 |  20 | deliver                 | ready   | generic | MiqAeEngine        ...
...1070 | 100 | create_request_tasks    | ready   | generic | AutomationRequest ...
...1069 | 100 | call_automate_event     | dequeue | generic | AutomationRequest ...
(3 rows)

   id   | pri |       method_name       |  state  | queue   |     class_name     ...
--------+-----+-------------------------+---------+---------+-------------------...
...1071 |  20 | deliver                 | ready   | generic | MiqAeEngine        ...
...1072 |  20 | deliver                 | ready   | generic | MiqAeEngine        ...
...1070 | 100 | create_request_tasks    | dequeue | generic | AutomationRequest ...
(3 rows)

   id   | pri | method_ | state | queue   |   class_name    | zone    | role
--------+-----+---------+-------+---------+-----------------+---------+-------...
...1071 |  20 | deliver | ready | generic | MiqAeEngine     | default | automa...
...1072 |  20 | deliver | ready | generic | MiqAeEngine     | default | automa...
...1073 | 100 | execute | ready | generic | AutomationTask  | default | automa...
(3 rows)

   id   | pri | method_ |  state  | queue   |   class_name    | zone    | ro...
--------+-----+---------+---------+---------+-----------------+---------+-----...
...1071 |  20 | deliver | dequeue | generic | MiqAeEngine     | default | auto...
...1073 | 100 | execute | dequeue | generic | AutomationTask  | default | auto...
(2 rows)

   id   | pri | method_ |  state  | queue   |   class_name    | zone    | ro...
--------+-----+---------+---------+---------+-----------------+---------+-----...
```

```
...1073 | 100 | execute | dequeue | generic | AutomationTask | default | auto...
(1 row)

 id | pri | method_name | state | queue_name | class_name | zone | role | msg_...
----+-----+-------------+-------+------------+------------+------+------+-----...
(0 rows)
```

We can search for any of these message IDs in *evm.log* and expand them to examine
the message content. For example, searching for `Message id: 1000000161070`
reveals:

```
MIQ(MiqQueue.put) Message id: [1000000161070], \
        id: [], \
        Zone: [default], \
        Role: [automate], \
        Server: [], \
        Ident: [generic], \
        Target id: [], \
        Instance id: [1000000000016], \
        Task id: [automation_request_1000000000016], \
        Command: [AutomationRequest.create_request_tasks], \
        Timeout: [3600], \
        Priority: [100], \
        State: [ready], \
        Deliver On: [], \
        Data: [], \
        Args: []

MIQ(MiqGenericWorker::Runner#get_message_via_drb) Message id: [1000000161070], \
        MiqWorker id: [1000000000503], \
        Zone: [default], \
        Role: [automate], \
        Server: [], \
        Ident: [generic], \
        Target id: [], \
        Instance id: [1000000000016], \
        Task id: [automation_request_1000000000016], \
        Command: [AutomationRequest.create_request_tasks], \
        Timeout: [3600], \
        Priority: [100], \
        State: [dequeue], \
        Deliver On: [], \
        Data: [], \
        Args: [], \
        Dequeued in: [5.622553094] seconds

Q-task_id([automation_request_1000000000016]) MIQ(MiqQueue#deliver) \
Message id: [1000000161070], Delivering...

Q-task_id([automation_request_1000000000016]) MIQ(MiqQueue#delivered) \
Message id: [1000000161070], State: [ok], Delivered in [1.866825831] seconds
```

This corresponds to the message queueing activity generated by the `execute` method
in the backend *vmdb/app/models/miq_request.rb*:

```
def execute
  task_check_on_execute

  deliver_on = nil
  if get_option(:schedule_type) == "schedule"
    deliver_on = get_option(:schedule_time).utc rescue nil
  end

  # self.create_request_tasks
  MiqQueue.put(
    :class_name  => self.class.name,
    :instance_id => id,
    :method_name => "create_request_tasks",
    :zone        => options.fetch(:miq_zone, my_zone),
    :role        => my_role,
    :task_id     => "#{self.class.name.underscore}_#{id}",
    :msg_timeout => 3600,
    :deliver_on  => deliver_on
  )
end
```

If we search the sources for `MiqQueue.put`, we see the extent to which the distributed nature of CloudForms is used.

Troubleshooting

As (by design) queued automation operations can be dequeued and run by any appliance in a zone with the Automation Engine role set, we cannot necessarily predict which appliance will run our code. This can make troubleshooting `$evm.log` output more challenging, as we may need to search *automation.log* on several appliances to find our method's log output. When we are tracing message passing, the enqueue `Miq Queue.put` and corresponding dequeue `Worker::Runner#get_message_via_drb` calls might even be on different appliances as well.

If Automate tasks are not being run in a distributed CloudForms installation, it is often worth examining the contents of the `miq_queue` table to see whether Automate messages are accumulating, and which zone the messages are targeted for (the `Zone:` [] field). If messages are not being dequeued as expected, then check that the Automation Engine role is set on at least one appliance in the zone.

We often see this when separating appliances into various role-specific zones, such as a WebUI zone and a Worker Appliance zone. Automation calls made using the RESTful API to an appliance in the WebUI zone will fail to run if the Automation Engine role is not enabled on any of the WebUI zone appliances or the RESTful call does not specify an alternative zone to run in.

Summary

In this chapter, we have studied the way that automation tasks can be distributed among multiple CloudForms appliances, which enables us to scale out our automation infrastructure as the workload increases. An approximate rule of thumb that is often used when planning a CloudForms deployment is to allow for one worker appliance per 300–500 managed virtual machines. However, in practice, this is workload-dependent. If we see automation tasks taking longer than expected to process, we can monitor the performance of each of our CloudForms worker appliances and check the number of outstanding requests in the miq_queue database table. This should give a good indication as to whether adding additional worker appliances will improve the overall performance, or whether we should look at individual workflow optimizations.

## CHAPTER 46

Argument Passing and Handling

Over the preceding chapters we have discovered several ways of calling Automate instances. In some cases we need to pass arguments into the instance's method, but the way that we pass arguments into methods, and receive them from inside the method, varies depending on how the instance is called. We need to consider this if we're writing code that can be called in several ways, such as from a button and/or from an API call.

In this chapter we'll look at how we pass arguments into instances and how we retrieve them from inside the method. We will call the same instance (*ObjectWalker*) four ways, passing two arguments each time: lunch and dinner. We can use *object_walker_reader* to show us where the arguments can be read from inside our called method.

Case 1: Calling from a Button

For this first case we call *ObjectWalker* (via */System/Process/Request/Call_Instance*) from a button. We create a button dialog that prompts for two text box fields (see Figure 46-1).

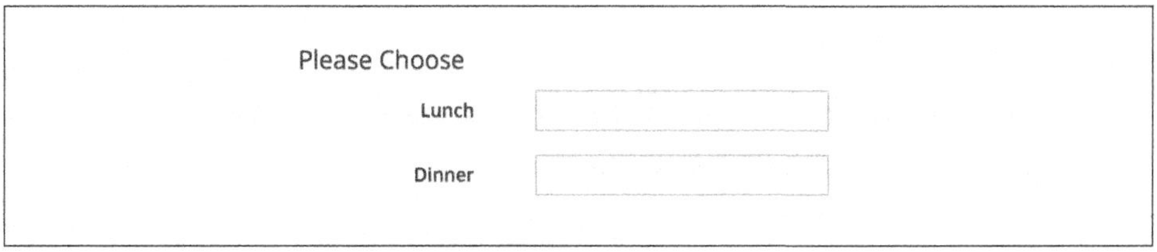

Please Choose		
Lunch		
Dinner		

Figure 46-1. Simple dialog to prompt for input values

We then add the button to a button group anywhere.

If we click on the button and enter the values `salad` and `pasta` into the dialog boxes, we see the dialog values appear in `$evm.root` in the receiving method, indexed by the key name prefixed by `dialog_`:

```
~/object_walker_reader.rb | grep -P "lunch|dinner"
     |    $evm.root['dialog_dinner'] = salad   (type: String)
     |    $evm.root['dialog_lunch'] = pasta    (type: String)
```

Case 2: Calling from the RESTful API

For this use case we have an external Ruby script that calls our internal CloudForms instance via the REST API:

```
url = "https://#{server}"

post_params = {
  :version => '1.1',
  :uri_parts => {
    :namespace => 'Stuff',
    :class => 'Methods',
    :instance => 'ObjectWalker'
  },
  :parameters => {
    :lunch => "sandwich",
    :dinner => "steak"
  },
  :requester => {
    :auto_approve => true
  }
}.to_json
query = "/api/automation_requests"

rest_return = RestClient::Request.execute(method: :post, url: url + query,
                                          :user => username,
                                          :password => password,
                                          :headers => {:accept => :json},
                                          :payload => post_params,
                                          verify_ssl: false)
result = JSON.parse(rest_return)
```

In the called method we see the arguments visible in several places: in the task's options hash as the `attrs` key, under `$evm.root` because this is the Instance that we launched when entering Automate, and under `$evm.object` because this is also our current object:

```
~/object_walker_reader.rb | grep -P "lunch|dinner"
     |    object_walker: $evm.root['automation_task'].options[:attrs] = \
     {:lunch=>"sandwich", :dinner=>"steak", :userid=>"admin"}  (type: Hash)
     object_walker: $evm.root['dinner'] = steak  (type: String)
     object_walker: $evm.root['lunch'] = sandwich  (type: String)
```

```
object_walker:  $evm.object['dinner'] = steak  (type: String)
object_walker:  $evm.object['lunch'] = sandwich  (type: String)
```

Case 3: Calling from a Relationship or Automate Datastore URI

When we call instances via a relationship (such as from a state machine), we specify the full URI of the instance. We can append arguments to this URI using standard web form query string syntax.

For this use case, we'll call *ObjectWalker* from an already running automation script, using $evm.instantiate. The argument to $evm.instantiate is the full URI of the instance to be launched, as follows:

```
$evm.instantiate("/Stuff/Methods/ObjectWalker?lunch=salad&dinner=spaghetti")
```

When instantiated in this way, the receiving method retrieves the arguments from $evm.object (one of our [grand]parent instances is $evm.root; our immediate caller is $evm.parent):

```
~/object_walker_reader.rb | grep -P "lunch|dinner"
    object_walker:  $evm.object['dinner'] = spaghetti  (type: String)
    object_walker:  $evm.object['lunch'] = salad  (type: String)
```

Case 4: Passing Arguments via the ws_values Hash During a VM Provision

We can pass our own custom values into the virtual machine provisioning process so that they can be interpreted by any method in the Provision VM from Template state machine.

The facility to do this is provided by the additional_values field in an */api/provision_requests* REST call (additionalValues in the original SOAP EVMProvisionRequestEx call) or from the sixth element in the argument list to an $evm.execute('create_provision_request',…) call (see Chapter 27).

For this use case we've edited the Provision VM from Template state machine to add a few extra stages (see Figure 46-2).

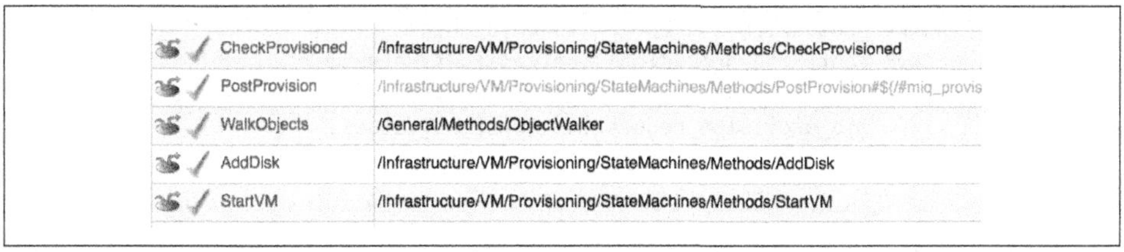

Figure 46-2. Calling ObjectWalker from the VmProvision_VM state machine

These stages could modify the provisioning process if required based on the custom values passed in. An example of this might be to specify the disk size for an additional disk to be added by the AddDisk stage.

For this example we're using a simple automation method to call $evm.exe cute('create_provision_request',...) to provision a new virtual machine. We specify the custom values in arg6:

```
# arg1 = version
args = ['1.1']

# arg2 = templateFields
args << {'name'         => 'rhel7-generic',
         'request_type' => 'template'}

# arg3 = vmFields
args << {'vm_name' => 'test10',
         'vlan'    => 'rhevm'}

# arg4 = requester
args << {'owner_email'      => 'pemcg@bit63.com',
         'owner_first_name' => 'Peter',
         'owner_last_name'  => 'McGowan'}

# arg5 = tags
args << nil

# arg6 = Web Service Values (ws_values)
args << {'lunch' => 'soup',
         'dinner' => 'chicken'}

# arg7 = emsCustomAttributes
args << nil

# arg8 = miqCustomAttributes
args << nil

request_id = $evm.execute('create_provision_request', *args)
```

When we call this method and the virtual machine provisioning process begins, we can retrieve the custom values at any stage from the miq_provision_request or miq_provision options hash using the ws_values key:

```
~/object_walker_reader.rb | grep -P "lunch|dinner"
     |    $evm.root['miq_provision'].options[:ws_values] = \
                         {:lunch=>"soup", :dinner=>"chicken"}   (type: Hash)
     |    |    miq_provision_request.options[:ws_values] = \
                         {:lunch=>"soup", :dinner=>"chicken"}   (type: Hash)
```

Passing Arguments When Calling a Method in the Same Class

When an instance (such as a state machine) calls a method in the same class as itself, it can pass key/value argument pairs in parentheses as input parameters with the call. We see the *VMProvision_VM* state machine do this when it calls *update_provision_status* during the processing of the On Entry, On Exit, and On Error (see Figure 46-3).

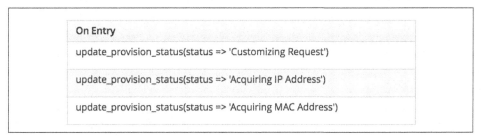

Figure 46-3. Text arguments passed to update_provision_status

When we create a method that accepts input parameters in this way, we need to specify the name and data type of each parameter in the method definition (see Figure 46-4).

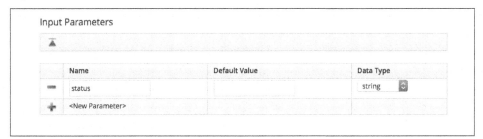

Figure 46-4. Specifying input parameters

The method then reads the parameters from $evm.inputs:

```
update_provision_status(status => 'pre1',status_state => 'on_entry')

# Get status from input field status
status = $evm.inputs['status']

# Get status_state ['on_entry', 'on_exit', 'on_error'] from input field
status_state = $evm.inputs['status_state']
```

Summary

This chapter shows how we can send arguments when we call instances and how we process them inside the method. The way that a method retrieves an argument depends on how the instance has been called, but we can use `$evm.root['vmdb_object_type']` as before to determine this, and access the argument in an appropriate manner.

## CHAPTER 47

Miscellaneous Tips

We've reached the final chapter in the book, and our journey toward automation mastery is almost complete. In this last chapter we'll cover some miscellaneous tips that can help us when we work with CloudForms Automate.

Updating the Appliance

When a minor update to CloudForms Management Engine is released and installed (e.g., 5.5.0 → 5.5.2), any changes to the Automate code are not automatically visible to the Automate Explorer.

Go to Import/Export, and "Reset all Datastore custom classes and instances to default" to get the updates added and visible (see Figure 47-1).

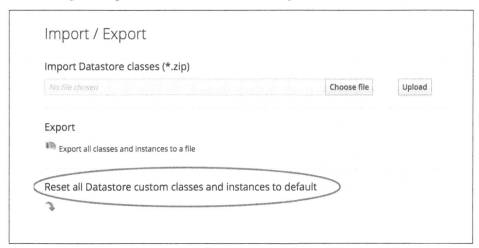

Figure 47-1. Resetting the locked domains after an appliance upgrade

This does not, as the wording might suggest, reset our custom domains; it merely reloads the ManageIQ and RedHat domains.

The ManageIQ Coding Style and Standards Guide

There is a ManageIQ Coding Style and Standards Guide (*http://bit.ly/1TWQbfa*) and a Ruby Style Guide (*http://bit.ly/1OeElk9*). Although the guides don't specifically refer to Automate coding style (they're more a guideline for ManageIQ code development), we can adopt the recommendations to keep our code clean and standards-compliant.

The guides recommend using snake_case for symbols, methods, and variables, and CamelCase for classes and modules. Although this doesn't explicitly refer to Automate Datastore classes and methods, we can adopt the same guidelines for our code.

The style guide doesn't currently mention whether we should name instances in CamelCase or snake_case. Although the examples in this book have used CamelCase naming for instances, it is likely that future versions of CloudForms will standardize on snake_case naming for both instances and methods.

Defensive Programming

The dynamic nature of the object structure means that we have to be more careful about testing for `nil` conditions, testing whether hash keys exist before we access them, testing whether variables are enumerable before we call `each` on them, and so on.

Some examples are:

```
if this_object.respond_to?(:attributes)
  if this_object.attributes.respond_to? :each
    this_object.attributes.each do |key, value|
      ...

user = $evm.root['user'] rescue nil
unless user.nil?
  ...

prov = $evm.root['miq_provision']
if prov.options.key?(:ws_values)
  ws_values = prov.options[:ws_values]
  ...
```

Catch Exceptions

As an extension of the tip "Defensive Programming" on page 386, we should also catch and handle exceptions wherever possible in our scripts. We have seen several examples of this in the scripts that we've studied in the book—for example:

```
begin
  ...
rescue RestClient::Exception => err
  unless err.response.nil?
    error = err.response
    $evm.log(:error, "The REST request failed with code: #{error.code}")
    $evm.log(:error, "The response body was:\n#{error.body.inspect}")
    $evm.root['ae_reason'] = "The REST request failed with code: #{error.code}"
  end
  $evm.root['ae_result'] = 'error'
  exit MIQ_STOP
rescue => err
  $evm.log(:error, "[#{err}]\n#{err.backtrace.join("\n")}")
  $evm.root['ae_reason'] = "Unspecified error, see automation.log for backtrace"
  $evm.root['ae_result'] = 'error'
  exit MIQ_STOP
end
```

Use an External IDE

The built-in WebUI code editor is fairly basic. It is often easier to develop in an external editor or IDE, and copy and paste code into the built-in editor when complete.

Version Control

There isn't any version control yet, although Git integration for the Automate Datastore is in development for a future release of CloudForms. In the meantime we should use our own Git repository, but this is a manual process, unfortunately.

Several of Red Hat's United States consultants have created an open source project for handling version control and continuous integration (CI) of CloudForms artifacts, such as Automate code and dialogs, across regions.[1]

The CI workflow is created using Jenkins. It provides a pipeline view that allows us to visualize which version of any of the artifacts is in any region at a given time. We can implement regions as lifecycle stages in our development process—such as DEV, TEST, and QA—and promote code through the lifecycle as our testing progresses (see Figure 47-2).

---

[1] The project code is located on Github (*https://github.com/rhtconsulting/miq-ci*).

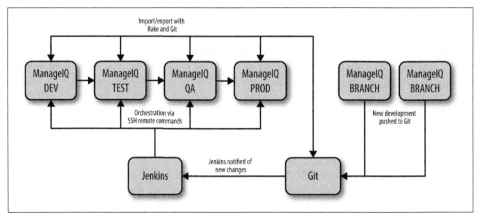

Figure 47-2. Continuous integration workflow for CloudForms automation development

Use Configuration Domains

We have seen several examples in the book in which system credentials have been retrieved from an instance schema, using $evm.object['attribute'].

When we work on larger projects and implement some kind of version control as previously described, we will have separate CloudForms installations for our various automation code lifecycle environments—DEV, TEST, and QA, for example. It is likely (and good practice) that the credentials to connect to our various integration services will be different for each lifecycle environment, but we want to be able to *promote* our code through each environment with minimal change.

In this case it can be useful to create a separate *configuration* domain for each lifecycle environment, containing purely the classes and instances that define the usernames, passwords, or URLs specific to that environment. The configuration domain typically contains no methods; these are in the *code* domain being tested. When a method calls $evm.object['attribute'], the attribute is retrieved from the running instance in the configuration domain, which has the highest priority.

The process of testing then becomes simpler as we cycle the code domain through each lifecycle environment, without having to modify any credentials; these are statically defined in the configuration domain. The process is illustrated in Table 47-1.

Table 47-1. Promoting code domains through lifecycle environments

Sprints/ environments	DEV	TEST	Q/A	PROD
Sprint1	Dev + Code_v4 domains	Test + Code_v3 domains	QA + Code_v2 domains	Prod + Code_v1 domains
Sprint2	Dev + Code_v5 domains	Test + Code_v4 domains	QA + Code_v3 domains	Prod + Code_v2 domains
Sprint3	Dev + Code_v6 domains	Test + Code_v5 domains	QA + Code_v4 domains	Prod + Code_v3 domains

Summary

This completes our study of the Automate capability of Red Hat CloudForms. Over the preceding chapters we have learned about the Automate Datastore and the entities that we use to create our automation scripts. We have taken a look behind the scenes at the objects that we work with and learned about their attributes, virtual columns, associations, and methods.

We discovered how these components come together to create the workflows that provision infrastructure virtual machines and cloud instances, and we have seen examples of how we can customize the provisioning state machines for our own purposes.

We created service catalogs to deploy servers both singly and in bundles, and we integrated our Automate workflows with an external Red Hat Satellite 6.1 server.

We have seen how CloudForms is able to manage our entire virtual machine lifcycle, including retirement, and we have studied the retirement process for virtual machines and services.

We looked at the integration capabilities of CloudForms Automate and saw how easily we can integrate our automation workflows with our wider enterprise.

Our journey toward automation mastery is now complete. All that is left is to practice, and start automating!

Index

Foreman host groups, 313

G

Git version control, 387
groups
    provisioning dialogs for, customizing, 202
    provisioning steps specific to, 142-143
        (see also provisioning profiles)

H

helper methods, Rails, 53-54
hostname variable, 189
hosts (hypervisors), 56
    (see also placement stage)
    active records for, 53
    attributes for, 56
    migrating virtual machines between, 69
hybrid cloud manager, 3
hypervisors (see hosts)

I

IaaS (Infrastructure as a Service), 3
IDE, 387
images, provisioning from, 142
Infrastructure as a Service (IaaS), 3
infrastructure providers, 5, 7-8
inline methods, 21
insight, 7-8
InspectMe tool, 81-82
instances, 20
    adding, 27-28, 34
    calling from RESTful API, 347-348, 350
    entry point for, creating, 44-45
    retiring, 335-337
    running from a button, 46-49
    running from alerts, 89-90
    running from control policy actions, 88
    running from dynamic service dialog elements, 90
    running from RESTful API, 88
    running in Simulation, 29-30, 36
integration, 9
internal events, 117, 125-127
IP address, adding to pool, 363-364

L

lifecycle environments
    configuration domains for, 388

dynamic elements for, 241
linux_host_name variable, 189
list_activationkeys method, 320
list_hostgroups method, 320
list_puppetclasses method, 321
list_smart_class_parameters method, 321
logging (see automation.log file)

M

ManageIQ Coding Style and Standards Guide, 386
ManageIQ domain, 15
ManageIQ project, xxiii, 11
management events, alerts for, 89-90, 128-129
Max Retries attribute, 105
Max Time attribute, 105
message fields, 111-113
methods, 20-21
    (see also specific methods by name)
    accessing attributes in, 35
    accessing custom attributes in, 43-44
    adding, 28-29
    for approval requests, 155-156
    argument passing and handling, 379-384
    in Automate Datastore, 20-21
    fields for, adding, 26-27
    helper methods, Rails, 53-54
    inline, 21
    naming conventions for, 386
    for placement, 195-198
    for retirement, 336-337, 342
    running context for, determining, 90
    of service model objects, 58
    for service reconfiguration, 319-324
Microsoft Azure, 5
Microsoft System Center Virtual Machine Manager, 5
microsoft_best_ methods, 196-198
MiqAeService class, 54-55
MIQ_ABORT exit code, 31
MIQ_ERROR exit code, 31
miq_force_unique_name variable, 189
MIQ_OK exit code, 31
miq_queue table, 372-377
MIQ_STOP exit code, 31
MIQ_WARN exit code, 31
MVC (model-view-controller), 52
MySQL database, 366-367
MySQL gem, 366-367

S

About the Author

Peter McGowan has worked for Red Hat in the United Kingdom since 2012, both as a consulting architect and, more recently, in the Systems Engineering team, where he works with Red Hat's Cloud Suite of products.

Peter started his IT career programming on PDP-11s, before weaving a trail through various Microsoft technologies and into open source software. For much of this time, he has specialized in enterprise systems management and automation.

When not programming Ruby, he can be found trying to locate the best cappuccinos and crate-digging for old records to play on his beloved Linn record player. He is step-dad to three wonderful grown-up children—Luke, Lucie, and Imogen—and husband to the very lovely Sarah.

Colophon

The animal on the cover of *Mastering CloudForms Automation* is a red-breasted goose (*Branta ruficollis*). It is part of the Anatidae family and can be found in Arctic Siberia on the Taymyr, Yamal, and Gydan peninsulas, as well as Azerbaijan when breeding. Bulgaria, Romania, and Ukraine are where most decide to winter. The species population appears to be in decline in all areas.

Both males and females look alike, with plummage of reddish-brown, black, and white. You can probably guess that the chest is red from the name, but so are the sides of their faces, outlined by white. There are also white patches between the eye and upper bill, as well as the upper legs, and parts of the wings, leaving the rest of the head, most of the wings, and back in black. Adults range in lengths from 21 to 22 inches, making them fairly small in size.

Red-breasted geese have a mostly vegetarian diet that consists of grass, leaves, shoots, aquatic plants, and other such items. They also eat barley, maize, and wheat when in more agricultural areas.

In the beginning of June, these geese nest near high and dry places, such as cliffs or rock outcrops, close to predatory birds, such as falcons and owls. The proximity helps protect their eggs from predators, such as the arctic fox. They begin breeding around 3 years of age, and each clutch consists of 3 to 8 eggs that are incubated for about 25 days.

Many of the animals on O'Reilly covers are endangered; all of them are important to the world. To learn more about how you can help, go to *animals.oreilly.com*.

The cover image is from *British Birds*. The cover fonts are URW Typewriter and Guardian Sans. The text font is Adobe Minion Pro; the heading font is Adobe Myriad Condensed; and the code font is Dalton Maag's Ubuntu Mono.

Short. Smart.
Seriously useful.

Free ebooks and reports from O'Reilly
at **oreil.ly/ops-perf**

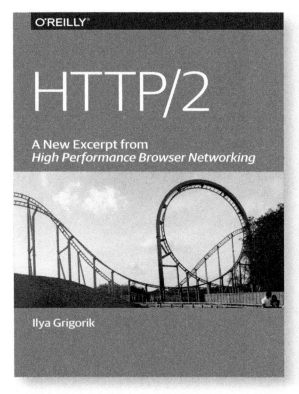

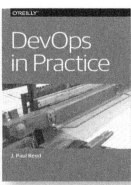

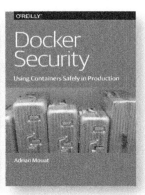

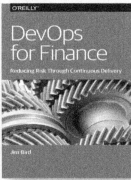

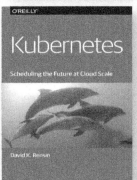

Get even more insights from industry experts
and stay current with the latest developments in
web operations, DevOps, and web performance
with free ebooks and reports from O'Reilly.

CPSIA information can be obtained
at www.ICGtesting.com
Printed in the USA
BVOW10s1223090916

461634BV00013B/76/P

9 781491 957226